About the Book

Charles (Chuck) Dixon wrote "Chasing a Whirlwind" to share his adventures during his life and career in aviation. His life is a story of ambition and determination to reach goals that were often challenging and adventurous. God, family, country, and aviation were the driving factors in his life.

Charles, an aerodynamicist, almost lost his life due to rogue whirlwinds or vortices created by powerful military aircraft early in his career. Vortices are necessary for an airplane to fly, and as an aerodynamicist, he was determined to learn how to maximize their effectiveness.

During his years working at two major aircraft companies Charles' revolutionary thinking created patents that enhanced his work for the rest of his career. His sense of adventure gave him many opportunities to explore the great outdoors and kept him fit during his long life.

After an early retirement, and the death of his wife Mary, Charles won two proposals. First to the Air Force to pursue the creation of a specialty software that could predict stability and control effects of most types of aircraft. The second proposal was marriage to Frieda who would be his lifelong partner in his new business and the editor of his life story.

Sharing his faith in God with co-workers and others became a cornerstone of Charles' life. His belief in the power of God to bring abundant life to everyone he met, inspired him to invite others to find God's peace in this world.

Much help for this book was provided by his second wife, Frieda, and by the members of the Christian Authors Guild and Word Weavers International.

Chasing a Whirlwind

My Life and Career in Aviation

CHARLES (CHUCK) DIXON
AND
FRIEDA DIXON

authorHOUSE

AuthorHouse™
1663 Liberty Drive
Bloomington, IN 47403
www.authorhouse.com
Phone: 833-262-8899

Published by AuthorHouse 11/30/2021

ISBN: 978-1-6655-4461-0 (sc)
ISBN: 978-1-6655-4460-3 (hc)
ISBN: 978-1-6655-4462-7 (e)

Library of Congress Control Number: 2021923396

Contents

Prologue

A wall plaque in my office reminds me that "FLYING IS THE SECOND GREATEST THRILL KNOWN TO MAN, BUT LANDING IS THE FIRST." That statement became a reality for me in 1970 during what was supposed to be a routine landing at Dobbins Air Force Base in Marietta, Georgia. I along with five other engineers from the Lockheed Martin Research Lab had flown to Dayton, Ohio on a Lockheed Beach 18. Our goal was to secure government research contracts for Lockheed from the Air Force Research Lab (AFRL). After our successful mission, we confidently boarded the plane for a smooth ride back to Marietta.

Typical Beech 18 Airplane

As we approached Dobbins, we saw a C-124 Globemaster and a C-5 cargo plane land safely on the runway. We were still twenty feet off the ground on the glide approach when we caught the lingering wake—which was like a horizontal tornado or vortex—from one of the planes. Our airplane pitched up and rolled 90° to the right. My aerobatic training in small aircraft did not prepare me for the fear in my gut as that airplane tossed around like a kite. Our experienced pilot hit that top rudder to regain control, straightened out the airplane, and set the Beach 18 down on its landing gear. Fortunately, the runway was 10,000 feet long which provided plenty of room to correct the flight and land safely. When we got to the ramp, we felt like getting down on our wobbly knees and kissing the ground. I thanked the Lord for saving our lives.

During a Monday morning quarterbacking session, my colleagues and I analyzed our near-crash experience. Some of my fellow engineers said they were going to ramp up their research on the trailing vortex flow that nearly caused our death. They wanted to solve the problem by destroying that trailing vortex.

I had a different thought process from the other engineers. I had gained some experience with vortex flow when I worked on fighter aircraft and believed that the trailing vortex flow or whirlwind that comes off the wing tip could be put to good use. I was determined to prove that those vortices could be made to work for us and not against us. I didn't know it at the time, but that became a turning point in my life. Flying and anything related to aircraft had been in my blood for as long as I could remember. But my "Aha" moment, born out of near disaster, would set the stage for the rest of my life and result in a new career after I retired.

One

Plum-n-Nelly

The Great Depression settled on Memphis, Tennessee and its environs like the thick, chilly fog that rose from the Mississippi River. Paddlewheel steamboats navigated the river daily carrying passengers and goods south to New Orleans and north to St. Louis. As the freewheeling money spending days of the Roaring Twenties screeched to a halt, the playground of Tom Sawyer and Huckleberry Finn just kept rolling along. The locals found solace in the newly popular jazz music that had its roots in Memphis and enjoyed visits to the Lowe's Palace to watch the first "talkie" movie, *The Jazz Singer*.

My parents lived in "Plum-n-Nelly"—also known as Whitehaven, Tennessee. Whitehaven got its nickname since it was "plum" out of Memphis and "nelly" into Mississippi. That small town, about 25 miles east of the Mississippi River, had two general stores, a drugstore, and a doctor's office. On November 25, 1930, the doctor delivered me at the home of my parents who gave me a good, sturdy English name—Charles James Dixon.

My older sister and I lived with our parents on a two-lane gravel road in a non-descript white-sided duplex. We called our parents Mother and Daddy. The haphazard additions to the shot-gun style house were typical of the era. Fruit trees—the cherry tree produced good switches—and a fig tree near the back porch adorned the two acres of our property. A vegetable garden provided fresh produce to be enjoyed in the hot summer and canned for the cold winters. Chickens roamed freely in the chicken yard

while they fattened up. My mother, an expert in ringing chickens' necks and plucking their feathers, served the bird Southern fried for Sunday dinner. When I was old enough, I cleaned the chicken house and spread the manure in the garden.

Our small house had one stove to heat the living room, dining room, and kitchen on the main level, and the small upstairs bedrooms. For many years, our bathroom was a two-hole outhouse until my parents added indoor plumbing to service both sides of the duplex. An outside well pumped water into the kitchen.

My paternal grandparents occupied the other side of our duplex. Three sets of aunts and uncles from my grandmother's first marriage lived in small houses on our same street. My father was born during my grandmother's second marriage. The children from her first marriage didn't get along with my father. My grandfather favored my father and only tolerated the children from the first marriage, which added to jealousy among the siblings.

My father, too, had a short-lived first marriage before he married a country girl born in Mayfield, Kentucky. Like my father, she was a stage performer. Vaudeville stage shows were a popular form of entertainment in the early 20th century. For several years, my father performed in Vaudeville as a black-face comedian and tap dancer. When Daddy left Vaudeville and brought Mother to live near his half-sisters, my aunts and uncles treated her like an outsider and the black sheep of the family. Performing on stage was not considered a moral vocation, so they falsely believed that my mother was a floosy.

I was born at the end of the first year of the Great Depression. Hard times were everywhere with money in short supply. In 1930, the age of radio was in its adolescence and talking movies were in their infancy. With stage shows on their way out, my father took jobs wherever he could—roofing houses and digging ditches.

My father worked hard, but he also drank hard and upset the family on more than one occasion with the ruckus he caused when drunk. My mother found work at a department store in Memphis, and between them my parents made sure we had plenty of food and the necessities of life. And somehow, we always found plenty of time for fun.

My earliest childhood memory occurred around age four. Mother

and Daddy invited two other married couples to our shotgun house. Bill and Eddie were firemen in the Memphis Fire Department. I am not sure where my dad and mother met Bill and his wife Bessie, but Eddie was one of Dad's partners in his Vaudeville career. Often, they got out the record player and our stack of 72 RPM vinyl records, found some good dance music, and performed the soft-shoe and tap dance together.

They loved to get my sister and me on the floor to dance the train dance with them. We followed my dad or Eddie in a line like freight train box cars with the leader acting as the steam engine. Our feet tapped on the floor making a train sound. We started slowly to get the cars rolling. Then we moved faster and faster, alternating between moving forward and backward. The tap dancing sounded like a train. My sister and I loved to do that until we had no more steam.

For me, however, those visits were not all fun. When it was time for us kids to go upstairs to get in our PJ's then come downstairs to say good night to all, Eddie or Bill would ask me if I knew who they worked for. I knew it was the Fire Department, but I could not say it, and they knew I couldn't. Every time I said "Fartin Partin," they had a good laugh at my expense. My red face showed my embarrassment. When I gave each one a good night hug, Eddie invariably pulled my pajama pants down causing me to moon everybody. I look back and laugh about this now, but then it made me very mad.

Another vivid memory occurred when I was between four and five years old. Since Mother and Daddy both had to work the same schedule to make ends meet, it was easy for them to take my sister and me to the other side of the duplex where my paternal grandparents lived. Since my sister was in school, I had to entertain myself with my wind-up train and track. My grandfather (Dada) helped me set up the track under grandmother's (Mama's) dinner table.

I carefully positioned the train on the track and got it running, but it kept jumping the track. After a few attempts to fix the problem, I cussed that train out— using some of Dada's favorite words. I said, "You g@# d*?@ train. Stay on the tracks!" Dada immediately got up from his favorite rocking chair and pulled me out from under the table. Then he proceeded to turn my bottom red with a spanking I will never forget. Mama came in and rescued me. She chided Dada a good bit, telling him I was just

copying him. Mama then rubbed milk on my bottom to ease the pain. I believe Dada and I learned something that day. I learned to be careful where I said those kinds of words, and Dada learned never to say those words around the family again. Sometimes he almost slipped up, but he would catch himself and say, "g--- gol darn it."

School Days

Despite teasing and nurturing by my parent's friends and my grandparents, I turned five years old and was old enough to go to first grade at Whitehaven Elementary School. I would not turn six until November of that year, and I was shorter than most of the kids that were already six years old. Somebody must have thought I was smart enough to keep up with the other kids. My memories of first grade are of receiving a prize for my cursive writing ability and being chosen as a page for the Memphis Cotton Carnival. Jane, the cutest girl in my class, was chosen to be my associate page.

The Memphis Cotton Carnival was organized during the Great Depression to promote interest in King Cotton and bring a sense of excitement and life back to the city of Memphis. It was Memphis' answer to Mardi Gras which was held down the River in New Orleans. There was a major parade, and Jane and I rode at the feet of the Cotton King and Queen on their float. I don't think either Jane or I realized at the time what a privilege it was to be a Page to the King and Queen and the royal court. In my mind Jane was my girlfriend, but I was bashful and never had the nerve to tell her. I don't know if she thought of me in that way or not but, before we got to the age of recognizing boy-girl attractions, she had moved away. I still had plenty of time to learn about girls, but in the meantime, I had to conquer the more important parts of growing up.

During my early childhood, my parents took me to church every Sunday, but my father's half-sister Vada had the most influence on

me when it came to spiritual matters. Aunt Vada was a very dedicated Christian, who showed her love for the Lord to both my sister and me. I believe her influence was the major source of my decision to become a Christian. When I was eight, a young preacher by the name of David Garland preached to us one Sunday. Things my aunt said, along with the young preacher's sermon, encouraged me to step up and say I wanted to be a Christian, and that I wanted to have Christ in my life. I was baptized in the Baptist Church even though I didn't understand all that meant. Once I became a Christian, I believed I really had to be good to be accepted by God. It didn't take long before I realized that being good was going be very hard. I was constantly afraid that I might do things wrong, and it made me very timid. This was good in a way because it kept me out of a lot of trouble, but it strongly affected my self-confidence.

One of my uncles who lived next door thought I needed to gain some confidence, so he taught me how to box. Since I was always shorter than my peers, he knew I should learn to defend myself. He was right. When I was in the second grade, my mother insisted that I wear a funny looking hat during the winter days. That hat looked like a court jester's hat straight out of the 16th century. It was red and black with pointed ear covers and a triangular front that came down toward my nose. To make things worse, I had to wear knickers for pants. On the playground at school, the bully type boys teased me about the hat, but I obeyed my mother and kept it on my head.

One day a boy jerked that hat off my head and ran away with it, so I chased him and knocked him down. He got up and came at me to start a fight. He figured I would run, but I remembered what my uncle had taught me and stood my ground. I put up my fists and started to fight. Soon there was a crowd circling around to cheer us on. After a few punches and a bloody nose, my short height and reach finally did me in. About that time, my bossy, older sister showed up, and to my embarrassment, stopped the fight. Well, I lost the battle, but I won the war. The teacher took both of us fighters inside to get the whole story. She took my side and punished the bully. I never had trouble with him again, and nobody tried to pick fights with me anymore.

I was extremely introverted through the seventh grade and not a particularly good student. Because of my strict raising, I was scared to do

anything that would get me in trouble at home or school, and I was afraid of discipline because it hurt. It took a humiliating experience to make me want to study and improve my grades. At a parent teachers' meeting, the teacher approached my mother to talk about my school grades. She told my mother I was not capable of learning and making good grades. Mother thought she meant I was stupid. That made me "fightin" mad, and I said, "I'll show her."

By the end of eighth grade, I was an "A" rather than a "C" student and excelled in introductory algebra and diagramming sentences. I liked American history, but didn't like medieval history or mythology, and literature was never my thing. In civics class I completed my assignments, but never enjoyed it. In high school, I took all the math and science I could get. I really enjoyed trigonometry, analytical geometry, and mechanical drawing, as well as chemistry and physics. I did all my homework during study hall and never took anything home. With my improved grades, I was inducted into the Beta Club—the highest academic honor in our school—and graduated in the top ten of my class.

I was a good student, but too short to be involved in sports. For a time in my junior year, I tried baseball, but I couldn't catch up to those with more experience. By my senior year, I finally grew tall enough to play football. I could pass and run with the best of the boys during our physical education classes. One day the football coach saw me and said, "Why don't you come out for football."

"I'm already a senior, and I wish I could," I told him. Then I explained to him that since my mother worked, I had many chores to do at home. I didn't get to play but being asked by the coach made me proud.

Three

Sprouting my Wings

Betsy

I n early 1940, a stray dog—I named her Betsy—showed up at our house. She was a beautiful German shepherd, very gentle and strong. We were inseparable. During that time, my father built a wagon for me. The wooden wagon had wheels with metal rims, hard rubber tires, and a metal steering bar. I attached Betsy to the front end to make it like a dogsled with wheels. We lived about a quarter mile from the high school, so I let her pull me towards the high school and then back to the house. One evening

Betsy and I were resting at the high school when my dad came by in his car. Betsy recognized that automobile and took off after it. She raced his car, pulling me in the wagon at around thirty miles an hour. When we reached the house, the dog didn't bother to go up the driveway. She went across the ditch, and of course, I got thrown into the ditch. I still have a visible scar on my leg from the bad cut I received from that rough landing.

World War II helped move America out of the Depression. In 1941, I was eleven years old and in the sixth grade when Pearl Harbor was bombed. The U. S. declared war on Japan, and Germany declared war on us. The movie news reels showed Germany overrunning Europe and Japan advancing in the Pacific. Those images made quite an impression on me.

My family did its part to support the war effort. Everything was rationed–gasoline, groceries, silk hose, and sugar. Every bit of scrap metal was saved to send to the collection point, where the metal was recycled into parts for new airplanes and guns. Bacon grease was also saved to help make ammunition and bombs. We had a victory garden and about two acres of land that we cultivated for our food. My grandfather was an expert planter and gardener.

My interest in aviation was piqued during the war years. My favorite playground and hideaway were at the end of the grass field behind my house where small airplanes occasionally landed. This grass field ran from the small woods behind our property all the way to Whitehaven High School— about 1500 feet. A pre-World War II Globe Swift attempted to land on the grass strip, but instead crashed into the trees in the woods. I remember seeing the airplane after the accident and realized that somebody had probably been hurt.

My friends and I had many adventures playing in those woods. But when the war came along that all changed, and the field became a much more exciting and fascinating playground. Squadrons of airplanes flew over my house and convoys of Army trucks and military equipment traveled down the two-lane highway. All the neighborhood boys gathered on the field behind our house with our wooden guns and acted like soldiers. We bought books on how to train to be soldiers and learned jujitsu. We practiced charging and dropping on the ground using our gun butts to support us as we fell.

To support the war effort and to train its students, the local high school

built a facility to teach military aircraft mechanics. The grass field near the school was filled with decommissioned airplanes that had to be taken apart and rebuilt. Most of those planes were outmoded and not up to the task of fighting the Germans and Japanese, but they were good for training mechanics. The planes were kept in an unrestricted area that my friends and I could access. We imagined we could fly in open cockpit trainers and pretended we were piloting bombers and fighters. Airplanes like the Bell Air-cobra P-39 fighter and Douglas A-20 light bomber were ready and waiting for our exploration. Even an old Stearman trainer biplane was there. The neighborhood boys and I imagined we were bombing Germans and Japanese just like we saw in the movies. I became an expert at shooting down enemy airplanes, making me an "Ace" before I was thirteen.

The government-built airfields everywhere, totally mobilizing the country for the war effort. Memphis airport became an Army/Air Force ferry command post. Our next-door neighbor, a captain in the Army Air Corps stationed at the Ferry Command, took me on a tour of many of those military planes. I later learned that women piloted those large and medium size bombers from the manufacturer to the deployment sites where the bombers were shipped overseas.

My dad encouraged my aviation interest. He used his creativity and expert building skills to create a fabric and balsa wood model of an early military fighter. It was a biplane like the Stearman biplane that was built to train military pilots. He added a scale model pilot and gunner and a tiny machine gun mounted in the rear seat. He painted the fuselage army olive drab and the wings orange. After displaying his work for all to see, he gave it to me. I believe my dad also had a secret desire to be involved in aviation.

Four

Dealing with Dad

E ven though my father did many good things like giving me the model airplane, I didn't often see his softer side. He was tough on me and my sister. I thought he was partial to her, and I had a difficult time feeling close to him. His expectations for me were quite high. Maybe he thought showing me affection would keep me from becoming a man. Due to the Christian influence of my Aunt Veda, I was active in church. Dad often said, "Charles has enough religion for the whole family."

That was not the only difference I had with my dad. His excessive drinking drove a wedge between us. Often, he came home from work after spending a lot of time in a "beer joint." He was not a pleasant man after drinking too much. During those times, I was scared. He and mother often got into fights–screaming and carrying on. Sometimes I saw evidence he had physically abused my mother. Dad's tendency toward a bad temper often got out of hand as evidenced by his throwing things across the room and breaking dishes. Sometimes he passed out and went into a state like an epileptic seizure. Mother, my sister, or I could usually revive him with a solution of water and ammonia which calmed him down. I didn't think he was an actual epileptic.

My mother, like so many women in her time, endured living with a drinking man. She drank too—especially when friends came over. But in my early years, she kept her drinking under control. She always took my side and did her best to protect me and my sister from my dad's abuse when he'd had too much. Mother worked hard to make sure I had as normal a

childhood as possible, even when things were anything but "normal" at home.

Despite our differences, Dad had a positive influence on my mechanical ability, which eventually led to my desire to be an engineer. He was a great carpenter and could fix about anything that broke down at home. For a long time, I really wanted a big "erector set", but didn't think I would ever get even a small one. An erector set was a collection of metal construction parts—girders, flat plates, screws, nuts, and all sorts of construction parts.

When I was around eleven, Dad really surprised me. It was close to my birthday and since I was sick, I was lying on the living room couch. Dad came down the stairs with this big red box. It did not take me long to figure out that inside that box was an erector set. That helped me to get better fast. Dad took the time to show me how to put the parts together to make a model elevator tower. Before long I was building cranes, trucks, and other industrial machines. At first, some of the moving parts didn't work well, but eventually I learned to carefully follow the directions and build with precision. It wanted to prove to my dad that I could accomplish any task I attempted.

When I was fourteen years old, my interest in the technical and mechanical things of life made me want to get a summer job as a stock boy in an auto parts business. Some of my friends were already working in a parts' place in Memphis near where my dad worked in an electro-plating shop. I believed that working hard was a good thing, and I liked the idea of having my own spending money. I told my father he could drop me off at the parts' store every day during the summer. My father did not see it that way. He was a proud man who wanted to control everyone, and he didn't want me to work and be independent. He thought he was supposed to bring home the income.

One evening during dinner, we began arguing about me going to work. If he could rant and rave, I could too. I got up from the table and picked up my chair and threw it across the room just like he had done on several occasions. I angrily stormed out of the house and headed to the field behind our house. I was so mad I didn't care about the consequences. Dad must have realized what a monster he had created since I was imitating his bad behavior. Later, he found me, apologized, and agreed I could work in the auto parts store during the summer. He even agreed to take me to my

job on the way to his shop. I think he finally realized that I was more of a man than he thought.

That summer, I learned a lot about auto parts and other things from some of my fellow employees. That helped me realize it could be a rough world when you are on your own. Most of the boys working there were older than me and as usual, I was smaller than all of them. Sometimes I got bullied, but I just ignored them and did my work. One of the guys tried to encourage me to get one of the worldly girls working there to teach me worldly ways. She was about three or four years older than I was and quite good looking. My mother and daddy, however, had taught me the dangers of getting involved with that kind of girl.

One of the good things I learned while working in the parts shop was to assert myself. The boss was careful not to make me move boxes or parts that were heavy. One day I went to the boss and asked, "Why don't you call me when you have some big lifting jobs?"

He sat in his big chair with all ten of his fingers together. He thought for a minute then said he thought I was too small to do the job, and that he didn't want me to get hurt. I told him I thought I was strong enough to try.

He relented and said, "I'll call you next time, but it won't be really heavy." Soon he had a load of things that needed to be put up, and he sent me to do it, along with the bigger boys. I learned early on that speaking up was an important part of growing up.

One of the problems in riding with my dad to work and back home was that he stopped at the beer joint every evening. I got bored while he drank and talked with other people. On occasion he would offer me a drink of beer, but I didn't like the taste. Not only was I bored, but I was afraid Dad would consume too much beer and go home with the wrong attitude. When I was with him, this didn't happen as often, and it helped for us to be together.

The next summer, Dad wanted me to come to work in the plating shop so he could teach me to be an electroplater. I wanted to learn new skills, so I agreed to try. It didn't take me long to discover that electroplating was a lot harder than it looked. The only part I enjoyed involved taking lamps apart, rewiring them, and putting them back together after they were electroplated.

Five

Love of Adventure

Some of my friends and I built model airplanes. My friends liked to build solid models that looked good on a display shelf. I looked at my display planes for a while, but that didn't excite me. I wanted adventure. My model airplanes had to fly. I started building rubber band powered airplanes out of balsa wood and special tissue paper.

I built several rubber-powered models. Most were scaled military airplanes like the Grumman F6F Hellcat, the North American AT-6 Texan, and the Ryan PT-19 training airplane. At the local theater, I saw all these planes in action during the WWII news reels. Sometimes to simulate more war-like realism, I took one of my worn models and put a firecracker in the fuselage. After getting the model ready to fly, I lit the firecracker and launched the plane, simulating it being shot down like I saw on the silver screen.

My skill as a model builder was in demand. Other people paid me to make display models for them. That experience helped nurture my desire to be an entrepreneur. I never dreamed one day I would train as a Navy taxi pilot riding in real airplanes like the models I had built.

As a Boy Scout, I liked camping, hiking, and any outdoor activity. I worked hard to earn the merit badges required to increase my rank. Military training was a part of scouting at the time, and all scouts wanted to be warriors. I became good at leading drills and marching. I rose to the rank of Star Scout before I transferred to the Sea Scouts, which was the boy's program affiliated with the Navy.

When I was seventeen years old, one of my best friends and Boy Scout partner, Donald, and I decided we would take an adventurous trip to Hardy, Arkansas. Neither of us had ever ridden a train, so that was an adventure. Since my father was born in Hardy, I had traveled there by car many times. My aunt and uncle were living on a ranch out in the countryside and Donald, and I were invited to stay with them. However, we were determined to camp out. Another compelling reason to go to Hardy was that I had some distant, good looking girl cousins living there. I was disappointed to learn from my mother that blood kin were off limits even if they were distant cousins. The picture I painted of those cousins might have been the real reason Donald agreed to go with me. The main reason was that we were good friends and both of us really liked to camp.

Donald and I had been Boy Scouts since we were twelve, and between us had plenty of camping experience. We bought jungle hammocks from the army surplus store for $3.50 each. Somehow, we managed to carry a load of camping equipment on the train, and we were prepared for whatever a few days in the woods would bring.

My parents drove us to the train station in downtown Memphis. With no parent or chaperone, we couldn't wait for the 150-mile train ride to begin. The trip was just as exciting as we thought it would be. Soon after we left the train station, we crossed the mighty Mississippi River onto the Arkansas Delta and saw the foothills of the Ozark Mountains. Riding the train through the mountains was a great thrill. I had been raised on flat land, and for some reason getting to high land was like magic to me. That stayed with me all my life, and to this day, I love being in the hills and mountains seeing God's creation spread before me. Perhaps that is why aviation also appealed to me.

Going around the mountains was exciting too. The train ran parallel to the beautiful Spring River which flowed past Hardy, Arkansas. We were fascinated by the clear water that looked green and the occasional waterfall coming down from the Ozark Mountains in Missouri. We finally reached Hardy. Aunt Vada and Uncle Sewell met us at the train station.

After a delicious meal and a good night's sleep at the ranch, we stocked up on food supplies and were ready for our outdoor adventure. Uncle Sewell took us to a mountain close to the river and left us to set up camp. We tied our jungle hammocks to sturdy trees and cleared a place for a fire

so we could prepare lunch. We fished and explored the river for safe places to swim. Both Donald and I were well trained in swimming and through Scouts had earned lifesaving badges.

Our next challenge was to rent a flat bottom boat and travel upriver to the Girl Scout camp to see one of the girls we knew from Whitehaven High School. We didn't expect the trip to be so difficult. Rowing was strenuous since we were going upstream but easier when we got out of the boat and towed it over the rapids. Navigating the rapids and small waterfalls required us to go around them or wade through them while towing the boat. A canoe would have been easier to manage.

Finally, after rowing and towing, we saw a pier where several girls were swimming and diving. The girls seemed as excited about seeing a couple of crazy boys in a flat bottom boat coming towards the pier as we were to get there. Although we were not football jocks, the girls recognized our adventurous spirit and welcomed us. We tied the boat to the pier and went swimming with them, since going ashore at the camp was off limits. Soon it was time to start back down the river to get to our campsite before dark. We were happy we had accomplished our mission and met some new girls. Going down river was more fun than coming upriver, but a bit more dangerous. As we picked up considerable speed, it was hard to control the boat. We were dumped out twice, but never lost the boat. We just hung on and stayed with it. After a few hours, we finally saw our campsite. It didn't take long to get to sleep that night.

That summer, my dad rebuilt an old bicycle for me, since we could not afford a new one. I was thrilled to get any kind of bike, especially such a rugged one. When I turned fifteen, I begged for a Sears & Roebuck modification kit that would motorize my bicycle. After much cajoling, I finally convinced Dad to buy the modification. I was thrilled when he took me to his shop and there was my old bicycle modified with a new wheel and motor. After a thorough check out, I enjoyed fun rides around our neighborhood, but I wanted to be able to carry a passenger. Dad helped me build a sheet metal seat on top of the engine. The eighteen by twelve-inch seat quickly got too hot, so we attached a cushion.

One day my grandmother called the high school office to tell them my dog, Betsy, was found at the state line about a mile away. When the principal called me into his office, I asked permission to leave school to

get my dog. "How are you going to do that," he asked. "I am going to ride the dog on my motorbike." I explained. "My dog rides on my bike all the time. She can balance on the seat I built and ride that way for hours."

"A boy's gotta have his dog, so go ahead," the principal said. I walked the quarter of a mile home, got on my bike, and rode the two-lane main highway to the Mississippi State line. Betsy jumped up on the seat, and we started down the highway. Other vehicles on the highway slowed down to watch us pass by. After I got a Cushman scooter, Betsy rode between my legs on the floorboard. Both Betsy and I agreed, "A boy's just gotta have his dog."

Six

Girlfriends

Because I was shorter than most of the boys and girls in my class, I had very few opportunities to date in high school. Girls I could attract were usually about two years younger than me. During my senior year, Joan agreed to date me. At sixteen, I was finally old enough to drive the family car. We went out a couple of times, but even though she was a nice, pretty girl, I didn't feel comfortable with her. She put the word out that she liked me, and it got back to my sister. My sister asked me, "Why didn't you kiss her goodnight? She really wants you to." But I never did. I believe it was because I was still too timid. Did I ever have a lot to learn!

I told my dad that I didn't care much for Joan, but my grandmother told me to really get acquainted with her because she was from a high-class family near my neighborhood. The last time we dated, I borrowed my dad's car, and on the way home, I hit another car's left rear bumper with my right front fender. It put a dent in our car but did not damage the other car, so we drove off. Nobody was hurt, but I was shaken up. I was going to have to tell Dad I wrecked the car.

My parents were in bed, so I knocked on their door, and said "I have something to tell you. I put a dent in the front fender of the car." Mother smiled a bit. I believe she was glad that I had arrived home safely.

Dad said, "I thought you didn't like that girl." And that was the last I heard about it.

After my graduation from high school, I was interested in Judy who lived a block down the street from me. She was the girlfriend of one of my

best friends, Steven. He really liked that girl, but after she met me, she invited me to come down to see her and meet her parents. I really liked Judy and her parents, and I hit it off with them. I asked Judy out even though I knew she was my best friend's girlfriend.

Steven was the most active Christian of the guys I ran around with. I believed that Judy was not particularly happy about that fact. Also, I was already out of high school and older than Steven and Joan. Steven took offense when Judy and I started to date. At the time, we were both Sea Scouts, and during one of our meetings the leader could see the animosity between us. The leader, who was a former boxer, saw that Steven was ready to battle it out with me. "Let's get the boxing gloves and go at it," the leader suggested. Steven was an undisciplined and untrained boxer, but my uncle's training finally paid off for me.

After I bloodied his nose, Steven and I shook hands and became best friends again. That was probably the result of us learning how fickle Judy was. She had already set her sights on Martin, a pal to both Steven and me.

I sat around daydreaming because Judy had broken my heart, but soon I realized she was playing all ends against the middle. She ended up marrying Martin who she dumped, too. During an overseas tour of duty with the Air Force, Martin received a Dear John letter from her. Fortunately, I met another wonderful girl and ended up marrying her.

Seven

Changing Times

E ven though WWII was "over there," everything about the war affected my teenage years. War related industries—aviation in particular— boomed and triggered my imagination of what I wanted to do after high school. When word came that Hitler had been defeated in April 1945 and that Japan had surrendered in August 1945, the people of Memphis erupted in celebration. Church bells rang, horns blew, and people shot off guns. There was singing and dancing in the streets. Only later did people begin to understand the devastation and genocide in Europe and learn of the atomic bomb that had fallen on Japan. Warfare had changed forever. At that point, no one gave much thought to how the end of the war and the shuttering of all the defense industries would affect the US economy and job opportunities.

At age seventeen, two years after the end of the war, I found a way to work on and fly in airplanes. The war in the skies had been a major influence in my life, so I joined the Naval Air Force Reserve. As with many young people, becoming a military pilot had been my dream for a long time. In the reserves I could only learn to maintain airplanes, but it would be a start. Flight training was still years away. I heard from some of my high school friends that I could also enroll in the Weekend Warrior program offered at the Memphis Naval Air Station in Millington, Tennessee.

Millington was only 28 miles from my home in Whitehaven, so being a Weekend Warrior didn't interfere with going to high school. As a

Weekend Warrior, I was required to attend training one weekend a month and take a two-week cruise each summer. Several of my high school friends also joined when I did, and all of us were eventually assigned to Naval Air Reserve squadron VF 791. We didn't know that squadron would be one of the first called to active duty in the Korean War.

We all had to go through boot camp training. Those of us who had spent several years in the Boy Scouts and Sea Scouts were well prepared. We had been taught to march, maintain discipline, and follow orders. Some of our Scout leaders had military experience they shared with us. When I was called to active duty during the Korean War, I discovered I had better marching, training, and leadership skills than those coming from the regular Navy. And as a Sea Scout, I also had experience and duty on a Navy ship.

I will never forget my first experience on a Navy Landing Ship Tank (LST) on the Mississippi River. The LST was an amphibious vessel designed to land battle-ready tanks, troops and supplies directly onto enemy shores. All of us Sea Scouts dressed in Navy dungarees and felt like we were real sailors. We had seen news reels of amphibious operations during World War II, and finally, we were a part of an actual Navy ship. We were made temporary crew members and were given important watch positions at the bow, the stern, and for the port and starboard watches. In Sea Scouts I had risen to the rank of Boatswains Mate Second Class. Maybe that is why I was assigned to the bridge to receive reports from each of the watches.

When Sea Scouts assigned to the watches saw something, they reported to me, and I passed it on to the Chief Boatswains Mate who reported to the Helmsman. If we had been in a real battle this would have been an important position. All we had to look for was logs or other floating debris and report it. After a few hours of idle chatter and good views of the river and small towns, I got a report of possible danger. The young Sea Scout on the bow watch called and said excitingly "there is a large log dead ahead off the starboard bow." I passed it on to the Navy Boatswains mate word for word.

He laughed a little and said, "Now which is it? Is it dead ahead or off the starboard bow? It can't be both."

Highly embarrassed, I called back to the bow watch and said, "Now

which is it? Is it dead ahead or off the starboard bow?" If we had been in the regular Navy, we would have been reprimanded by the Chief Boatswain Mate. This was a good lesson for me to learn. Think before speaking. This was not my last time to make a mistake in my naval career, but each time I used my mistake to help me become a better sailor and aircraft mechanic.

My next experience on a ship would be on an aircraft carrier. In the meantime, there were several turning points in my life before I was called to active duty during the Korean War.

I was still going to high school and in the Reserves, interested in going to college, and getting a scholarship through Naval ROTC. I was very conscientious about my studies, always did my homework, and did very well in school. My interest was in mathematics and physics, and I really wanted to be a mechanical engineer or architect. I was in the Beta Club, which was an honorary club for high school students, and graduated with honors from high school in June 1948. But my grades and schoolwork were not good enough for earning the NROTC scholarship. Taking tests under pressure never was my strong point, and I froze when it came time to take the test and didn't get a high enough score.

I was extremely disappointed to not have a scholarship, and my parents couldn't afford to send me to college. They did not encourage me to get a BS, and in fact, strongly opposed the idea. My father thought it was a waste of time and money, and he had little respect for those who got degrees. He believed in working with his hands and thought that was what a man did to support his family. In the late 1940s going to college wasn't common like it is today.

To keep my parents happy and because I had no other options, I decided to work full time with my dad as an electroplater. I had worked two summers with him in the downtown shop of Memphis Plating Company. Then Dad decided to open his own electroplating business in the backyard of our house, so we didn't have far to go to work.

Electroplating was a dangerous job. I worked with several toxic chemicals–muriatic acid, cyanide, and strong lye solutions. Also, I had to run powerful polishing machines, which sometimes caught the articles that we were polishing, and gave us nicks on our hands. If I splashed some of the chemicals in the little nicks, my hands ached all night long.

Once day, I was working in the shop by myself. I was polishing the brass

parts of an old antique lamp. One of the parts was a circle that was about 5 inches in diameter. The metal of that part was only on the outer edge of the circle, and it was about one quarter of an inch wide. It was very sharp on the inside of the circle. The polishing wheel caught it and my fingers at the same time. My hand was lacerated, and I thought I was going to lose a finger. I made it to the front door of the house to show my mother what I had done. She immediately got some antiseptic and started wrapping my hand. Then I passed out and slid down the door. Mother revived me and got me onto the couch to lie down while she worked on my hand. She did a good job and thought it wasn't necessary to get stitches. I was unable to work for a long time while my hand healed.

I really enjoyed taking an old piece of metal and turning it into something else. A friend of mine said he wanted me to look at an old silver service to see if I could restore it. I asked him how much he wanted and couldn't resist his three-dollar offer. The set consisted of a teapot, cream and sugar pots, and a coffeepot. The pieces were filthy and covered with coal dust, so I had to dip them in lye and clean them well. The top to the teapot was missing, so I used the coffeepot top to make a mold that I used to make a lid for the teapot. It took me about a year in my spare time to go through the process of cleaning the silver service and then silver-plating it to make it beautiful again. When I finished it, I gave it to my mother because I owed her about $75. She gladly accepted that as payment for the loan. She hung on to that silver service for many years and one day she sent it to me as a gift. It is now worth about $2000.

Some of the other items that we repaired and electroplated were brass lamps and other antiques. We used silver, brass, nickel, and chrome plating. Since alcoholic beverages were still prohibited in the state of Mississippi and other nearby states, Dad often received handguns from whiskey runners to electroplate. With no prohibition in Tennessee, it was legal for us to repair those guns. The whiskey runners were very particular about their finished guns. They had to look perfect and perform up to their standards.

Since I didn't particularly enjoy the electroplating work, I was glad for a change of pace to serve as a Weekend Warrior at Millington. I eagerly looked forward to a long break and my first two weeks cruise with the Naval Reserve. The two weeks cruise training was mostly boot camp training, but I did get to ride in an airplane for the first time in my life.

I had three flights in a "Consolidated PBY Catalina."—an amphibious aircraft which was quite popular during World War II as a rescue aircraft. It didn't ride very well—much like riding on an umbrella in turbulent weather. An old expression goes like this, "The airplane cruised 100 Knots (115 miles an hour) and went up and down at 100 knots." Most of us young recruits sat in the back with our heads in a bucket, which made it an uncomfortable flight. In the three flights I made in this airplane, I had motion sickness, but eventually learned to conquer that problem.

While in the Naval Reserve, I was encouraged to take the entrance exam for the Naval Academy at Annapolis, Maryland. I wanted to try but knew it would be a daunting task with four days of testing about everything that I knew or didn't know. The most unfair thing about it was that if I had received a Congressional appointment, I would have only had to take two days of testing. If I'd had two years of college, I would only have had three days of testing. If I had received a Congressional appointment and had two years of college, I would only have had one day of testing. During my four days of testing, I tried but realized it was way beyond my capabilities. I was disappointed not to have passed, but later realized it wasn't meant to be and that God had other plans for me.

My next two-week cruise began about June 1949. For this trip, I was selected to ride in a naval transport aircraft called an R4D along with many other recruits. This airplane was like the Douglas DC-3 and like the Douglas C-47, which was used extensively in World War II to transport troops, cargo, and paratroopers. It also was an extremely popular airline aircraft but had been transformed into a Naval Reserve aircraft with the words US NAVY emblazoned on the body and a big red painted stripe wrapped around the fuselage. I was excited to pack my gear and head to the Naval Air Station at Pensacola, Florida. That was my first time to get a feel of real Navy life.

My best memory of that trip was a one-day trip on the aircraft carrier, USS John Cabot. The USS *Cabot* (CVL-28/AVT-3) was an Independence-class aircraft carrier in the United States Navy—the second ship to carry the name. The *Cabot* was commissioned in 1943 and served until 1947 and then re-commissioned as a training carrier from 1948 to 1955.

We put out to sea in the Gulf of Mexico and got far enough for the carrier to begin flight operations. It was the first time for some of the flight

cadets to make a carrier landing. The airplane they flew was the North American SNJ Trainer. My eyes were opened during that trip as I watched the landing exercises.

Navy carrier aircraft had a tail hook on the aft fuselage of the plane. This tail hook was extended on landing and supposed to catch one of several wires. One of the students touched down on the deck but did not catch any of the wires. The plane went off the side of the deck, not off the ship but just to the edge. One wheel hung over the side, but the pilot was able to get out and get back on the ship. Several crew members went out to the airplane and crawled onto the wing sticking up in the air and tilted the airplane back onto the ship. They saved the airplane, but there were some scary moments. The men were awfully close to the ship's edge and could have fallen into the water.

All ended well, and we saw no more accidents that day. We returned to the dock and went to our rooms to think about what had happened. I realized that potential dangers were ahead, but it still didn't deter me from wanting to fly. "Someday I will learn to fly," I told myself. "I don't know if it will be for the Navy, but I WILL learn to fly."

The Pensacola Naval Air Station was a great place to have reserve duty for two weeks. The white sandy beaches and beautiful Gulf of Mexico offered fun-filled recreation when I was not on the job. I was careful in the water and avoided the stinging jellyfish, but some in my group were not so fortunate. We had to work hard while at Pensacola, and there was not much play time. Our job was to train to take care of airplanes. My group learned how to refuel the planes and manage other maintenance functions. I was sad when the two weeks came to an end, and I had to return to the electroplating job.

Eight

Turning Points

During 1949 and 1950, two turning points changed the direction of my life. I had been out of high school for over year when I met Mary Gibson at a high school football game. I was almost nineteen years old, but Mary was only sixteen and still in the tenth grade. She was with a couple of girls that I already knew—one of whom was a former girlfriend. After getting Mary's telephone number, we dated often and soon found ourselves talking about a future together. By today's standards, we were both young, but in the late 1940s many young people married at an early age.

Mary was one of seven siblings. Her two older sisters, Clara and Otis were married with families of their own. Her living brothers were Fred, Ed, and Richard. Another brother, Al, endured some of the fiercest fighting in Europe during World War II, but was killed in a motorcycle accident when he returned home. Since all three of her brothers were interested in aviation and flying, we had a lot in common. Richard and I became close friends after I started dating Mary. She was well protected by her brothers, but they trusted me to go out with their sister since I had a good reputation for respecting girls. I enjoyed doing things with her brothers like learning tricks on the monkey bars. We also had fun tearing up an old Crosley car while driving and dodging trees in the backyard of their place. When we banged up the radiator, we put a bucket full of water in the front and kept driving it until the car fell apart.

Mary learned she had diabetes when she was thirteen years old. There was nothing about Mary's appearance that indicated she had a physical

problem. She managed well and took good care of herself, except that she had to take shots every day. My grandmother warned me several times that Mary's diabetes could become an issue if we decided to get married. Love is blind, and I decided to trust our future to the Lord.

While courting Mary, my unhappiness in working for my father as an electroplater grew stronger. In November 1949, I decided to go on active duty with the Naval Reserve. I became a full time Station Keeper at the Millington, Tennessee Naval Air Station. I thought I would get a chance to spend more time working with airplanes. Just like in the other branches of the military, a Navy recruit didn't get desired duty until he had proven himself. I was assigned to work in the hydraulics shop in the hangar. I helped to change gigantic aircraft tires which was a backbreaking job for me since I was still small. I did my best and worked hard at it until I got a toothache one day and reported to the Navy dentist. He pulled my tooth and sent me back to duty. The leading enlisted man allowed me to sit down while they worked. When an officer came by, I didn't stand up at attention until prodded by another airman. The leading enlisted man told the officer that I just had a tooth pulled. "That's okay," the officer said, "Sit back down." I was fortunate that I didn't get into trouble. That experience taught me to respect the officers no matter how badly I felt. If I had been in battle, I couldn't have stopped fighting because I had a toothache or other minor malady.

Even though I worked hard at my job, I was still not happy. I decided to talk to the top Chief Petty Officer. He told me to sit down and asked about my situation. "I want to work on airplanes and get out on the flight line so that I can learn how aircraft operate," I explained.

"Well, I don't really have an opening right now," he said, "but I'll keep you in mind." That talk helped my self-confidence, and I think he respected me for speaking up.

At the end of every workday—about 1630 hours—I heard this announcement from the hanger speaker, "Now hear this, clean sweep down fore and aft, empty all spit kits, and paint pots." This meant it was time to find a broom and start sweeping down the hangar to clean out all foreign objects. Every day I grabbed that broom and swept as thoroughly as possible. One day I heard an announcement over the loudspeaker, "Airman Charles Dixon report to the top Chief Petty Officer immediately." I hurried to his office wondering what I had done wrong.

"Airman Dixon," he said, "I've been watching you carefully and you appear to be a hard worker. I want you to report to the flight line tomorrow."

"Thank you, sir. I'll be there."

"Don't call me sir. It's Chief."

I worked on the flight line for about three months. Since the Navy didn't have fuel to fly those airplanes, they were often grounded. I did get to run the engines to keep them from freezing up, but there was not much else to do. In the Navy, however, they want you to keep busy, so I washed and waxed airplanes until I felt waxed. Once again, I was bored and still not learning much about airplanes. If that was what the Navy was going to be like, I much preferred resigning my station keeper duties and going back to being a naval reserve "weekend warrior." Since my status was active reserve, I had a right to do this, but the personal officer did not like it. He said, "you told me you wanted to make the Navy a career. I have to let you out, but I will get you back as soon as I can." I didn't know it at the time, but the peacetime Navy was not going to last. God had other exciting plans for me, and the Navy was not through with me yet.

I felt I had no other choice than to go back to work for my dad. I think my dad was happy, but I was disappointed. It appeared it was my destiny to work for him and take over his shop someday, so I went back home to live and work. It was not all bad since I had more time with Mary, who was good for my morale.

Our relationship was growing, and we realized that we were very much in love. Mary and I talked seriously about getting married. We were young, but I knew I could hold a good job and be a good provider. Mary was concerned about telling her parents, and since she was only sixteen years old, we thought we'd better wait. Meanwhile, the world was changing and the unrest in Korea was growing.

In early 1950, I learned the Navy had activated my old squadron VF 791. Mary and I knew that it wouldn't be long before I would have to report for active duty. Like many young people during World War II, we thought getting married was the right thing to do before I went off to war. We had unrealistic high hopes that I might be able to take her with me if I wasn't ordered overseas. We nervously waited for the official paperwork. I was ordered to report on October 5, 1950, which gave us some time to tell our parents and make wedding plans.

Nine

Wedding Bells

M ary was still nervous about approaching her parents, and she suggested we elope. I knew people who had gone to Hernando, Mississippi to get married by a justice of peace. Hernando was not far from us just across the Mississippi state line. We started to drive to Hernando, but I grew uneasy with the idea of eloping. I told Mary I would go talk to her father so that we could get married the right way. She agreed.

When the time came for us to talk to Mr. Gibson, Mary was afraid and went inside. I sat down on the porch with her father and explained that I had been called to active duty and that we wanted to get married before I left. To my surprise her father said, "Well, her mother and I have been expecting this. But let me tell you one important thing. You are making a vow to God—not to Mary, not to yourself, not to us, but to God—that you will be married for a lifetime." I told him that I agreed with him and planned to stick to that.

Then it was time to face my parents. The next day, Mary and I went to my house and told my parents that we were getting married. They also said, "We've been expecting this. When's it going to happen?" Since I would be leaving in October, we knew that we had to get busy planning the wedding. We set the date for July 31, 1950. There was no time or money to plan a big wedding. We would exchange our vows in Mary's home.

When I returned to the Naval Reserve as a weekend warrior, they put me in a different reserve squadron than the VF791. It was fortunate for me since the VF 791 squadron reported to active duty in July 1950.

I still had to take a two-week cruise in June. Before the cruise I was an Airman First Class, which meant I wore three green stripes on my uniform. Because I outranked many of the other cruise members, I was selected to ride to Pensacola Naval Air Station on a Grumman TBM Avenger. That type of airplane had dropped many torpedoes during World War II, and many young pilots had lost their lives in that kind of plane.

The TBM could carry four crewmen besides the pilot. Since I was given first choice of a seat, I chose the gunners seat of the airplane, which was inside of a bubble on top of the airplane. There were two younger airmen below me. They had not flown very much, if any. I was sure I'd gotten over my airsickness, but just in case, I drank a Coca-Cola before the flight, which settled my stomach. It was a good thing, because the two airmen below were airsick, and the smell was terrible. I pulled up my legs to my stomach and tightened my belt, and I didn't get sick. The trip down to Pensacola was good otherwise. It was a thrill to watch a group of Grumman F6F Hellcat's flying formation beside us.

After arriving at the Pensacola Naval Air Station, we got our duty assignments. I was assigned to an F6F Hellcat to keep it refueled and help with loading ordnance. At the end of the first week, I was riding on the running board of a pickup truck that was taking us to our airplane. The truck came close to the plane and slowed down enough for me to jump off while it was still moving. It was moving faster than I thought. I rolled down on my left shoulder and was unable to stand up. Someone said, "Don't raise your left arm," but it was too late. My cracked collarbone hurt so bad I passed out, and the next thing I knew I was in the hospital. The medics put my arm in a sling and told me the collarbone would heal itself. I could not put on my Navy white jumper because I couldn't raise my arm. The jumper had to be cut out so I could pull it over my head.

Several other airmen were also injured on that cruise. The Navy arranged for a transport airplane, an R4D, to take us all back to Millington Naval Air Station. Some of the old Navy hands had unflattering names for us, but let's just say they called us misfits. I spent two weeks in the Navy hospital at Millington before they let me go back home to my job as an electroplater. The Navy hospital is not like a regular hospital. If you can move, they put you to work. I could still walk and use one arm, so they made me sweep and swab the floor. I was not too happy about that.

I could have recovered at home, but the Navy wanted to make sure I was getting well before they let me go. I couldn't move that left arm very well for about two months, so I couldn't work much for my dad.

Mary and I spent a lot of time together counting the days until our wedding on July 31. The joyous day finally arrived and since neither one of us had been to East Tennessee, we decided to take our honeymoon in Chattanooga. I had seen a few smaller mountains in Texas and wanted to see the higher mountains of East Tennessee. My old, high-mileage 1940 Chevrolet sedan made the long drive to Chattanooga from Memphis. The first night we stayed in a large hotel and were rather disturbed when they put us in a room with twin beds. We were so young the attendant at the registration desk thought we were brother and sister. We convinced him we were married, and he put us in a room with one bed. The price was too high for us to stay in that hotel for more than one night, so we found a nice little cabin at the foothills of Lookout Mountain. It was quiet and—I guess you'd say—a romantic place.

After one week, we ran out of money and headed for home. We didn't travel far before the battery ran down and we had to find a mechanic to fix the problem. It wasn't the battery; it was a problem with the voltage regulator. The shady mechanic sold us a battery and didn't tell us about the voltage regulator. We continued toward home, and the battery started to go down again. Once again, we got the battery charged and continued on our way. After sunset, our lights began to dim, so we found another service station to get help. I had run out of cash and only had one dollar in my checking account. I was able to convince the service station manager to charge our battery for a dollar, and I wrote him a check. I was broke, but we made it home safely. What a way to start a marriage!

Mary and I moved into a small garage apartment near my former house, which was now my place of employment. It was only about a quarter of a mile away—as the crow flies—with a cow pasture in between. It was the same pasture where I had played soldier with my friends during the war. I could almost see my old house from my new one.

Now that the vacation part of the honeymoon was over, we had three months to learn about married life before I had to report for active duty. My salary was sufficient to support our marriage and the garage apartment for the three months. Once we were living on an Airman First Class pay,

it was going to be a problem. We decided that when I was deployed, Mary would move back home with her parents. I hoped to arrange for her to be with me if I was assigned stateside, but the possibility was slim. My friends that stayed in the VF 791 squadron had already been assigned to a Carrier Air Group of the USS Boxer aircraft carrier. They were on their way to Korea.

Mary's family struggled financially more than mine. They were not saints, but they were active Christians and a joy to be with. My parents, by this time, were both alcoholics and difficult to be around. In addition, my mother was having a hard time letting her little boy go. She made it difficult for Mary, since she thought that Mary was not good enough for me. I look back now and believe that if we had lived around my parents much longer, we would have divorced. I loved my parents but putting up with their drinking was a severe problem. To make matters worse, we had to move out of our apartment and live with them for a short time.

While we were still in the garage apartment, we encountered a serious problem. My family knew the people who owned the house adjacent to our garage apartment, and nobody dreamed we would ever have a problem with them. One day while I was at work, the man of the house came to visit. Mary was an attractive and sweet young lady, and she never thought that this man would try to take advantage of her. He grabbed her and was out of control before she broke loose from him and ran to the car to get away. She came to the shop where I was working with my father and told us what happened. My father knew the man and didn't want to believe he would do such a thing. He finally came around after seeing how shook-up Mary was. He and Mother said that we would have to move out and stay with them until I left for the Navy. We had no alternative. It was for the best, but it was a difficult month.

During that time, my parents planned a trip to New Orleans to visit my sister and her husband, and we were invited to go along. Mary also had a sister living in Mississippi—only fifty miles from New Orleans. We thought we would have a chance to see both sisters. My father drove, and we sat in the back enjoying the eight-hour trip. We stayed with my sister one night and then I asked my dad if Mary and I could borrow the car to drive to Picayune, Mississippi to see Mary's sister.

We had a nice visit with Mary's sister and got back late in the evening

the next day to discover that my parents had been out drinking with some other folks. I learned that my dad had consumed a bottle of gin, and as usual when he was drunk, took out his anger on me. He told me I didn't care anything about my own family—only Mary's. He was so mad he slapped me and almost knocked me down. I knew it was the liquor talking, so I just took it. The trip back to Memphis was not very enjoyable, especially for Mary. I'm sure she wondered if she was going to have to put up with that the rest of her life. We were thankful there were only a few more days before I would leave, and she could go back to live with her parents.

Ten

For Duty or Further Transfer

On October 5, 1950, I packed my sea bag and caught a ride to Millington, Naval Air Station to join up with my group that was headed for active duty. They separated us into smaller groups of around ten to fifteen men. Two men in my group were World War II veterans who had stayed in the Naval Reserve to give them a little extra funding for school while on the G.I. Bill. A first-class petty officer was selected to lead our group. Since World War II, he had earned a law degree and was practicing law. I don't believe he was very happy about being recalled. However, he was a good man, and I trusted his leadership.

Everyone in our group was given the same orders, "for duty or further transfer at the Naval Air Station Alameda, California." Our leader passed out our American Airlines tickets and told us what day and time to arrive at the airport for our flight to California. That gave me a couple more days to go home and say goodbye again. I was sad to leave and quite scared for my future since I was surely headed to Korea.

Once on the plane, I found a place to settle down. Most military passengers were given two seats. Like the World War II veterans, we were treated with respect and given special privileges. At that time, most airplanes that flew to the West coast had to make multiple stops for fuel and to pick up additional passengers. After one fuel stop, we were given blankets and pillows so we could go to sleep when we got back in the air. I remember one attractive stewardess came over and tucked me in. I enjoyed the special treatment, but it made me sad knowing I was leaving Mary.

Since I didn't know where I was going, I wasn't very optimistic about seeing her again anytime soon.

We landed at the San Francisco airport across the bay from the Alameda Naval Air Station and boarded a bus. Under other circumstances, riding around San Francisco would have been fun. It was different from any place I'd seen before with lots of hills and strange buildings. I could see the Golden Gate Bridge as we traveled across the Bay Bridge to Treasure Island. There was a naval base at Treasure Island which was used to ship out recruits for duty in Korea. Our group got off the bus and what I saw made me nervous. The fellows there didn't look very happy about shipping out. My group was told to get on another bus with the destination of the Alameda Naval Air Station.

The Alameda Naval Air Station was a better-looking place. We were driven to the enlisted men's quarters where we found our bunks and lockers for our sea bags and personal equipment. We had chow in the mess hall before turning in for the night. We were awakened early and told to dress in working clothes, then after breakfast we were briefed and told where to report. I was assigned to the flight line chief at the hangar for Fleet Aircraft Service Squadron 8 (FASRON 8). That was great news! I knew it would not be as boring as the flight line at the Millington Naval Air Station. Since we were at war, there would be plenty of aircraft operations.

FASRON 8 was a good squadron for me to learn about a lot of airplanes. That was what I had wanted for a long time. Most naval aircraft squadrons had only one or two types of airplanes, but my squadron served many airplanes. We helped support many of the Carrier Aircraft Groups that were headed for Korea. During the early part of the Korean War, most of the airplanes in service were World War II fighter aircraft.

Two of our aircraft were Grumman F6 F Hellcat's. These aircraft were used as the utility aircraft for our pilots to get their required time in the air. After a while on the flight line, I was chosen to be plane captain for one of those aircraft. A plane captain had to make sure the airplane was air worthy. That job required me to perform all regular maintenance, clean the plane, and make sure it was ready to fly on a moment's notice.

When I began my service in FASRON 8, my military rank was Airman First Class. FASRON 8 was not only a maintenance squadron for airplanes, but it was also a transition squadron for personnel. For the

two years I worked there, my orders said, "for duty or further transfer." Whenever an aircraft carrier arrived at Alameda Naval Air Station, I got nervous. Usually, those carriers were looking for personnel and airplanes. During my second week in FASRON 8, the aircraft carrier Princeton docked and announced they were looking for petty officers. Since I was still an airman first class, I got to stay on duty in Alameda.

I decided to take a big risk and send for Mary, not knowing when I might be called for duty on a carrier. I didn't have money to pay for her trip to California, but I didn't let that stop me. I was fortunate to have good friends who were willing to lend me money and agreed that I could pay them back later. I sent Mary the money to fly from Memphis to San Francisco with a little extra for expenses. Within three weeks after arriving in Alameda, California, I had my bride on her way to be with me.

Mary had never been on an airplane before. In 1950, airline flying was mostly reserved for the financially well off or military personnel in transit. Mary was getting a rare privilege for people with our standard of living. Flying all the way to the West coast by herself was a scary event, but she really wanted to be with me, even if it was only for a few days or weeks.

Mary's ticket was with Trans World Airlines (TWA) on the beautiful Lockheed Constellation (Connie). The Connie was a propeller-driven airliner with a curved fuselage and a streamline shape. It was powered by four 18-cylinder radial Wright R-3350 engines and distinguished by a triple-tail design and dolphin-shaped fuselage. It had four engines running when Mary left Memphis for San Francisco, but one of them quit before reaching its destination. For a young lady on her first flight, this was very traumatic. The pilot diverted to Phoenix, Arizona and landed safely. I didn't know that her arrival had been delayed when my friend and I left Alameda to head to the San Francisco airport.

Kent was a true friend to help me any time I needed it. He wanted to share the joyous experience of seeing me reunited with my bride. We had an interesting trip to the San Francisco airport, since we had no car and relied on the bus system.

Since Kent and I couldn't afford a hotel in downtown San Francisco, we registered at the YMCA and quickly settled into our room before exploring Market Street. There were stores to see in every direction we walked. We came across one store that looked like a pawn shop. In the

window there was a box filled with jewelry–watches, bracelets, necklaces, and rings. Since they all looked good, I paid $50 for the whole box. I only had $50 to spare and since I wanted to have something for Mary when she arrived, I bought the box of jewelry. After I returned to the Y and was resting on my bunk, I thought about my impulsiveness. I couldn't afford that jewelry but later discovered it was a good purchase.

The next morning, we caught a bus for the thirty-minute ride to the airport. Mary's plane was scheduled to arrive at 11 o'clock. Kent and I managed to travel without any luggage, so all I had to carry was that box of jewelry. I did have a toothbrush that I put it in the laces in the back of my official Navy uniform pants. My pants were the old-fashioned type with thirteen buttons in the front—representing the 13 original colonies—and a crisscross shoelace on the back that I tightened to make my pants fit my waist. As I was getting off the bus, my jumper rose up and showed the toothbrush in my laces. I heard someone say, "He sure is traveling light." That's the kind of thing a sailor did during my Navy days.

Mary's airplane was delayed for an hour, and that delay seemed to last forever. When I saw her get off the plane, it was a joyous moment. The three of us boarded a bus for San Francisco and then caught another bus for Alameda. After an awfully long ride, we arrived at the Naval Air Station. I had arranged for living quarters on the base for us in Carrier Courts which was named for the many aircraft carriers that arrived and departed the station. It had been a long trip for Mary, and she was not feeling very well. The main thing was she was there with me, and we were both incredibly happy. We were off on a brand-new adventure!

It did not take long for us to learn how poor we were. To live in California on an Airman First Class pay was difficult—if not impossible. Living in Carrier Courts was expensive. I was able to get some subsistence pay for being married, but it didn't help much. We had to walk about a mile to get groceries, and since we couldn't carry much at a time, we had to make repeat trips every week. We had no automobile. We were poor and homesick—which made us lean on each other for support. It was difficult for Mary when I had to stay at the base every fourth weekend. My job was to stand watch, so I slept and ate on the base. It was also depressing to stand watch in the inclement weather. The year I arrived, it rained or

drizzled constantly from October to March of the following year. After March, the weather began to improve.

To help our homesickness, Mary and I decided to visit a distant relative of Mary's who lived in Daly City near San Francisco. We learned to navigate the public transportation system. First, we had to catch a bus to cross the Oakland Bay Bridge into San Francisco. Then we had to catch a streetcar that traveled down Market Street and through the tunnel of Twin Peaks to Daly City on the other side.

Mary's relative was a cousin who had never married. We never considered her an old maid, for she was a young acting and gracious person. She cheerfully welcomed us and was glad to hear about her relatives back in our hometown. Back in the early 1950s, people didn't travel much, and the 2000 miles cross country trip to Memphis was difficult. The visit with Mary's cousin was uplifting and helped to alleviate our homesickness.

The types of homes in much of the San Francisco area seemed very strange to us. Many of them were Spanish in architecture—adobe-like homes with no separation between them. Property in San Francisco was expensive, so every inch of land was used, especially in the urban areas. The home of Mary's cousin was nice inside, but it was an attached home.

I soon realized that I had to advance in rank to make more money. My goal was to pass the test to become a Petty Officer Third Class. It took a lot of studying to advance to the next rank. Since we needed to find another place to live, I found military housing off base that was much cheaper. Then I needed to find an automobile. I had a good friend who was shipping out, and he let me buy his old 1933 Chevrolet for $75. It was not much of an automobile, but it worked. In its day, it was a very deluxe automobile. It had fancy wheels in the front fenders and a spare wheel on the back. The rag top sometimes leaked when it rained, but it was tolerable. It was painted a very faded dark green, but it was transportation. Hallelujah! It would've been very difficult, if we had moved before I got a car.

Petty Officer 3rd Class Charles J. Dixon

Our new apartment was at 1107C Eagle Avenue. It was upstairs and above a very cranky old woman who bumped her ceiling with a broom handle to let us know we were being too noisy. Most of the other neighbors were very friendly and helpful. They made us feel at home, and we needed that badly. One of our neighbors was a Navy cook who invited us over for delicious shrimp boils. The other military wives were helpful to Mary when I was off on duty. Many times, she relied on those women for encouragement and support.

One of our neighbors was an experienced automobile mechanic. He had been in World War II and was still in the Naval Reserves when he got called up to active duty. He helped me keep that old car going, and I learned a lot from him. I was already a good aircraft mechanic, so it wasn't hard to learn something about automobiles.

Even though Mary and I were not active Christians during our time in California, I believe the Lord was watching out for us. We did go to church occasionally but found it difficult to get active in a church since my orders still read "for duty or further transfer." We lived with the uncertainty that I might have to ship out to serve on the next aircraft carrier on a moment's notice. Nevertheless, I believe that the Lord was working on our behalf during our time in California. While I was still an Airman First Class, several aircraft carriers came into port at Alameda to pick up a new crew to prepare for the next tour. Some of the aircraft carriers were the Boxer, the Antietam, the Princeton, and Bonhomie Richard. Once again, they

recruited petty officers, so I didn't get called to ship out on an aircraft carrier.

I worked hard to advance in rank and received my promotion to Third Class Petty Officer Aviation Engine Mechanic in 1951. This promotion helped our finances considerably. When I learned that Mary was pregnant, I started studying for the next advance in rank to Second Class Petty Officer.

Eleven

Exciting and Frightening Events

When I was assigned to work on active aircraft, it was the opportunity I had been waiting for. I was finally part of the action. My squadron, FASRON 8, had numerous airplanes on the ramp that had seen or were going to see action in Korea. Some had come from the overhaul and repair facility located on the Alameda Naval Air Station. Some were being repaired in our squadron's hanger by the engineering airman and petty officers.

As a flight line mechanic, my duties were pre-flight the repaired aircraft before their required flight tests. In the Navy, the duties were like civilian general aviation pilot duties before flight. The pre-flight checklist had to be followed exactly to make it possible for a pilot to jump in very quickly for an emergency flight. I took my job seriously because I knew if the pilot got in trouble while in flight, I might get blamed.

I also served as plane captain or maintenance officer for a Grumman F6F Hellcat. The Hellcat was a renowned fighter airplane during World War II, but during my Navy career served as a utility aircraft for pilots to maintain their flight time.

Different types of engines required different procedures for starting and shutting down the engine. For example, the Douglas AD Skyraider had a Wright 3350 cubic inch radial engine. It had a different kind of carburetor than the F6F, and I had to be careful not to push the throttle all the way forward to shut it down. If fuel was left in the cylinders, the next person might find the engine jumping into full RPM. In one case,

an engine was completely pulled off an airplane. The last person who ran the AD had pushed the throttle forward and then brought it back. When I tried to start it, it began to run away. I cut my hand trying to find switches to shut down the engine. I did shut it down before it ran away, but I was so shaken up I had to sit in the cockpit for a while until my nerves relaxed. I reported the event to the flight line chief. It was a good thing that the Chief was a nice guy, or I could have gotten in serious trouble.

My next assignment was for night watch on the flight line. The late arriving planes had to be serviced and prepared for the next day's flight. A Twin-Engine Beechcraft SNB was used for night flying, and it was my job to top off the fuel. For our own safety, the night crews were told not to take a shortcut by crawling over the cockpit from one wing to the other. One night when I was in a hurry, I got careless, crawled over the cockpit, and put my knee through the windshield leaving a big crack and grounding that airplane until it could be repaired. I immediately went to the hangar to find a replacement windshield, but none was available. The worst part was that I had to wait until the next day to tell the chief on the flight line. I didn't sleep that night.

When I reported the accident to the Master Chief the next morning, he called my Chief Petty Officer and ordered us to go to the junkyard to find a new windshield. The way he said it made me believe I was in big trouble if we came back without one. I was really sweating it out when we came back empty-handed. All I got was a dressing down and told it better not happen again. I believe the Chief gave me the benefit of the doubt because I always worked hard and performed to the best of my ability.

Navy SNB-2—1950s Instrument Trainer

(A photograph of a 1950s twin-engine Navy SNB is provided. This type of airplane had a significant influence in my life. Not only did I make sure the airplane was airworthy before flight, but I also often became a crew member as an observer during instrument training flights. As discussed in the introduction of this book, I almost lost my life in a newer version of this type of airplane.)

As Plane Captain of a F6F, it was my responsibility to check everything on that airplane before it was to fly the next time. The plane was due for a 100-hour check in the hangar. After the engineering group checked it over thoroughly, the chief engineering officer called me in to show me the loose exhaust stack. I had overlooked it on my watch, and it could have caused a serious fire in flight. Again, I was just given a warning and told to be more careful during future inspections. I learned a good lesson and from that point on investigated every little item on all the airplanes on my watch. The safety of the pilot was at stake and my own pride wouldn't allow me to make any more mistakes.

My duties as a flight line mechanic became more interesting after I made Third Class Petty Officer and was trained to be a Navy taxi pilot. Before that, all I could do was sit in an airplane and rev and idle the engine. Now I could leave the tail untied and taxi the airplane out to

the compass row. At the compass row I taxied to the cup in the center of the compass row and put one wheel in a cup in the center of the compass. That maneuver held the airplane at the cup while the other wheel taxied around the compass row. My assistant directed me around the compass and had me stop at every cardinal point of the compass. I checked the magnetic compass with the actual heading in the airplane to see if it agreed. Normally, it should not agree because of the deviation of the magnetic compass from the real direction. I recorded that deviation on a chart attached to the magnetic compass. That was a tremendously important job since I didn't want to cause a navigation error which could cause an airplane to get lost. I did my best to make it right.

There were only two taxi pilots in my squadron, and I was glad to be chosen to do that important job. The other taxi pilot was a well-experienced World War II veteran. I learned a lot from him and soon was able to taxi many types of planes. Being a taxi pilot was about as close as I was going to get to being a Navy pilot. That experience gave me great training for the day I would learn to fly as a civilian pilot.

One day, our First-Class Petty Officer test pilot asked me if I wanted to fly with him on the T2V—a Navy jet trainer with two seats. I didn't hesitate because I knew he was a very safe pilot. On one occasion I watched him land an F9F jet in an emergency. The nose gear wouldn't come down, but fortunately, there was a dive break in front of the nose gear housing. He was able to deploy the dive break and use it as emergency landing gear. Sparks flew during the landing, but only the dive break was damaged.

Navy Lockheed T2V Airplane

In my Navy days, I didn't receive a lot of training for high altitude flight. The pilot just sat me down in the airplane and explained the oxygen mask, the ejection seat, parachute operation, and other good things to know in case of emergency. One of my jobs was to watch the warning light for low fuel and tell the pilot if that light came on. I think that job was mainly to make me feel important.

After the pilot climbed into the plane and fastened his seat belt, we were ready to go. The flight tower radioed instructions to taxi to the active runway. Once the tower gave clearance, the pilot turned onto the runway and accelerated for takeoff. I didn't realize how fast that airplane had to travel before lifting off. Much to my surprise, the plane traveled up to 130 knots or 149 mph and was still on the ground before we finally lifted off. As we climbed into the air, I could see the cities of San Francisco and Oakland beneath the wings. When our altitude reached around 30,000 feet, I could see the Sierra Nevada Mountains in the distance. On that beautiful day, the view of the snowcapped mountains was a sight to behold, and I completely forgot to watch for the flashing light. I was fortunate to fly in a jet airplane. Today that's an everyday occurrence, but back then it was phenomenal. Not only did I have a wonderful view, but I got to take the controls. That was definitely a highlight of my time in the Navy.

My flight on the jet was thrilling but was soon followed by a frightening event with serious consequences. My job as plane captain for the F6F was

to get one of two planes ready to fly. Two young pilots were going out for early morning flight training and a little fun. Three hours after takeoff, only one of the planes returned to the tarmac, and it was not my airplane. I asked the other pilot. "What happened to my airplane and pilot?" He said, "We went into some clouds and I didn't see what happened to him." I was scared to death. *Was it my fault! Did the airplane crash! Was he coming back?*

I checked out the airplane that made it back by looking at the cockpit instruments. Nothing seemed amiss until I noticed the G meter was showing about nine G's which was too high for that airplane. That meant the pilot was pulling loads nine times the weight of the airplane. On closer inspection, it looked like one of the wings was buckled. It soon became obvious that something disastrous happened to my airplane. The one that returned was extremely lucky.

That happened on a Friday, and I was off for the weekend, which was probably the worst few days I had spent in my life. Mary knew something was bothering me, so I told her my concerns. I heard nothing about the missing plane until I went back to the base on Monday. At first, no one told me what happened since the incident was still under investigation. It was eventually determined to be an accident attributed to pilot error. The two planes were doing aerobatics that exceeded the capability of the airplanes, and my plane crashed in the little town of Vacaville, California. The pilot did not survive. Much to my relief, I was never blamed for anything.

During my off hours, Mary and I explored California in our old 1933 Chevrolet. We drove across the Oakland Bay Bridge to San Francisco and Market Street where the streetcar tracks ran down the middle of the street. My narrow car tires just fit in in the streetcar track so we could follow the trolley down the hill. That old car took us up over Twin Peaks, down to the fisherman's wharf, and across the Golden Gate Bridge to Sausalito. We even drove it up into the mountains east of Oakland to Mount Diablo, which is Spanish for Devil's Mountain. The terrain was remote and arid. On the way up, we were shocked to come across hundreds of hairy, giant tarantulas crossing the road. We stayed in the car. Once those ugly spiders passed to the other side, we turned around and headed back down the mountain.

I thought it would be fun to put the old car into freewheeling mode while we drove down the hill. Freewheeling meant that the engine was no

longer connected to the wheels, and everything was free to let the wheels roll. It was not like the cars of today when you put them in overdrive, and you still have some braking. The Chevy's cooling fan was not running either on that hot day. The radiator went off like Old Faithful and sprayed rusty water all over the car. We were not far from a place to get water, but it took a while to clean that windshield so we could drive home. Even when the car had its problems and rain leaked through the rag roof, it was a blessing to us. Today, I am much more cautious and wouldn't go to the places we went in that old car. Since we didn't have much money, we created our own adventures and fun and didn't think too much about the consequences.

Our constant concern was that I would be shipped out. My sea bag stayed packed in case an incoming carrier needed a Third-Class Petty Officer. However, most of the carriers that came to port were looking for Airman and not Petty Officers, and I escaped deployment again.

My task of towing airplanes to the aircraft carrier Boxer, however, almost got me and another petty officer assigned to that ship. At lunch time we went to the officer of the deck who was on the gangplank and asked permission to get chow in the ship's mess hall. We told him we had been loading airplanes and had missed our lunch time. We were wearing our work dungarees and baseball hats, which was not the right attire for the ship. We ate a good lunch and then attempted to go ashore. The new officer of the day on the gangplank said we were not dressed appropriately to leave the ship. We tried to explain to him what happened, but our pleas fell on deaf ears, and we wondered if we were about to be shipped out. We were rescued when the Boatswain's Mate that was on duty earlier returned and explained our situation to the officer who then let us off. There seemed to be many ways that I could get in trouble, but I usually came out okay.

Charles and Mary

It was 1952, and I was about to become a father. Making Second Class Petty Officer helped somewhat to ease our financial worries and finding new friends at our apartment complex helped ease our homesickness. The ladies in our apartment complex who were experienced at having babies were a big help to Mary. Of course, the baby decided to come when I was on duty at the air base. The neighbors got Mary to the Naval Hospital and the doctors began to deliver the baby. When I received word from the ladies, I was not too sure I would get liberty to go be with her. I told my Chief Petty Officer, and he barked, "What are you doing here." When he heard my reason, he said, "You go right away to the Master Chief and tell him that your wife is having a baby, and that you need special liberty to go to the hospital."

When I arrived at the hospital, Mary was in labor, and they would not let me be with her like they do today. I had to sit outside and listen to her screams. It was a terrible and frightening time. When it was over, the doctor came out to me to tell me it was a boy, but the baby had died. It was a breech birth and the child had been deformed. Mary survived, but the pain of that loss left scars that affected her mentally for the rest of her life. She blamed herself and her diabetes since she had to inject herself with insulin every day. The insulin attacked the baby and caused his death. That meant we could not have our own children. That was tough for both of us to take, but much harder for Mary than for me. It was the worst part of my two years on active duty in the Navy.

Twelve

Our Kicks on Route 66

One of the great benefits of my time in the Navy was having thirty days of annual leave. During December 1951, Mary and I traveled back to Memphis. Since we couldn't afford to fly, we bought Trailways' bus tickets and left two weeks before Christmas. The bus route took us from Oakland, California to Arizona. The warm desert was interesting and new to us especially the tall Joshua trees that lined the road. The treacherous road from the desert up over the mountains into Kingman, AZ set our teeth on edge. We feared the bus would plunge thousands of feet into the valley. When we reached Route 66 heading east, we finally relaxed.

We got our "Kicks on Route 66" five years after that song was published and long before the TV show of the same name débuted. Route 66 traveled from Barstow, California through Arizona, New Mexico, Texas, Oklahoma, Missouri, and Illinois. It would have been fun to visit the Grand Canyon as we passed through Arizona, but the bus only stopped to pick up passengers and for meals.

In Gallup, New Mexico we stepped out of the bus to -5°F, which was very cold for a couple from California. It was also our first time to see Native Americans or Indians as we called them back then. The route took us almost 13,000 feet into the mountains past Albuquerque. The next major stop was in cold, snowy Amarillo, Texas. After being on the road day and night, we finally arrived in Oklahoma City, changed buses, and headed toward Memphis. After traveling around the clock for over two

thousand miles, we reached Whitehaven, Tennessee and were home for the holidays.

I hoped my father would put me to work in his electro-plating shop since I needed money to get back to California. Even though I didn't like that work, I had no choice but to accept his offer. Most of the time we stayed with my parents because his shop was in the backyard, but we did spend some time with Mary's parents also. We decided not to ride the bus back, so we needed to figure out how to return to the Navy base.

During the fifties, automobile dealers sent used cars to California because the prices were much higher in California. It was cheaper to lend used vehicles to drivers going to California than it was to ship them. I found a dealer that arranged for me to drive a 1949 Chrysler—a very fancy car—all the way to the West coast. Since I was young and eager to please, I did not read all the fine print in the agreement. I found out later, much to my chagrin, I was responsible for any repairs or damage made to the automobile.

We had a great Christmas, since I had our return trip all lined up. Since we had a large car and lots of room, my sister and Mary's sister decided to ride to California with us. I was not looking forward to driving five days with three women in the car, but we took turns driving. I was too nervous to close my eyes when one of them drove. We had our differences, but mostly we had a ball traveling in such a good automobile. At first, the going was slow as we rode through the small cities in Arkansas.

After we got to Oklahoma and back on Route 66, the cities were a little further apart and we made rather good time. Even though Route 66 was a two-lane road, we drove fast through Texas, but had to slow down when we got to Amarillo and the mountains around Albuquerque, New Mexico. Once the road straightened out, we could see miles ahead with no other cars in sight. None of us had ever ridden more than 70 miles an hour, but soon we were going at least 90. My sister liked to put her driving foot flat on the floor.

In Arizona, we started having trouble with the fuel pump. We managed to get off the road and get the pump fixed before it was too late. I had to fork over $13 which was a lot of money back then. I found out when we delivered the car to the California dealer that my money wasn't going to be

refunded. I learned a good lesson, but instead of complaining, I praised the Lord that we made it safely back to California with no further incidents.

I'd asked a friend to watch my old 1933 Chevrolet while we were back East. He forgot to crank the car and the battery died. I jump started the engine, went for supper, and forgot that it was running. When we were in bed, I heard something that sounded like a chicken clucking — "pluck cluck, pluck cluck." It finally dawned on me that the battery was fully charged, and the car was running.

Even though that old car enabled us to have a lot of fun, we needed something more dependable. A used car was all we could afford, and I finally found a 1941 Chevrolet sedan that looked in good shape. I had dreams of driving that car back to Memphis one day, but soon realized that car wasn't in good shape after all and needed a new engine. Sears had a rebuilt engine I could afford.

Mary and I made one more trip to Memphis during our two years in California. We decided we'd better not try to drive the car, so once again we rode the bus to Memphis with no idea how we would get back to the Navy base. I searched the newspapers and found a listing from a lady that needed someone to drive her car to California. That was ideal and much better than assuming liability for a dealer's car. The lady was going to California to meet her husband, an officer in the Army. She didn't want to drive the long distance alone, so our chauffeuring was a perfect fit for all of us. After adjusting to each other's unique personalities, we enjoyed one another's company.

Because it was winter, we drove the southern route back to California, which took us through El Paso, Tucson, and on to San Diego. It was wonderful to see new parts of the country for the first time. We visited Carlsbad Caverns and drove through the white sands of New Mexico. We toured Old Tucson, watched the Wild West shows, and the shootout at OK Corral. Hollywood was filming a Wild West movie on the site with superstars Darren McGavin and Joseph Cotton.

Our next destination was Davis-Monthan Air Force Base because Mary's brother was stationed there. The base played a strategic role in WWII as a storage facility for Army Air Force planes. In 1946, the newly activated Strategic Air Command (SAC) assumed control of the base. It had a high military classification and required visitors to be escorted

onto the base. As we drove around the back side of the base, I noticed old airplanes from WWII parked outside the gate, and then I saw another entrance to the base.

I pulled up to the entrance and asked the guard how to get to the main entrance. He noticed the sticker on the window of the car that showed it was owned by a commissioned officer. He said, "Just go right straight through here." I said, "OK" and proceeded to drive along the road taking me to the front entrance.

It was strange to see strategic bombers, like B-29s and B-50s, outside of the main gate. When I realized we were inside the base, I nervously approached a second guard to ask directions to the main entrance. The Air Force aviation policeman on duty demanded to see my credentials.

"What are you doing on the base?" he barked.

"We're here to see my brother-in-law." I showed him my naval military papers and explained that the guard at the rear entrance had let us in.

"The Visitor Center is about a mile up the road. Stop there and call your brother-in-law. You're not allowed to be on this base. I'm only letting you go because you are military."

I felt sorry for the guard that let us onto the base. I'm sure he was reprimanded and punished for allowing an unauthorized vehicle to enter a Strategic Air Command base.

The rest of our trip back to California was uneventful. We safely delivered our passenger and returned to our apartment. After such a long trip—with so many adventures—our little apartment in Alameda looked good to us. Now it was time to start planning my future.

Thirteen

College Bound

Since my two years of active duty in the Navy were ending, I began to dream again about going to college. I was twenty-two years old, had a wife to support, no money in the bank, and wondered how I could make it happen. On more than one occasion, I had young Navy Ensigns come to the flight line to fly one of the planes I had just taken through pre-flight. Most of them were not much older than I was, but they had advanced education. I knew that without college I could never be a naval aviator. Mary and I decided I should take advantage of the GI Bill to get an education. Mary also wanted to graduate from high school. We knew it wouldn't be easy and would be a struggle just to buy groceries.

When I told friends about my interest in college, some of the younger fellows gave me some good advice. Since I was going back to the South after my discharge, they gave me names of several engineering colleges such as Georgia Tech and the University of Tennessee. I knew I couldn't afford Georgia Tech's out-of-state tuition, and even though UT was in my home state, it was more than I could afford. One friend suggested Mississippi State College. It was out of state, but close to my hometown of Memphis. I applied and was accepted at MSC starting with the fall semester in September 1952. One problem remained. I was not due to be discharged from the Navy until October 1952. My Master Chief helped to arrange an early discharge, and I was able to report to college just two weeks after the semester began. Because I was a veteran, MSC was helpful in adjusting my schedule.

Our first place to live was in the college town of Starkville, Mississippi. We rented rooms in a house about three miles from the campus that was owned by a nice single woman. We only had a little kitchen, a bedroom, and a bathroom, but it was sufficient until we could find a cheaper place. The college had converted some old-World War II barracks into married couple's apartments. We put our names on a waiting list, and during my sophomore year, we were able to move into one of those apartments.

After we moved in, we met other married couples and veterans. We all worked hard but also enjoyed doing fun things together on holidays and weekends. We all had our own stories to tell, and sometimes we studied together. When some of the younger students came over to study with us, we encouraged them. They, in turn, respected us for overcoming the obstacles we faced in going to college.

In the four years since I had graduated from high school, I had forgotten a lot and needed to take remedial courses in Algebra and English. The Algebra came back to me quickly, but I had to work harder in English. I used my experiences in the Navy as topics for all the papers and reports I had to write for the English class. I believe I gave the English professor a good course in airplane mechanics and how to operate Navy fighter aircraft. These remedial courses put me behind schedule, so I had to take classes during the next year's summer semester. But by the end of that semester, I was caught up and ready to move into the aeronautical engineering school.

To help with expenses, I found a part-time job in the engineering lab. Professor Edwards, who was the department head, helped me land the job and continued to encourage me in many ways during my college years. He was impressed with my naval aircraft mechanic experience and wanted to use me to help build up the aircraft engine testing lab as well as complete the new wind tunnel.

The challenge was to make the wind tunnel fan fit properly into the tunnel. The clearance between the circular wall of the wind tunnel and the propeller blades had to be just the right distance. A lot of carpentry work and difficult sanding was required. My boss, Mr. Fultz, who worked for the laboratory as a full-time mechanic, was a patient man. Any time I made a mistake and worried about it, he said, "You'll never know the difference

100 years from now." Going to school and working was a full-time effort, so I was thankful for a stress-free job.

I wasn't the only one working hard. Mary took a part-time job in the school laundry to help with our finances. The laundry was an extremely hot facility, especially during the Mississippi summers. She received the incoming laundry and sometimes had to help with the cleaning and ironing. She earned a whopping 50 cents per hour during my first two years of college. I was getting rich earning 75 cents an hour at the aeronautical lab. With my $136 each month from the G.I. Bill and our two jobs, we were able to get by. We received no financial help or any other support during my four years of college, and we could honestly say we did it all ourselves. It was almost all work and no play. By the end of the first year, Mary completed her high school diploma, and I was in the groove of being back in school and organizing my time to get it all done.

We didn't have much time to socialize with the other students on the MSU campus. Most of them were single and hadn't been in military service. Our goals were different—work and study—and it showed up in the classroom. The professors recognized that I was there to get an education and not play. I was quite embarrassed in one of my classes when the professor chided the young college kids for not studying. He pointed me out and said, "You folks should be like Charles." I guess that's what you have to put up with when you work hard.

My sophomore year became more interesting and the studies harder. I was also given an interesting job in the lab. Mr. Fultz and I had the task of building up the aircraft engine laboratory. We started with an empty building made from concrete blocks which had two rooms about 20 x 15 feet in size. We built a small interior control room and mounted the engine in the outer room. A safety glass window separated the two rooms, allowing the running engine to be observed from the control room. The first challenge involved building the engine mounting system and welding it together. Arc welding was a new skill I had to learn and a fun thing to do. I was proud when I finally got my first engine mounted and running.

Professor Edwards was quite a collector of old aircraft engines, mountings, and many other airplane parts. The mezzanine floor of the laboratory was devoted to the storage of all his equipment. It was fun to go up there and search for an engine and the appropriate mount. I was

thrilled when I found two that matched. Then I had to locate the right carburetor and a club propeller to mount on the engine propeller shaft. The engine was a five-cylinder radial engine, the same type I had worked on in the Navy. My goal was to get it mounted and running and mount parts in the control room.

We rigged up a control panel, mixture controls, throttles, and other levers necessary to operate the engine. Connections to those controls ran down to the floor and under the wall in a channel between the two rooms to the engine. It was fun to scrounge for the parts and get them to work. We even had to make special tools for the project because we were not an engine shop. One tool was like a circular protractor that mounted around the shaft of the prop. It was marked off in degrees so we could set the timing of the engine.

The day finally came to start the engine. We filled up the fuel tank, put oil in the engine, and made sure everything was tightened down properly before we entered the control room and pushed the starter button. The engine stuttered, blasted out a bit of oil-soaked smoke, and sputtered to life. This feat did wonders for my confidence and boosted my determination to learn how to design better engines. My long-term goal at that time was to design aircraft power plants and make them more efficient. I already had experience in the Navy working with jet power plants and hoped my future career path involved working on those engines.

Some of my fellow students and professors in the aeronautical engineering department urged me to join the student branch of the National Institute for Aeronautical Sciences (IAS). Because of my leadership and experience in the Navy, it wasn't long before I was elected president of the local IAS group. I knew that job would mean more work, and I was already stretched to my limit. I had a hard time saying no to doing more than I should, especially when it involved aviation. It was common knowledge that if you wanted to get something done, find a busy person to do it.

In college, I was required to take a machine shop course which taught me how to use a lathe and how to put threads on bolts and screws. I made a variety of other parts using almost every other machine in the shop. That didn't make me a machinist, but it helped me learn what was involved in designing something as an engineer. I enjoyed building things with my

hands by using the proper tools, but it couldn't compete with the challenge of mathematics.

I took all the mathematics courses I could take in four years of college and made my best grades in those subjects. I was urged to become a member of honorary societies such as Kappa Mu Epsilon—the honorary mathematics society— and Phi Kappa Phi, for excelling in most other subjects. To my delight I was selected for the honorary engineering society, Tau Beta Pi. The initiation into that society was quite demanding.

The Tau Beta Pi initiation didn't involve any hazing, but we were required to perform a difficult task. I was given a block of wood and told to carve an extremely complicated scale model of the Tau Beta Pi symbol. I was given the choice of a cedar or mahogany wood block. I could use a pocketknife, sandpaper, and a micrometer. Upon completion, my scaled model would have to have the required dimensions with small tolerances. I chose the cedar wood because I thought it would be softer and easier to work with. That was a big mistake. Mahogany isn't that hard to carve, and it is less likely to break or crack.

Charles' Tau Beta Pi Symbol

I took the task seriously and spent two intense weeks trying to make the symbol as accurate as possible. Just as I finished, it cracked and broke.

The senior members of Tau Beta Pi were lenient with me, allowed me to glue it back together, and approved my task. A photograph of my actual completed model is shown in the previous figure.

After completing my sophomore year, I was tempted to become a military pilot by joining the Air National Guard in Meridian, Mississippi. That meant I would go on full-time active duty for at least four years with the Air National Guard. As a veteran of the Korean War, I was eligible for an officer's commission. Being a pilot in the Air Force wasn't the same as being a Naval Aviator, but it came pretty close. Another of my fellow students, who was a US Army veteran, wanted to fly as much as I did. I wanted to discuss this with my mentor, Professor Edwards before I decided,

During my lengthy appointment with Professor Edwards, we discussed all the pros and cons. He was convinced that I was doing too well in school to quit now. He told me that if I trained to be a pilot with the Air National Guard, I would never go back to college. I recalled how much he had done to help me with my education and decided to stay in college. The professor was so right.

My U.S. Army friend, Troy, joined the Air National Guard but soon became inactive. He told me the planes he was learning to fly were not well maintained and were dangerous. Troy got a private pilot license and bought a small private airplane. While flying, he was caught in a storm, the plane crashed, and he was killed.

Later I realized it was very providential that I did not join the Air National Guard. I would have been flying F-4 Phantom jets during the Vietnam War. Instead, I designed airplanes during that time and didn't risk becoming a POW in Vietnam. Thanks, Professor Edwards!

Learning to fly was still a top priority, so I joined the college glider flying club. As a Navy crew member, I had some stick time and knew a little bit about flying, but not as a pilot. Training to fly a glider was unique. The club had one training glider–a Sweitzer 119. It had a single wheel in the fuselage, and the wings had to be held up before the airplane started to move. A tow truck bed was stripped of its sideboards, and a seat for the instructor was attached to the truck bed. A 100-foot short towline was hooked to the glider at its release point.

The truck moved just fast enough for us to raise the wings and keep

them level while still rolling on the single wheel attached to the middle of the fuselage. Once that was mastered, the towline was lengthened, and we were towed faster until we began to fly on a straight runway. At the end of each of these operations, we released the towing cable. Before releasing the cable, we pushed the control stick forward to counteract a very severe pitch-up. Then the towline was made longer, and we were able to climb higher, but not too high, so we could land on the same runway we started on.

Schweizer 1-119 Glider

The runways on that old WWII Air Force base were exceptionally long. After we mastered these steps, we released the rope and flew a short distance before turning onto another runway that was about 45 degrees from the take-off runway. I finally rose about 20 feet off the ground and stalled the airplane which meant that the glider was out of control. I hit the ground hard, and the wheel was torn from under the airplane. I was not injured, but my pride was. My back was a little sore, but I helped tow the airplane back to the hangar.

After the glider was repaired, I, along with the rest of the club, went back to flying. Soon I was flying well enough to soar—if I could catch a thermal to help me climb. A thermal is a small whirlwind that forms under cumulus clouds that are near to your location. One day, I caught a thermal and managed to get about 1000 feet above the runway before starting to circle. I wanted to continue to climb. As I looked down at the ground, I saw my instructor walking in circles. I thought he was trying to tell me to come back and land because there are others waiting to fly.

When I landed, the instructor walked up to me, pulled out a great big wet towel and hit me over the head with it. He said, "Why didn't you keep circling and go on up?"

"I thought you meant for me to land," I said. I never caught a thermal again before graduating from college. My next opportunity to learn to fly would be after finishing college and going to work.

Fourteen

My Junior Year

In 1953, Redstone Arsenal in Huntsville, Alabama buzzed with activity. Many of the world's top rocket scientists, including the famous German Werner von Braun relocated there. Von Braun and his team surrendered to the U.S. military at the end of World War II to ensure that they were not captured by the advancing Soviets or shot by the Nazis.

After my second year at MSC, Mary and I headed to Huntsville where I worked as a co-op engineer. My project focused on research and aerodynamic analysis of a new type of Army missile for its ground troops. I didn't work directly with von Braun but was thrilled to be at the same location.

Huntsville experienced a population explosion after the end of World War II. A severe housing shortage meant that Mary and I had a tough time finding a place to live. First, I moved into a small room in a boarding house while Mary stayed back in Starkville, Mississippi. I finally found a tiny apartment in the old Cotton Mill Village that had at one time housed cotton mill workers. Our civil service pay didn't cover rent for a better place, but it didn't matter to us as long as we were together.

My assigned work group had just organized, and there were no desks to spare. I ended up working on the corner of Bob's desk. Bob didn't mind sharing his desk with me and seemed happy to have me there. What a great opportunity to receive on-the-job aeronautical engineering training from an experienced engineer.

Bob, a World War II veteran, had seen real action in Germany near

the end of the war. His U.S. 45[th] Infantry Division entered and liberated the Dachau Concentration Camp on April 29, 1945. He showed me a documentary book of the atrocities that were committed by the German SS troops. Bob had tears in his eyes as he showed me the pictures. I had seen Holocaust pictures in the movie news reels, but what I saw in the book made me sick. My emotions from the War were still raw, and I struggled to respect the Germans working at Redstone Arsenal.

Many of my colleagues considered the German scientists to be egotistical. They wondered if the U.S. could accomplish anything by working with them. I learned later that gossip couldn't be trusted and that the U.S. profited from their good work. I also gained a better understanding of the character of Werner von Braun. I like to brag that I had lunch with him, even though I ate on one side of the cafeteria, and he ate on the other side. Some of my associates in Huntsville told me that Von Braun professed to be a Christian. Later, I learned that von Braun often quoted the words of Abraham Lincoln, *"It is no longer enough that we pray that God may be on our side. We must learn again to pray that we may be on God's side."*

Mary and I needed to pray more to be on God's side. Although we were professing Christians while living in Huntsville, we were not active. We attended church occasionally— just enough to say that we had not forgotten our upbringing. Going to college and working part time kept us busy. I am convinced that God looked out for us, and that we were a part of his plan. It was a miracle that we were going to college. We were totally without resources when I left the Navy. Two years later, one door after another had opened, making it possible to for me to dream of my graduation and future career.

Even though I worked full time at Redstone, we spent our off days learning about our surroundings. We liked to take nighttime drives to the top of Mount Sano where we could look down on the city of Huntsville. Under a clear sky, we could see the bright lights spread before us and identify some of the landmarks. We had done the same thing when we climbed the hills near Alameda on the east side of Oakland, California to view the bay area. I had grown up on the flat lands of Tennessee and seeing mountain top vistas thrilled me. I also knew that von Braun and his family lived on Mount Sano, and I wanted to advance in the scientific community just like him.

After a much-needed respite from my studies during the summer of 1953, time came to move back to Mississippi State and buckle down for my junior year of college. Mary and I packed all our belongings in our 1941 Chevrolet and returned to Starkville.

My last few semesters of college proved to be difficult, and Mary struggled to finish her high school classes. My courses required intense studying and tests, including a tough final exam for every course. Somehow with Mary's support and tolerance, I managed to get through it all and maintain exceptional grades and rapport with both my fellow students and professors. Mathematics and engineering courses were my favorites, but I struggled with English and Chemistry.

Both of us were fortunate to find part time work in the Aero Physics Department (APD). My aeronautical engineering professors recommended me for the position of hangar mechanic. Mary knew someone in the APD who helped her find a job plotting flight test data. Most of the work in my junior year involved drilling holes in the wings of airplanes. These holes were carefully placed to allow boundary layer control by sucking air through the holes.

Boundary layer control prevented the air flow from separating from the wing. All aircraft were limited in their minimum speed by this flow separation. With boundary layer control, this minimum speed can be reduced. That means the airplane can take off and land at a lower speed, resulting in shorter take-off and landing distances. The APD had contracts from the Office of Naval Research that supported their research. I helped get the planes in the air for flight testing, and Mary analyzed the test data. Well known scientist Dr. August Raspet directed the work.

Although Raspet's close friends called him Gus, his students didn't dare take such liberties. We called him Dr. Raspet. Much of the original boundary layer flight test research was conducted on sailplanes at APD. Dr. Raspet had become a well-known sailplane research scientist, and in 1949, he became the sailplane projects leader for the engineering station at Mississippi State College. From 1953 until his untimely death in 1960, he served as Head of the Aero Physics Department at MSC. The Flight Research Laboratory at Mississippi State University is named for him.

A highlight of my college career came when I worked for Dr. Raspet from 1954 through 1956 during my junior and senior years in college. The

work interested me, and I met some of the most well-known scientists and test pilots of the industry

Dr. Raspet suggested I participate in a wind tunnel test to receive college credit. The Aeronautical Engineering Department had two wind tunnels built for student training. The one I used for my project was a blow-through tunnel housed in a former military barracks. Air was drawn in from one end of the building and blown out the other end. The test section, in the center of the building, measured about 4 feet by 4 feet. After training and a thorough check out, I ran the tunnel and collected the data. Most of the time I worked by myself.

I correlated the level of drag noise inside of a cavity caused by air blowing over the cavity. This simulated an open bay door of a bomber or any other hole in the fuselage of an airplane. To keep the test simple, I built a cavity in the shape of a cylindrical tube with an adjustable plug that could be moved to change the depth of the circular cavity. I cut a circular hole in the middle of the floor of the test section where I inserted my circular cavity. Then I placed a microphone in center of the plug in the cylinder and connected it to an analog recorder to correlate with the drag of the cavity.

A wake rake, a series of small tubes mounted normal to the wind tunnel floor, measured the drag. It measured total and static pressures which determined momentum drag. This rake was set at a series of stations across the wind tunnel and downstream of the cavity. This method took days to complete. After a successful test, I completed a paper for presentation at a student Institute of Aeronautics Science (IAS) meeting. The report was titled "Correlation of Sound Level and Drag of a Cavity."

The IAS meeting held at Virginia Polytechnic Institute in Blacksburg, Virginia gave me my first experience at writing and presenting a technical paper. I recall I did OK, but I didn't win any awards. I realized I still had a lot to learn. I made the mistake of changing the name of the report just before presenting the paper. My plain old Navy no-nonsense way was still with me. I thought it more practical to change the word *cavity* to *hole*. One of the judges asked why I changed the name. I said, "That's what it is, a circular hole."

Dr. Raspet chided me for making the change, since the word cavity relates to the aviation world. I have presented many technical papers since then at IAS meetings— now called American Institute of Aeronautics and

64

Astronautics, AIAA—and I am still learning about writing and presenting papers.

Dr. Raspet didn't give up on me. He and some the other college professors recommended me to be awarded the Snedden Scholarship. I received $500.00 to further my education— a lot of money in 1954. I did some soul searching as to what I wanted to do with the money. Since I had been offered another summer co-op job, this time with Boeing Airplane Company in Seattle, that option rose to the top of my list. I wanted to go back to the West Coast and Boeing gave me that opportunity. My decision didn't please Dr. Raspet. Perhaps he didn't think I made a wise decision, or maybe he wanted me to spend my summer working with him. But I had made up my mind to go. I believed I would gain a lot of practical experience that would help me find a good engineering position after graduation.

After making the decision, I had to figure out how Mary & I would get from Starkville to Seattle. I looked for a more dependable car than my 1941 Chevrolet and settled on a used and worn 1952 Ford sedan. I planned to drive it all the way to Seattle but didn't consider the problems that could occur with such a well-worn car. I just forged ahead.

Fifteen

Washington Bound

My adventurous mother-in-law was determined to travel with us. As a young girl, Mrs. Gibson had lost her mother, along with many other family members, during a flu epidemic. Her father had already died leaving her and her siblings without guardians. Her brothers and sisters were separated and sent to various places. One of her sisters now lived to the eastern part of Washington State. Our trip provided a great opportunity for Mrs. Gibson to visit her sister.

Mary and I gathered our few belongings and proceeded to Memphis to pick up Mrs. Gibson. None of us had seen the northwestern part of the United States, and since it was summer, we decided to drive that route. We planned to travel through South Dakota, Montana, Idaho, and finally into Washington.

After leaving Tennessee, we crossed into Arkansas and headed north following the Missouri River. Although we were not on the river itself, we charted a path like the Lewis and Clark expedition. We travelled to Sioux City, Iowa, on to Sioux Falls, South Dakota, and headed to Rapid City so we could visit Mount Rushmore. As we traveled through the Badlands, I recalled the many Westerns I had seen where the outlaws had hidden in the desolate brown hills.

Mount Rushmore impressed us with its grander. As we looked up at the carvings of some of the greatest presidents of this country, we were spellbound. When we reached Montana, we saw signs for the Little Bighorn Battlefield where General Custer made his last stand. When I

saw the big field at this historical site, I visualized the battle between the Indians and soldiers I had seen portrayed in the movies.

Somewhere in Montana the car started rattling and kept getting worse the more we drove. We made it to a city where a mechanic told us the driveshaft bearing was wearing out. If the driveshaft had fallen off, we would have been in real trouble. After repairs were made, we continued our trip. Once again, I could see how God had helped us in our time of need.

Interstate highways were still in the future when we made this trip. In retrospect, we saw a lot more beauty than we would have on any interstate. I imagined the challenges that the early pioneers faced driving their horses and wagons over such rough trails. We were often surprised when we looked into the distance and thought we would arrive at our next destination in about 30 minutes. Then a canyon would appear, and it took an hour to drive down into the canyon before making our way up to the other side. Many years later, I flew over the same area, and I looked down at those canyons and remembered the long trips through them.

We crossed the Bitterroot Mountains then headed toward Spokane, Washington. We saw many beautiful vistas of God's creation in the distance—lush valleys and snowcapped mountains. After crossing over the mountains, we finally arrived in Spokane, which looked more like a desert. We did not see greenery again until we reached the Cascade Mountains east of Seattle.

Our next stop was Yakima, Washington where Mrs. Gibson's was reunited with her sister. It was a great reunion for them since it been many years since they had seen each other. They were raised in different homes and had searched for each other for a long time. It was obvious that her sister had a lot of Native American in her. No doubt there was some intermarriage with the Cherokee or Choctaws in past generations. After a day or two in Yakima, we said goodbye to Mrs. Gibson and her family and headed toward Seattle to begin our adventure with the Boeing Airplane Company

As we crossed over the Cascade Mountains the scenery began to green up again. Unlike the dry Spokane area, the land west of the Cascade Mountains was well-watered and warmer in the winter than other parts of the country at the same latitude. The Japanese Current in the Pacific Ocean flows in that area making western Washington a bit warmer and

wetter in the spring and summertime. We were surprised, however, to experience temperatures around 98 degrees. This unexpected phenomenon surprised the engineers who had designed the highways and bridges. The highways buckled, and the rotating bridge across Lake Washington locked up due to the expansion. I guess we Southerners brought the heat with us.

Finding a place to live became our top priority. We looked in the newspapers until we found a little apartment located on the east side of Beacon Hill, not too far from Boeing. Our landlord and his family were nice people who liked to take their boat salmon fishing. They shared a lot of their catch with us—our first introduction to salmon country.

Sixteen

Boeing Aircraft Company

Several other co-op students and I finally started to work. Boeing required us to attend an orientation course to learn how to be an employee. One of the nice things they did for us was to host a salmon barbecue for our families. We all decided there was nothing better anywhere than barbecue salmon from the Northwest. Every time I've returned to Seattle on business, I've always found time to feast on salmon and halibut.

In 1955, the Boeing military division of the company was still building B-52s and some B 47s. I was assigned to the B-52 power plant engineering group. As a co-op I was assigned some mundane, repetitive work that wasn't at all exciting. I plotted a lot of power curves and learned pretty quickly that if I was going to work in the power plant part of the aircraft business, I would have to join a company that designed and manufactured the engines. I began to look around Boeing to see what other kind of work was available.

One of the disciplines that appealed to me was working as a manufacturer's representative to the airplane maintenance companies. I told the Boeing department that handled that effort I might be interested in working with them. They told me to give them a call after graduation if I wanted to apply. Although I didn't particularly like my internship, I still worked hard and tried to learn as much as I could. The people I met and the experiences I had proved to be of great help in my future.

My experience with one employee, whom I will call Jim, was not so good. One day Jim asked me to go flying with him. A free airplane ride in

Jim's Fairchild PT 19 sounded exciting. The PT 19 was primarily a trainer used by the military to train beginning pilots. The airplane was a low-wing monoplane with two open cockpits. I had been in many airplanes in the Navy but had never flown in an open cockpit aircraft. The surplus airplane had been rebuilt and looked good.

When we arrived at the airport, the weather was quite nice, at least on the ground. I was told to bring a warm coat for much cooler weather. Jim gave me a parachute to wear, and then we crawled into the plane and locked the seatbelt in place. We lifted off into the blue sky. I was surprised to learn that he was taking me flying around Mount Rainier at about 10,000 feet. The snow-capped mountain was a beautiful and thrilling sight to see from the open cockpit. At that moment I couldn't have been happier, even though I was extremely cold at 10,000 feet. Soon we headed back to the airport and did a few unusual maneuvers, just for fun of it, before landing safely.

Fairchild PT-19

Mt. Rainier
15000-foot Altitude

As I unbuckled my seatbelt and took off my parachute, Jim surprised me when he said, "Normally, when I have people fly with me, we share the cost."

I was shocked at his inconsiderate statement. He should have told me that before we took off and not after we'd landed. As a co-op student, I was paid little, and it was a stretch to pay for food and rent. He told me I owed him $3.00, which was a lot of money at the time. It wasn't so much the money, but rather the principle behind it. I learned a couple of lessons from that experience—to find out upfront the cost before I start something and to not expect those I take flying to help foot the bill.

It is enough to see somebody enjoy the thrill of flying. I've flown many people since that day, and I never charged a penny. Flying around Mount Rainier in an open cockpit airplane was a fantastic experience. I would have gladly paid Jim $3.00 for the opportunity if he had told me his expectations up front.

Mary and I had many great experiences the summer of 1955 while we lived in Seattle. We attended the unlimited Gold Cup boat racing at Lake Washington along with about 10,000 other people. Suddenly our eyes turned from the water to a spectacular sight in the air. Right over the lake, Tex Johnson—Boeing's test pilot—rolled a 367-80 airplane. He made a

complete and perfect roll of the prototype of Boeing's new 707 jet airliner. No test pilot had ever done a maneuver like that with such a large airliner, and I got to see it up close and personal. When I tell people, especially one of today's Boeing employees, about my experience their eyes get big and they exclaim, "You were there?!"

Boeing Airplane Company and Douglas Aircraft Company were in a big competition to sell their first major jetliner to the airlines. Part of the reason Boeing came out on top was Tex Johnson's unusual effort "to sell airplanes." Years later when I was working for Douglas Aircraft Company, I got a different story. I was told Boeing pulled ahead because the wing sweep of the 707 was slightly higher than that of the DC-8. The DC-8 was more stable, but the 707-cruise drag was less than the DC-8. I learned over the years that fuel savings and better range were more important to the pilot and the airline companies than how easily the plane flies.

During my free time away from work, Mary and I enjoyed self-directed sightseeing tours. We wanted to see everything Washington State had to offer. We drove as far south as Mount Rainier and as far north as the Canadian border. At over 14,000 feet, Mount Rainier is considered one of the most dangerous volcanoes in the world, but we were determined to walk on it. We drove the 100 miles from Seattle to the mountain, enjoying beautiful vistas along the way. In the 1950s the glacier had descended to around 6,000 feet. We got out of our car and walked on the glacier—a very thrilling experience. After returning to Seattle, we could still see Mount Rainier hovering over the city.

On another trip, we drove north to see old friends from our Navy days. Tony was a Navy cook who made us delicious, broiled shrimp and then invited us to go waterskiing. Mary was not interested, but I decided to give it a try. The freezing mountain lake was a shock to my system, and skiing was a lot harder than it looked. I took many tumbles into the icy water before I decided I was a candidate for hypothermia.

The biggest problem we had while living in Seattle was the constant drizzling rain. It never seemed to rain and be done with it. I was told that if you lived there long enough you got used to it and could enjoy the surrounding beauty despite the rain. I wanted to stay longer in Seattle, but summer was about over for us. It was time for us to get back to Mississippi State.

My job was not all that stimulating, but I worked hard so that no one

would think I was lazy. I gathered as much information as I could from fellow Boeing employees, who gave me a lot to mull over regarding my future career.

Our trip back to Mississippi allowed us to see more of the natural wonders of the country. Our number one goal was to go through Yellowstone National Park. We arrived at Yellowstone Park after dark and couldn't find a place to stay until we saw a sign pointing to a lodge. It was scary to drive up the dark hill into the woods to find the lodge. After a long day on the road, we were so glad to find a place. We checked in and went to sleep.

The next morning, we discovered we were the only visitors at the lodge. An older gentleman who was the manager served us breakfast and told us about all about Yellowstone Park. He told us that by driving at night we had missed some beautiful scenery. He introduced himself and asked if we recognized his name. Then he proceeded to tell us he was the grandson of Buffalo Bill Cody and that his mother was Buffalo Bill's daughter. We were not sure we believed him, so he told us to visit the museum in the town of Cody, Wyoming and see for ourselves. Sure enough, when we visited the museum the next day, we saw his picture along with the rest of his family.

We also planned our trip so we could go through Milwaukee, Wisconsin to see an old friend from my childhood. Bill Adams had been living in Milwaukee since he had graduated from high school in Whitehaven, Tennessee. We thought it strange he had picked up the local Swedish accent and didn't sound Southern at all.

The rest of our trip was uneventful and exceedingly long. After we drove through Chicago, we just wanted to get home. We made a brief stop in Memphis to visit both sets of parents and then headed for Mississippi State College in Starkville.

As I reflected on my adventurous summer and the beautiful scenery we had seen, I recalled a poem written by Henry Wadsworth Longfellow. The verse from that poem that caught my attention was, "Glorious indeed is the world of God around us, but more glorious is the word of God within us."

I understood the first part of the quote, since I was constantly awed by the grandeur of God's creation, but at that time, the second part of the quote and the need for God to be within me, was still not a reality. I knew I still had some changes to make in my life, but first I just wanted to get through college.

Seventeen

My Senior Year

My senior year was tough, but I really enjoyed my subjects. I still needed some math, but most of my courses were in aeronautics. I studied aircraft structures and airplane design under professor, Dr. Chuck. He was a good instructor who motivated his students to learn. In our design class, the airplane I chose to design was a Korean War era North American F-86 Saber. I was determined to make all "As" during my senior year and hoped my design class project would earn a top grade. When I received an A in design, I was on top of the world and ready to graduate with a BS in Aeronautical Engineering.

But graduation meant giving up my job in the Mississippi State Aero Physics Department working under Dr. August Raspet. Before I left, Dr. Raspet had one more job for me. My assigned task was to reduce the after body drag of the rear cockpit canopy on a Cessna L-19 "Bird Dog." The L-19 airplane had been ordered by the military to be used as a forward observer for the artillery, giving it the Bird Dog title. The rear of the cockpit was a flat rectangular Plexiglas canopy between the fuselage and the wing. The design gave the pilot better observation but, since the canopy was blunt, it was not a good shape from an aerodynamics point of view. My task was to design a more streamlined shape for the canopy.

First, I had to measure the existing drag of the canopy by drilling about 200 tiny holes in the plastic shield. Then I measured the pressures at each hole during flight. Then after modifying the aft body canopy of the cockpit, I had to do it all over again to see if the pressure changed enough

to reduce the drag. The time it took to build a new canopy and drill the new holes was tedious and boring.

Cessna L-19 Bird Dog

My favorite part of the task was taking measurements during the twelve hours of flying time. The tests had to be conducted in smooth air. On more than one occasion, we climbed extremely high to find an altitude that was less turbulent before beginning our experiments.

Sometimes we flew at very scary altitudes. One day, our pilot flew through overcast skies up to 12,000 feet to find clear non-turbulent air. As we topped the clouds, another airplane came up behind us. I saw it because I was turned aft, but the pilot didn't see it at first. The airplane was an Air Force North American AT-6 Texan that must have come from the Air Force Base in Columbus, Mississippi. I knew that plane was used for training new pilots, and I thought for sure we were in big trouble because we were not on a flight plan. The Air Force plane tailed us for a while, probably taking down our numbers. Since our plane was military surplus, no trouble came from that near miss. The tests were successful, and we finally got the hoped for drag reduction.

Dr. Raspet and I disagreed somewhat about the expected outcome of our experiment. I thought we would only discover the drag reduction between the old and the new canopy. Dr. Raspet finally convinced me

that the tests also showed the actual drag of the canopy before and after modification.

I shared our conversation with Dr. Joe Collins, who at that time, was assistant Head of the Aero Physics Department. Dr. Joe's answer to me was, "If Dr. Raspet tells you to stick your head through a screen door, stick your head through a screen door." In other words, he was the boss, and most of the time, he was right.

I wrote and presented a paper at the Student Institute of Aeronautical Sciences at Virginia Polytechnic Institute in Blacksburg, Virginia. I didn't win an award or get special credit for the paper since the judges felt I'd had too much professional help. I was okay with that, since it was such a good learning experience, and we had achieved good results.

I often wondered why I was assigned to do the research on the after body of the cockpit. Later, I learned that Cessna L19 was going to be converted to a boundary layer control airplane and needed a good drag reduction increment before starting the modification. The plan was to remove the airplane wings so students could drill thousands of holes into the upper surface. Suction would be applied through those holes to reduce the boundary layer thickness and prevent flow separation. The only problem was that the power for the suction came from the power of the engine that propelled the airplane. If the engine quit at a low speed, the airplane could stall and crash.

This became an unfortunate reality a few years after I graduated. I heard Dr. Raspet was involved in a plane crash during a demonstration of a light airplane with suction boundary layer control. This accident occurred above Mississippi's Bryan Field Airport. He, along with one other person, died while he was demonstrating the amazing slow flying ability of the airplane. It was quite upsetting to me because he had done so much for me.

Later in life, I heard another story about one of the leaders of the APD. I don't know if it was true, but it's a good story. He was a great observer of birds in flight and used his sailplanes to study the birds' flying techniques. Dick Johnson was a well-known sailplane pilot, who had won many awards for his flying expertise. One day, Dick was chasing a big buzzard that was riding a thermal. Dick was in contact with the APD leader on the ground who said, "Go after that bird." As he followed the bird, he took pictures

and described to the APD leader exactly how the bird was flying. The bird flew out of the thermal and Dick asked the APD leader, "Do you want me to continue following?"

The APD leader said, "Yes." So, Dick followed the buzzard for quite a while. He called back again and said, "He's turning back now, shall I follow him?" The APD leader said, "Yes!"

This went on for several times before Dick Johnson said, "He's landing in a tree. Should I still follow him?"

As I reflect on that time in my life, I realize God was taking care of me. I believe it was providential that my project was to reduce the after body drag of an airplane. That valuable experience prepared me for my future career working with wing aerodynamics and studying after body drag reduction on a variety of airplanes. I believe God not only kept me safe but was also teaching me step by step to rely on Him for my future. However, I still had a lot to learn.

The hard work of getting through college was finally over. I received a good education and practical training in the Aero Physics department. That, along with my naval experience, led to some top job offers. Boeing, Northrup, North American Aviation, Pratt & Whitney, NASA, Grumman Aircraft, and Douglas Aircraft all offered me jobs. I was finally ready to step out into the real world of aeronautical engineering. Boeing Airplane Company offered me a position in their field service division. I did not accept it because it was associated with the Strategic Air Command, and I'd have to travel weeks at a time. Neither Mary nor I wanted that.

In the end, I chose Douglas Aircraft located in El Segundo, California. I had three good reasons for choosing Douglas Aircraft: theirs was the highest monetary offer, I would be working with the Navy division of Douglas, and Mary and I wanted to go back to California. Instead of just maintaining and taxiing Navy planes, I would be designing Navy aircraft as a member of the Advanced Design Group. I never regretted my choice of Douglas Aircraft. The work there gave me a great foundation for the rest of my career.

The next thing we had to do was decide how to get to California. The answer was simple. We would buy a new car, pack it up, and go. We had a fair trade-in with our 1952 Ford. I knew I had a good paying job

waiting, and we could afford financing. We were thrilled to buy our first brand new car—a custom line 1956 Ford. After stopping in Tennessee to see our parents and friends, we once again headed west on Route 66. Our destination was greater Los Angeles—2000 miles away. We wanted to do some sightseeing, but the lack of funds kept us pressing forward toward LA. The Grand Canyon had to wait until another time.

Eighteen

Douglas Aircraft

For a young couple from the flatlands of Tennessee, moving to Southern California for my first real job was thrilling. Mary and I had eaten lot of beans and bread during the four years I was in college, and we could not wait for our first paycheck. Our struggles and hard work were about to pay off.

Our apartment search in the Los Angeles suburbs led us to Gardena, which was five miles from Douglas Aircraft in El Segundo. After settling in our apartment, I discovered another Douglas co-worker lived in the same complex. We decided to share the daily commute, and other engineers would eventually join us. One of the drivers had a fancy 1956 Chevrolet, which today is considered a classic. He liked to show off his "hot car" and took risks on the road. I told him one morning that he was going to get caught. He bragged that he could find cops anywhere. Sure enough, that very afternoon the cops stopped him and gave him a ticket.

The Douglas plant was located on the south side of Los Angeles Airport next to North American Aviation. Housed in those hangars were the Navy airplanes that Douglas and North American were manufacturing or upgrading at the time. Among them were the A4D Skyhawk and the F4D Skyray. I learned a lot about those planes during my early days as a Douglas employee.

The Skyray fighter had quite a reputation. The new high-speed Delta wing plane was known for its high rate of climb on takeoff. During an early test flight, the plane suddenly climbed straight up, and the test pilot

found himself inverted at approximately 44,000 feet. The experienced pilot managed to deal with that scary event and brought the plane back under control.

The A4D Skyhawk was a popular attack class aircraft. The nickname for it was "Heinemann's Hot-Rod, the Ferrari of Airplanes." Edward Henry Heinemann was highly revered at Douglas Aircraft. He had been the chief engineer for many years but had retired before I came to work at Douglas. The first flight of the Skyhawk was in 1954.

Since a lot of the original design work on the Skyhawk was completed, I was assigned to work on modifications. We were always trying to see how many more bombs we could load on the airplane and it still fly. The main title of my work was Carrier Suitability. My assigned job was to conduct wind tunnel tests to find the change in lift, drag, and stability of the plane when loaded with varying numbers of bombs. Since those airplanes were launched by catapult, I also studied the catapult systems of various aircraft carriers and safe landing approaches. A lot of this was grunt work, but it was still interesting.

The working conditions at Douglas were quite good compared to some of the places I had worked as a co-op. Ten of us worked in a 30' x 30' room that was dedicated to the Advanced Design Department. We each had a specific job or specialty. The other three floors of the building housed the Performance, Stability and Control, and Structures Departments. The people I worked for and worked with were top notch, and that was only the Navy division of Douglas Aircraft. The Commercial Division and Missiles Division were located in Santa Monica, and the Air Force Division was in Long Beach.

Many types of airplanes came out of those divisions. There was the well-known DC-3, also known as the C-47, which had served the military during World War II. During my time at Douglas, the DC-8 and DC-9 aircraft were being designed and produced. The DC-8 airplane was in competition with the Boeing 707. Both were four engine jet airplanes designed for airline operation. The DC-8 eventually lost out to the Boeing 707, but the DC-9 continued production for many years.

Although the Navy division didn't normally work on the DC versions of airplanes, I got involved for a couple of reasons. The engineers at the Commercial Division came up with unique design methods for the

wings of the DC-8. I was only one of two engineers to use those same methods to design some proposed planes for the Navy. The other reason I got involved was the commercial division needed information about designing leading-edge slats for the DC-9. Most of the naval carrier aircraft designed by Douglas had leading-edge slats for high lift capabilities, and that knowledge could be applied to the DC-9.

Working on those leading-edge slats was my first responsibility. As with all the other designs that Douglas had made, the leading-edge slats were automatic. This was an overly complex design but necessary to slow the airplane down when landing. After the tedious work with slats, I began to study many theoretical concepts that helped us design wings in the future. Some of those theoretical concepts, with a combination of experimental data, were used to design a new wing for a proposed Navy airplane. The airplane had to be capable of loitering for a long time around the fleet to serve as an early warning of enemy submarines. We were excited when the Douglas proposal won the contract but disappointed when the Navy later decided to cancel it. The contract loss was not all bad because we were able to use the same design for another new plane being designed in Italy.

Douglas and Piaggio Aerospace of Genoa, Italy had joined forces to design and build a new executive jet aircraft. The Advanced Design Group at Douglas was assigned to accomplish all of the aerodynamic design, which included wind tunnel tests. That was right down my alley. My partner and I upgraded our wing design and applied it to the airplane. The airplane was supposed to cruise at 0.8 Mach number or 80% of the speed of sound. Douglas presented the design to Piaggio Aerospace with hopes they would soon build the airplane. We waited and waited. It took two years before they came up with the airplane. By that time, other companies had pulled way ahead of them in the commercial executive jet market. The Piaggio 808 was eventually completed, but due to their delay in design and manufacture, they did not produce very many. We were still pleased that the airplane performed well and met our design specifications.

In the late 1950s, Southern California was a pleasant and scenic place to live. After living in the San Francisco area—where it was rainy and cool most of the time—sunny southern California appealed to us. Clear days were mostly limited to the cooler fall and winter months. In the hot

summertime, the smog could be as deep as 6,000 feet along the mountain range. On those clear days, Mary and I enjoyed driving down the Pacific Coast Highway toward the beach and past the foothills of the Palos Verdes Mountain. After climbing the mountain, we were rewarded with great views. In the distance, we could see the great blue Pacific Ocean and Santa Catalina Island–twenty-six miles across the sea. From the summit, Los Angeles and Orange Counties, with their Japanese farms and orange groves, were spread before us.

From our bird's eye perch, we could see Torrance and the Louis Zamperini Airport, which was named after a famous World War II hero. I told Mary my goal was to take flying lessons at that airport. Another interesting view from the mountain was the Harbor Freeway–one of the oldest freeways in the Los Angeles area. The Harbor Freeway extended north and south from San Pedro Harbor to Pasadena. We couldn't wait to explore the exciting and interesting places we had observed from the mountain summit. When we did, we often found ourselves traveling on the Harbor Freeway.

I worked hard at Douglas with good leaders and peers that inspired me. My immediate supervisor, Claude Arnold, had tremendous knowledge about takeoff and landing on carriers. Most of what he knew was written in a type of shorthand on the backs of envelopes. When I filled in for him, I often got questions from somebody in the company about how to fix something. I knew the answer was somewhere on one of those envelopes, so I searched and hoped to find something to give me insight. That motivated me to start writing down what I was learning. Most questions were about takeoff and landing on aircraft carriers or on the ground. I made up charts that helped eliminate time-consuming equations and helped me get better answers.

Military airplanes were always being updated with a new device hanging on the outside of the airplane. I was constantly asked by other engineers about how the new device would affect the flight characteristics. They wanted a quick response. Many of the devices not only caused changes in drag, but also changes in the lift and pitching moment. A better method to answer those questions was needed, so I began to write a report on predicting lift, drag, and pitching moment. I studied reports from the National Advisory Committee for Aeronautics to help me come up with an

empirical method to predict the answers. I spent many hours at Douglas putting all this together in a report, which was similar to writing a master's thesis. Examples in the report showed that the empirical method (from observation or experience) could reasonably and accurately predict the lift and drag and pitching moment of some of the airplanes like the Skyhawk and the DC-8. Some of the people in our group used that report, but it was never published.

Four more interesting projects were assigned to me during my years at Douglas. Two were related to short takeoff and landing aircraft (STOL) or vertical takeoff and landing (VTOL.) The other two were related to ground effects flying machines. My first attempt in obtaining a patent was a joint effort by my group leader and me. It was based on an innovative control method for ground effects flying machines. All my experiences and the practical knowledge that I gained at Douglas was a great help in pushing me to new heights in my career.

Nineteen

New Experiences

While I was involved in many exciting efforts during my employment at Douglas Aircraft, my life away from work was moving in new directions. By 1958, I was being encouraged by my immediate supervisor, Claude Arnold, to get a graduate degree. My partner on many projects was a female engineer named Doris. Doris was older than I was—attractive, professional, and a pleasant person to work with. She was a good bit taller than I was and more experienced in aeronautical engineering, so I looked up to her in several ways. She was the first to suggest that I go to the University of California at Los Angeles (UCLA) to begin working on a master's degree. I was eager to get started once Doris helped me secure a scholarship from Douglas. I soon learned that my professor at UCLA was going to be my boss, Kenneth Van Avery, the chief aerodynamicist of Douglas Aircraft. He was an intelligent engineer and a good manager.

That was like being stuck between a rock and a hard place. My coursework was Practical Aerodynamics, all of which I could use at work. I had plenty of homework, and the tests kept me busy studying. I needed to keep my job and do well in class. Doris graded my homework and test papers and there was no favoritism. I must have done well, because every time I finished learning something in my course, I wound up with a job that required the use of that knowledge. It was like going to college and having on-the-job training all at once.

After I finished the course work with Kenneth Van Avery, I transferred to the University of Southern California (USC) where I wouldn't be

required to write a masters' thesis. With going to school three nights a week and working full time, I felt that it would be better if I did not have to write a thesis. I transferred to USC and began working towards a Masters' Degree in Aeronautical Engineering. I took courses in theoretical aerodynamics, stability and control, and airplane design.

With all this going on Mary, and I decided that since we couldn't have biological children, we would adopt. Shortly after I started at USC, we applied for adoption through the Los Angeles County Adoption Agency. We learned the process would be long and require many visits from social workers. I had to sacrifice much study time, and I was beginning to wonder how I would manage.

Mary had also started a full-time secretarial job at Rohr Industries. I signed up for flying lessons in September 1957, so I could learn how to fly powered airplanes. During that time, we also moved into our first house in Torrance, California. It was at the foot of Palos Verdes Mountain and not far from the Torrance Airport. All those changes were important, but none were more important than the spiritual changes in my life.

Shortly after Mary and I moved to California, we began to look for a church. We didn't expect to find anything similar to the churches we had attended in the South but were pleasantly surprised when we found Calvary Baptist Church at Hawthorne, California—not far from where we lived. We had not been active in church during our early married life, but we believed now was the time to get serious about our spiritual lives and active in our new church.

We had a wonderful pastor by the name of Guy Bradley. Guy and his sons were outdoorsmen. They loved hiking, fishing, and many other sports. Even though his son Joe was younger than I was, we became close because we both liked similar adventures. After being around the Bradley family awhile, I realized there was something missing in my life.

Even though I had gone to church a lot when I was young and had been baptized when I was eight years old, I was not sure about my spiritual life. I first thought I was not serving or working hard enough as a Christian. The pastor and other members of Calvary Baptist Church explained to me that I could never work hard enough to get to heaven. They taught me that I could not be saved by works but only by faith as explained in the book of Ephesians.

"For it is by grace you have been saved, through faith—and this is not from yourselves, it is the gift of God— not by works, so that no one can boast. For we are God's handiwork, created in Christ Jesus to do good works, which God prepared in advance for us to do." (Ephesians 8:9-10 NIV)

I finally understood that faith in Jesus Christ and not my good works would get me into heaven. I also believed that God had good works planned for me, and that he was going to use my love of aviation to serve him. With this new revelation, I went before the church in late 1957 and rededicated my life to Jesus Christ as my Savior and Lord.

As a rededicated Christian, I had a mentor by the name of Joe Weber. Joe and his wife were members of Calvary Baptist Church and were great examples of the Christian life. You could see and hear the peace and joy in their lives. I wanted people to see those characteristics in me, not as a fanatic, but as a friend with concern for them. I began to put my newly discovered faith into practice in the workplace by working hard and helping people on the job.

Our lives were not all work and no play. Mary and I found time to have a lot of fun individually and as a couple. While Mary was enjoying various activities with her church friends, I took up diving with my friends and a black Labrador retriever that Mary and I adopted. That dog loved to dive and didn't seem to mind the cold Pacific Ocean. I, on the other hand, wore a full wetsuit to protect me from the chilly ocean water. I tried scuba equipment one time but preferred snorkeling. It was great exercise and good for my health.

My buddies and I practiced our diving on the beautiful rocky shores of the Pacific Ocean. Getting in and out of the water over the rocks was quite tricky. After getting scratched and beat up a few times and getting sea urchins stuck in our hands, we learned how to get in and off the rocks. It was a matter of timing the waves as they crashed. As a wave was going out, we went with it, and then dove before another wave hit. As we came in, we kept our faces looking down in the water and used our gloved hands to guide us over the rocks. We only did that when the waves were gentle. If they were high and treacherous, we went to the sandy beach and body surfed.

The marine growth and fish near the rocks were colorful and beautiful. Diving for abalone was the most fun of all, since the right kind of abalone

was good to eat. We were equipped with weights on our wetsuits that allowed us to float neutrally. We carried large knives to pry the abalone from the rocks. We each had an inner tube with a burlap bag tied to it. The bag was used to store the catch, and the inner tube was tied to us so we wouldn't lose it during the dive. One January, Jack and I spent two hours in the water off Palos Verdes Mountain in San Pedro Harbor. We had picked a spot to dive away from the boats. Both of us were so proficient we could dive to about forty feet just by snorkeling. We didn't find any abalone, but the exercise and comradery were great. I suspect that his wife and Mary were enjoying each other's company too.

Our diving hobby was not without hazard. I read in some diving magazines that seals liked to play with divers. I guess they thought a diver wearing a wetsuit looked like a seal. Being curious, they bumped and tried to roll the diver. We didn't see seals very often, but when we saw them in the water, we got out. When one of them came up on the rocks near us—barking like he was talking to us—we made a beeline for the shore.

Sharks were another potential hazard. We never saw any sharks while we were diving, but one time we got a scare. As we were coming out of the water heading for the beach, a fisherman said, "Did you see those two big sharks following you?" We were surprised, since normally only the smaller leopard sharks came near the shore. But that didn't stop us from diving.

My friend Joe and I liked to go hiking and fishing in the Sierra Nevada Mountains. Joe had a friend that lived in Fresno who was an expert in hiking the Sierras. One July, we met him in Fresno, and he showed us how to pack for hiking in the mountains. We planned a one-week camping trip to the high Sierra's. We could carry only twenty-five pounds on our backs since we would be climbing from 8,000 to 11,000 feet to see the lakes.

Joe and I left the Los Angeles area and drove up to Mineral King, which was at 8,000 feet. The next morning, we got up and began the hike to the top. I did not realize how difficult the climb would be. I had started smoking when I was in the Navy and was still hooked on cigarettes when I made the hike. Although I was in fairly good shape, smoking hurt my climbing, and I started getting sick about halfway up the trail. Even though my head hurt, I still could climb. We stopped often to rest and to drink plenty of fresh water coming from the mountain streams. After

reaching the 11,000-foot pass, we descended 1,000 feet to see the lakes, which we had heard were full of golden trout.

Our Fresno friend hiked up the mountain with us then left Joe and me there alone. We picked a camping spot and unloaded our gear. Our back packs consisted of a rack and equipment covered by a large poncho. The poncho was waterproof, so it was used as a makeshift tent. Packed in the poncho were our sleeping bag, food supply, and fishing equipment. Our fishing rod was fastened to the outside of the rack. We didn't have much food in our packs, so we had to catch lots of fish in order to survive. We snagged hungry golden trout on every hook we threw in the water. Their pink meat tasted like salmon. We managed to eat like kings and survive the whole week. We had golden trout cooked every way imaginable. After we caught them, we cleaned them and hung them up in a tree to dry. Sometimes an agile animal climbed up the tree to snatch a snack. We were glad to share and relieved that we were not on the menu.

Rain is a given in the mountains. When it poured, we got under our ponchos and waited it out. It was a rugged trip, and despite my altitude headache, we made it safely through the week. We were exhilarated by our nature adventure. By the end of the week, we looked like bums, and I had a rather good beard. We were both tired and looking forward to a milkshake and hamburger at McDonald's, which was a long hike down the mountain.

First, we had to navigate the trail back up and over a pass filled with huge boulders. We had to jump from one boulder to another all the way down, which was difficult after a week in the wilderness. We left that place determined to come back the next summer. But for now, it was time for me to go back to work and for Joe to return to school.

Twenty

Parenthood

On the home front, our family and church life kept us extremely busy. Both Mary and I were anxious to proceed with the adoption. We didn't know it at that time, but a boy had been born on May 1, 1957 that would soon become ours. In the summer of 1959, the adoption agency finally agreed he belonged in our home. The poor little fellow had been tossed from one foster home to another for twenty-two months and was still called "little boy," since no one had given him a name. Darrell Clay Dixon officially became the third member of our family in April 1959.

Much of his character had already been formed. He was somewhat a loner, and it took a while for him to get used to being our son. Parenting him was mostly a joy, but there were difficulties as well. Darrell and our black Labrador retriever didn't get along. Darrell was hyperactive, and the dog didn't like his constant motion. When the dog nipped him near his eye, Mary sadly said, "We have to get rid of the dog." That decision was painful, since I loved that dog. However, I knew she was right, and the black lab was taken to the pound.

It was helpful and rewarding to be involved with other young parents in our church who were also struggling with the challenges of parenthood. One of the things we enjoyed doing together was visiting in the homes of our church visitors. Some of the visits were good and productive, and some were unpleasant and difficult. The good visits, like with Brad and Sheila Smith and their young child, made it all worthwhile. Brad also worked at Douglas aircraft and had been a Navy fighter pilot with lots

of aircraft carrier experience. I had wanted to be a Navy pilot but wasn't successful in that pursuit. My flying experience in small general aviation airplanes, as well as my aircraft mechanic experience, however, gave us much in common. Brad eventually dropped out of Navy flying because he developed diabetes. Both Sheila and I were care givers for our diabetic spouses.

The Smiths became continually active Christians and members of our church. They were growing in their spiritual lives along with us. The church must have agreed, because Brad and I were asked to be Bible teachers and deacons. It wasn't all work and no play since the Smiths and Dixons found plenty of opportunities for fun.

Both families decided to go camping in the Sierra Nevada Mountains. Brad and I informed our bosses and co-workers at Douglas Aircraft that we would be gone for a week. We needed them to be aware of our wilderness adventure in case we ran into an emergency. After all, it is not unusual to have fires or earthquakes in California.

We headed deep into the wilderness in my two-year old 1956 Ford. The car was packed with camping gear for four adults and two small children. We headed north of Los Angeles through Palmdale, Lancaster, and the Mojave Desert. Then Highway 395 took us up the east side of the Sierra Nevada Mountains to Bridgeport and then toward the mountains and the Sonora Pass. It took us about seven hours to reach Pinecrest Lake near Strawberry, CA at the peak of the Sonora Pass. We were thrilled to have found such a beautiful place to camp.

Since we had left early on a Saturday, we made it to the lake in time to set up our tents and have a meal before sunset. We were all tired especially our three-year old's Darrell and Candy. Brad and I did most of the set up while Mary and Sheila cooked and took care of the children. Camping with little ones was not easy; however, the kids seemed to enjoy the outdoors.

The second night in the woods, we awoke to the sound of something stomping through our campground. It sounded like a moose or a large elk, but we were scared and didn't look. Nothing came of the event, but it made us tightly close our food supplies.

Our campground was in a lush green setting and the air was refreshing compared to the city. Our week of fishing and enjoying the beautiful

scenery soon came to an end. We packed the cars, broke camp early Saturday morning and headed home, expecting to be back at work on Monday. We soon learned that was not going to happen.

As I drove down the mountain, I shifted into second gear several times to keep from going too fast on the steep road. In the process, something gave way in the transmission, and it locked up in second gear. The car was still drivable, and there was only one thing we could do—keep driving and pray we made it down safely. God answered or prayers when we pulled into Bridgeport, CA.

We found the only mechanic's shop in Bridgeport and made it there without having to shift into reverse. It was going to take two or three hours to determine the problem, so we borrowed a loaner car from the mechanic's shop and found a restaurant and fed our starving kids. When we went back to the shop to hear the verdict, the good news was they had found the problem and the bad news was they needed to order parts. It was going to take three days to get the parts from San Francisco. That was depressing news for Mary and Sheila, and Brad and I were not shouting for joy. After a spirited discussion, we decided we would rent another car and go back up the mountain road to find another camping spot. Before we left, Brad said he would call his office at Douglas Aircraft to inform his co-workers he would be delayed in returning to work. He asked his office to call my office to give them the same news.

Our camp was by a small stream of water that was not far from Bridgeport, so we could get supplies and keep check on the car repair. The campground was poorly maintained and extremely dusty. The kids were dirty, and we all very tired. On the third day the wind started blowing and blew our tent down on top of Mary and Darrell. I was outside when I heard Darrell yelling and Mary yelling back, "Oh, shut up Darrell and go back to sleep." They both just stayed in the tent while Brad and I raised it again.

Finally, the car was fixed, and we made it home. When I reported to work, everybody asked, "Where have you been? We knew you had gone to the mountains and were afraid you had had an accident or driven off the mountain. We were about ready to call a rescue team." I explained that Brad had called his office and they were supposed to notify my office. I learned my lesson. If I was able, I needed to make my own calls. Thankfully, my boss and peers didn't stay unhappy with me too long.

Mary and I had another fun adventure visiting the Lawrence Welk Show. His famous band was considered one of the last big bands of the 1940s and 1950s. We hoped to be one of the couples chosen to dance on his television show. We lined up with a lot of other folks hoping to get in. I learned the selection criteria eliminated bald men because the lights reflected off their heads. The man in front of me was bald, and he and his wife were not chosen. Instead, the selectors chose Mary and me to be on stage, probably because of my abundance of dark hair.

Mary and I were thrilled to dance with the Lawrence Welk band. My show-business father had taught me not to have stage fright, so Mary and I danced to every song the band played. We were really "cutting the rug" when Lawrence Welk himself squatted down to be close to us. He was clapping his hands and encouraging us to keep it up. That was on national TV and broadcast throughout the world. My parents and other friends in Memphis were already exited we were going to the show, but that was icing on the cake.

If you wonder why a Baptist deacon was dancing on national TV, you wouldn't be the only one. The Sunday after the Lawrence Welk show aired, we went to church as usual. One of the leading deacons said to me, "Dancing was one thing, but did you have to do it in front of the whole world." From that point on, I was called the Dancing Deacon. I believe that dancing, like anything else, can be used for immoral or good purposes. For me, dancing was a way to express my love of music, to enjoy a beautiful art form, and to get great exercise.

Twenty One

Learning to Fly

Dancing in the ballroom was enjoyable, but I wanted to return to dancing in the sky. On September 2, 1957, I began my flight training in a powered airplane at Zamperini Field. That experience was much more exhilarating than my flight in the Navy jet trainer at 30,000 feet or my first soaring flight in a glider at Mississippi State College.

It thrilled me to be back in the air and in a Champ. With a control stick in my hand and my instructor by my side, I made that airplane dance in the sky. My feelings were best summed up in the poem, *High Flight*, written by John Gillespie Magee, Jr. of the Royal Canadian Air Force.

Oh! I have slipped the surly bonds of Earth
And danced the skies on laughter-silvered wings;
Sunward I've climbed, and joined the tumbling mirth
Of sun-split clouds, — and done a hundred things
You have not dreamed of — wheeled and soared and swung
High in the sunlit silence...

My instructor had a difficult time teaching me to use the power of the engine and its propeller to land. I wanted to glide into a landing, but I knew how helpful it was to use power. Often the air was turbulent as it came over the Palos Verde Mountain before tumbling down toward the airport. Many times, we did a lot of dancing on the mountain-split air

while landing. This was great training, especially in a tail dragger like the Champ.

After ten hours of practicing stalls, steep turns, climbs, take-offs, landings, and forward slips, I soloed in the Champ. For my first supervised solo, the instructor was on the ground watching my take offs and landings. After two more supervised solos and another hour of flying, the instructor signed me off to fly on my own. But since I still had much to learn, the instructor continued to fly with me many more times.

One time, we took off and climbed up over Palos Verde and headed out to sea. On that windy day, I saw huge waves hit the shore and rocks where the mountain met the sea. That was intimidating because the instructor had me doing steep stalls. I learned how to get into a stall and quickly recover by pulling the control stick back to my lap and holding it there. The only way I could keep the airplane from rolling over and heading for the sea was to use the rudder. When we started to roll right or left, I pushed the opposite rudder and kept the airplane under control. As we were getting closer and closer to those large waves, I began to wonder if the instructor had suicidal tendencies. He finally told me to nose it down, use the rudder to control the plane, and then give it power to pull out of the stall.

Ailerons—little flaps at the wing trailing edge near the outboard wing tip—are normally used to control the airplane roll, but not when the wing stalls. On some airplanes, using the ailerons in a stall can put the airplane in an unrecoverable spin. That stall problem led me to research life-saving devices that could be used to control spin-stalls.

I had a second scary event while flying the Champ. The tower controllers at the Torrance Airport used lights to control the traffic. Pilots received control directions by steady or flashing green or red lights from the tower. One time as I was landing, I missed seeing a flashing red light. It meant the airport was unsafe for landing. Because I was distracted by another airplane, I missed seeing the red flashing light. It was a windy day, and the airplane preparing to land was out of control and headed for the pea patch at the end of the runway. I decided to climb and continue over the airport. I didn't know that another airplane had been given clearance to take off. That was another time that the Lord was looking after me. As I looked to the right and below, I saw that plane taking off and heading

straight for me. I quickly made a climbing left turn and avoided a midair collision. Later when I safely returned to the airport, I was invited to come to the tower for a serious discussion about airplane protocol.

Although I continued flying off and on for several months after that scary event, I was not getting enough flying time. There was too much going on in my personal life at home. Graduate work kept me busy, and the demands of parenthood took a lot of my time and energy. There wasn't enough time to fly and stay proficient. So, in the first part of December1958—after logging 19 hours—I stopped flying. It would be eight long years before I would once again dance in the sky.

Twenty Two

Burning the Candle

My professors at USC told me about the von Karman Institute for Fluid Dynamics located in Saint-Genesius-Rhodes, Belgium. They encouraged me to apply to this renowned school for experimental aerodynamics. As a non-profit educational and scientific organization, it specialized in three aerospace fields: aeronautics and aerospace, environmental and applied fluid dynamics, and turbomachinery and propulsion. Professor Theodore von Kármán had proposed the establishment of an institute devoted to training and research in aerodynamics that would be open to young engineers and scientists of the NATO nations.

Since I qualified as one of those engineers, I explored how to enroll in that school and experience life in Belgium and Europe. When I researched the qualifications for going to the school, I learned I needed a completed master's degree in Aerodynamics. I lacked one semester of classes to graduate. I shared my disappointment with Delores, my supervisor. She came to my rescue by suggesting, "Why don't you just call von Karman. He lives in Pasadena."

"Who me? Call von Karman?" His theories had made him one of the greatest aerodynamic scientists in the world. I had studied some of his works in college and knew I would never rise to his level. His many accomplishments included directing the Guggenheim Aeronautical Laboratory at the California Institute of Technology (GALCIT) and helping to establish the Jet Propulsion Laboratory (JPL) in Pasadena. I

had participated in several wind tunnel tests at GALCIT but knew that wouldn't help me contact von Karman.

Delores insisted. "He is just another person like you. Don't be intimidated." I remembered the lesson I had leaned in the Navy. It worked when I had asked for a better job from the Master Chief Petty Officer. *Why shouldn't it work now?*

I found von Karman's number and called him. His Hungarian and Austrian accent made him difficult to understand on the telephone. Somehow, I managed to tell my story and asked if he would authorize admittance for me to enter the von Karman Institute for Fluid Dynamics. He said, "Yes!" He probably thought that anyone who qualified and boldly called him deserved an invitation. He turned me over to his secretary— who I could understand—to give me the information I needed to sign up. She explained one caveat that could have kept me from getting into the school—my company was required to share the cost of the NATO funding. I contacted Douglas about the scholarship allocations.

Much to my disappointment, Douglas had run out of scholarship funding. Since Douglas had paid for my schooling at USC, I didn't want to push them any harder for funding. Although I didn't get to attend the von Karman School of Fluid Dynamics, I benefitted from the experience. I talked with Theodore von Kármán! I learned once again not to be intimidated by high level persons but to be well prepared to present my ideas, desires, and opinions at the right time.

The responsibilities of parenthood, working all day at Douglas, and going to school three nights a week affected my ability to study and maintain good grades at USC. In addition, we adopted our second child. Cheryl Valyn Dixon, born on August 17, 1960, became Darrell's baby sister. Mary and I now had a family as large as we wanted. With Mary's diabetic problems and my career and school, we decided two children were enough.

Graduating with a master's degree required that I maintain a B average. When I made a C in my theoretical aerodynamics course, I knew I had to work even harder in my other courses to make an A. With a lot of hard work and Mary's help, I managed to graduate from USC in 1961 with a master's degree in Aeronautical Engineering. A graduation highlight was California Senator Richard Nixon giving the commencement address.

In 1962, Douglas hired Arnold to work with me. We worked well together on an interesting engineering project. During the early stages of the Vietnam War, the Navy sent out a proposal to design, develop, and produce a small, Short Take-off and Landing (STOL) airplane for transporting South Vietnamese soldiers. The airplanes had to land in the rough terrain of the jungle and allow soldiers to quickly load through the back of the airplane fuselage. In addition, the design called for a twin boom airplane with two large propellers mounted on the nose of the booms. Those propellers were mounted ahead of the wings to obtain the high lift needed for STOL. Arty and I were given the task of designing the wings and the high lift flap system and determining the take-off and landing requirements.

Several years earlier, Douglas had developed a great high-lift, double-slotted-flap airfoil. We chose that two-dimensional airfoil for our wing. Earlier, I had developed methods to compute three-dimensional airplane characteristics from two-dimensional airfoil data. We also had developed methods to predict the effect of propeller slipstream deflection on the high lift characteristics. With those methods, we had the capability to design a very efficient STOL airplane.

After making all the preliminary design estimates, the twin boom configuration created too much drag to meet the performance requirements. The drag analysis experts insisted we eliminate the twin boom concept and go back to a conventional fuselage with an aft body door like that of the C-130 cargo airplane. Eliminating twin booms also helped improve the high-lift characteristics. All the design work changed the conventional fuselage concept. We developed a new way to store the landing gear, since it could no longer be stored in the twin booms. The conventional fuselage configuration had to have very short-spanned wings on the bottom of the fuselage to store the landing gear. After many dead ends and design changes, we designed, built, and tested a wind tunnel model. Arnold and I headed to United Technologies Research Center in East Hartford, Connecticut to oversee the wind tunnel test.

The test lasted a long time because we were getting some bad directional stability from the wind tunnel model that would be dangerous in flight. When we gave a report to our bosses back in California, we told them about the problem. My boss simply said, "Don't come back home until

you solve the problem." After making many model changes and running more tests, we finally removed the gear pods, and the problem was solved. The pods were redesigned, no further problems occurred, and the tests were successful.

While working at my desk in the control room of the wind tunnel, I overheard a disturbing remark about me. One of the secretaries whispered to someone that I looked just like Edward G. Robinson. Robinson was a well-known Hollywood actor. He probably was a nice man off screen, but most of the time he played the part of a tough gangster. Robinson was short and moderately overweight. During the previous year, I had gained 30 pounds. That was way too much for my height of 5'7" inches. My feelings were hurt, but I knew I needed to do something about my weight. But with everything else going on, I wasn't ready to deal with that yet.

Arty and I spent a lot of time together during our month at the wind tunnel. We had a good working relationship, but his personal lifestyle concerned me. Arnold came from the tough south side of Chicago. He had a short, stocky frame and he cursed worse than most sailors. He must have come from a middle-class family because he had a college degree; but if he had any interest in spiritual matters, it was not apparent to me. It hadn't been long since I had rededicated my life to Jesus Christ. My faith in God had grown as I saw the ways he had directed my life. Because I saw how God blessed my life, I wanted to share my faith with others. I soon had that opportunity.

I believed God told me to share my faith with Arnold, and that I would be shown how to do it. I talked with him a little at a time, believing the Holy Spirit would provide me with the right words at the right time. Arnold respected me as a military veteran and admired the difficult time I'd had getting through college. He knew that during my Navy days I could have used some pretty rough and crude language, too. I think the fact I had changed and now lived a different life became obvious to him. After about a year of working with him at Douglas and subtly but firmly sharing my faith, a wonderful thing happened.

In 1963, the Southern California Billy Graham Crusade drew in crowds night after night. I asked Arnold if he would go with me one evening after work. He surprised me by saying, "Yes." That night, Billy Graham talked about the parable of the lost sheep. When he gave the

call for people to come forward, I asked Arnold if he wanted to go down and give his life to Christ. Again, he said "Yes." As we continued to work together, it became obvious that Arnold life had changed.

With all my job responsibilities and travel, Mary assumed most of the responsibility for maintaining our home and caring for the kids. The month I spent at the wind tunnel proved to be challenging for her. Both Darrell and Cheryl had mumps during that time. If I had stayed home, I could have caught the mumps, which I'd never had as a child. Mumps can cause many complications in adults, so once again I felt God guiding and protecting my life. I made it up to Mary by taking the family out to eat at Marie Calendar's, a new Los Angeles area family restaurant. We ate Marie's soup and pies so often that we helped her business thrive. No wonder I couldn't lose any weight.

Twenty Three

Getting in Shape

The year preceding the wind tunnel test at United Technologies, Douglas Aircraft made the decision to move its Navy operations from El Segundo to its Air Force plant at Long Beach. That turned out to be a good thing for me and my family. We had been trying to sell our house at Torrance for four years. It was like a white elephant that nobody wanted, since it was on the frontage roadside of the Pacific Coast Highway. The highway noise turned off potential buyers. In God's timing our house sold—just in time for us to relocate to Huntington Beach, which was close to the Long Beach Plant. I wasn't thrilled with the accommodations for the engineers at the plant but was pleased with the nice home we bought about three miles inland.

We qualified for a VA low-interest rate loan on our home mortgage of $22,000. We lived on Baffin Bay in a subdivision where most of the streets were named after some bay in the world. Our ranch house foundation, built on a concrete slab, was covered in tile and carpet. It sat on a postage-sized piece of land, so tiny that I could stretch out my arms and touch our house and the neighbor's next door. I worked hard in that small yard to grow flowers and ground cover so that I didn't have to cut grass. The climate and rich dirt made it possible to grow almost anything. After tilling, I could stick a geranium in the ground, and it would grow. I really loved the beautiful bougainvillea vines that grew on my garage wall.

Our subdivision was close to the Navy Seal Beach Munitions area and surrounded by a lot of green space, so we weren't bothered by the noise.

That close to the beach, we did get some occasional fog, but we could drive out of it quickly. For the most part, the weather was ideal. It usually got cool at night so that even in the summertime a sweater felt good.

Soon after settling down at Huntington Beach, we looked for another Bible believing church like we'd had in Hawthorne, California. We were led to visit the Garden Grove Baptist Church. It was not far from the Crystal Cathedral that was founded by Robert H. Schuller. The Crystal Cathedral promoted its unique drive-in services, but we were looking for a church where we could get involved. It didn't take long to make new Christian friends at Garden Grove and for Mary and me to begin working with youth. I taught a group of teen-age boys in Sunday School. We met outside under a shade tree year-round since the weather was so mild. The boys loved it when we went snorkeling in the ocean at Laguna Beach. Working with those boys led me to change my life again.

One Sunday, the lesson was from I Corinthians 6:19. *"Do you not know that your bodies are temples of the Holy Spirit, who is in you, whom you have received from God? You are not your own." NIV*

That verse hit me hard since I was still smoking and knew it wasn't good for me. Every time I tried to quit, I started back with a vengeance. When I read that verse, I knew I couldn't teach teenage boys and continue to smoke. So, I quit cold turkey and never picked up a cigarette again. I am alive today and in good health because of that decision.

I began eating more to compensate for my desire to smoke, and the weight just kept creeping up. I went from one bad habit to another. I was thirty pounds overweight. I knew my body was the temple of God and something had to be done. After we got back from the wind tunnel test, Arnold and I both agreed we needed to do something about our weight. He didn't have to lose as much as I did, but he wanted to encourage me. We decided that we would sponsor a contest at Douglas Aircraft to see who could lose the most weight. We asked others at work to join us, including Delores. Like good engineers, we plotted our weight loss each day on a chart that we pinned to a bulletin board. At the end of three months, the winner would receive an Italian dinner paid for by the other participants.

I was determined to win that contest. With the help of a calorie counting book, I limited myself to no more than 500 calories per meal. My hunger was kept under control with good low calorie healthy foods

like fruits and vegetables which I hadn't eaten before. Three months later, I was 30 pounds slimmer and declared the contest winner. I bought a new wardrobe, and thoroughly enjoyed that Italian meal. Delores and others complemented me on my new suit. The next health-related task was to get back to exercising, so I resumed ocean diving. That continued for as long as we lived in California. Thank you, Miss Secretary at United Technologies.

Upon our return from Connecticut, Arnold and I had presented our findings to our boss, explaining that the aerodynamic characteristics and the take-off and landing performance of the test plane were well confirmed. Finally, the proposal for the Douglas D-855 was summited to the Navy. All of us thought our version of the airplane without the twin booms was a winner. Our model met all the performance requirements because it had lower drag than that of the twin boom version. After the Navy proposal was submitted, I came down with the flu and stayed in bed for two days. Then I got a call from my boss at Douglas. He said he hated to bother me, but he had an emergency. The Navy had asked for someone responsible for the STOL analysis to come to the Naval Air Systems Command in Washington, DC for a conference and discussion.

My boss said he wanted me to catch a Red Eye flight and be in DC for a meeting the next day at 8:30 am. He said I could fly back home as soon as the meeting was over. I felt honored that the bosses at Douglas thought I could solve the problem, but I felt awful and wondered if I would survive. I guess my college struggles and my military training in perseverance paid off. I told my boss I would do my best and to sign me up.

John, one of Douglas' local "DC" Marketing experts, picked me up at the airport at 7:30 am and we proceeded to the Naval Air Systems command. I guess I didn't smell too bad, and my clothes weren't too disheveled because the meeting went well. I felt good that I had answered the naval engineers' questions. After the meeting, John and I met to discuss the results. He told me I did a good job and that he had a special gift for me. He gave me a silver-colored pen and pencil set with Douglas Aircraft Company engraved on them. I really appreciated the gift, but what I really wanted was two weeks off with pay. John took me back to the airport and somewhere on the return flight the adrenaline wore off. I was completely exhausted when the plane landed at Los Angeles Airport.

The Navy and the Marines had their minds set on the twin boom

version of the prototype aircraft and North American, not Douglas, won the contract. The final production aircraft was the twin boom version, which is now called "The North American Rockwell OV-10 Bronco." After a comprehensive flight test of that aircraft, the airplane did not perform as expected and incurred penalties for the North American Airplane Company.

My coworkers and I were disappointed in our loss, but I knew it was time for me to move on. Late in 1964, after eight years with Douglas, a fellow aeronautical graduate from Mississippi State College contacted me. He said he was recommending me to his supervisors as a potential manager for Brown Engineering Company in Huntsville, Alabama. He said my leadership skills with students at the university and my work resume was appealing to his supervisors. It seemed to be a great opportunity for me and my family to return to our roots in the South.

Twenty Four

Back to the Southeast

Mary and I had liked living in sunny California and moving back to the Southeast presented some challenges. Darrell—now in second grade—would have to adjust to a new school. Mary and I had lived and worked in Huntsville, Alabama during my junior year at Mississippi State College. We had not been impressed with that experience, and we hoped that this time would be different. However, the move would put us closer to our aging parents and extended family. I could also have the opportunity to test my skills as a manager at Brown Engineering.

As we packed for our move to Alabama, we experienced some interesting family events. Mary was driving our 1961 Ford Falcon Sport when she stopped behind a gray car with sporty red leather upholstery that waited for the light to change. A large Lincoln sedan that was a car length behind suddenly accelerated and ran into her. The impact drove Mary's car into the gray car and turned our Ford Falcon into an accordion.

Both Mary and Darrell were injured, but we didn't think it was serious. Darrell had some scratches, but Mary suffered a whiplash. That injury caused back problems for her the rest of her life. The long trips we enjoyed became difficult for her. Soon after the accident, she developed diabetic neuropathy in her back which greatly added to her discomfort.

We thought the Falcon would be totaled, but the insurance company thought differently. The unibody construction of the1961 Ford meant it had no body frame like earlier cars. The body shop agreed with the insurance adjuster and repaired the car. Keeping the wheels aligned on that

car had been a problem, and I was afraid it would be worse after repair. The body shop did such a great job I never had a problem again with the wheel alignment.

We drove that car to Huntsville and kept it for several more years. Before leaving California, Mary faced another challenge with that car. She was driving towards Huntington Beach and following a vehicle with a surfboard on top. The surfboard worked loose and flew right into Mary's windshield. She was not hurt, but the Ford Falcon had to return to the body shop once again.

Another of Mary's experiences with cars was funnier than scary. My work car was a used Ford Falcon station wagon with radiator problems. I pulled the radiator and put in the trunk of our other car to take it for repairs. Since it was late in the evening, I had planned to take it to the shop when I went to work the next day. I made two mistakes. First, I put the hood down on the station wagon; second, I didn't tell Mary what I had done to the car. She thought it was fixed and she could drive it to the grocery store. She drove less than a half a mile when steam began to bellow out from under the hood. She stopped at the closest gas station, and the serviceman came out to help. She told him there was something wrong with the motor. When she opened the hood so he could have a look, he announced in a loud voice, "Lady, you do have a problem. There is no radiator!" The engine wasn't damaged, but there was little peace around our house for the next week.

Another experience that affected Mary involved a trip she took to Memphis to introduce Cheryl, our adopted daughter, to our families. While she was gone, my plan was to take Darrell on one last hiking and camping trip in the Sierra Nevada Mountains. I dropped Mary off at the Los Angeles airport for a two-stop flight to Memphis. Mary was shocked when she saw her brother, Fred, at the Dallas, Texas airport. Fred was on his way back from Vietnam after serving a tour there with the Air Force. When they boarded the same flight for Memphis, they were so excited the flight attendant had to calm them down. The fact that Fred was coming home intact was God's blessing, but meeting Mary was icing on his cake.

Fred was a happy-go-lucky guy who loved to play pranks on other folks. After he got acquainted with Cheryl, he came up with a trick to pull on his wife and the rest of his family when the plane landed at the

Memphis airport. The family had no idea Mary and Fred were on the same flight. The trick was for Fred to get off the airplane first carrying Cheryl. That was one nasty trick to play on his wife, but there was more to it than coming home with a toddler in his arms.

When we adopted Cheryl, we were told that her background was French and English, and that was all we knew about her ethnicity. She had darker skin and black hair that made her look more Hispanic than English. We thought it was due to her Caribbean-French background. The point is that by the time she was two years old she looked more Asian than Caucasian. Fred snuck up behind his wife and surprised her. She turned around and almost passed out when she saw Cheryl. She thought Fred had brought his Vietnamese love child home with him. Before things got too far out of hand, Mary stepped in to clear up the confusion. All was well again with Fred and his wife, but our family faced a new challenge.

We moved back to the Southeast in the early Sixties when racial tensions were high. Our families had a hard time accepting our adoption of a child with darker skin. Our families thought she had a mixture of African American blood, and that was not acceptable to many in the South. It was obvious that we, along with Cheryl, would have to overcome that problem. Despite those concerns, we were soon on our way to Huntsville, Alabama.

Twenty Five

Disappointing News

Our house in Huntington Beach sold in three weeks without a realtor—a miracle since it had taken four years to sell our previous house. We also sold the Falcon station wagon and drove the rebuilt 1961 Falcon Sport to Huntsville. Brown Engineering Company promised to pay all our moving expenses; we only had to find a place to live. After settling in, I started my new job.

By1964 a major part of the Redstone Arsenal had been transferred to NASA's George C. Marshall Space Flight Center (MSFC). The German Missile Specialists, led by Wernher von Braun, still worked there. Von Braun and the other specialists had become U.S. citizens. As Chief of the Guided Missile Development Division, Von Braun received much credit for developing the Explorer I—the first successful orbiting satellite for the U.S.

The next project involved the development of the Saturn V rocket, which would take the manned Apollo module to the moon. This huge task required the effort of many companies and thousands of engineers. The MSFC obtained most of its employees by signing contracts with companies who then hired their new workers. My employer, Brown Engineering, had one of those mission-support contracts.

The first day on the job, my assignment was to work as a contract engineer for the Mission Space Flight Center (MSFC) under a NASA manager. My job description said quite the opposite. I was hired—or so I thought—to be a supervisor of other Brown Engineering employees

at MSFC. The NASA manager did not want to work through a Brown Engineering supervisor. His interest was in structures, which had nothing to do with aerodynamics— my specialty. I soon realized I had been misled about the job.

Every day I reported to work and had nothing to do. I hated that warm-body job, and my family knew it. Here we were trying to get settled in a new place, but the uncertain job had us wondering if we were going to stay in Huntsville or go back to California. Since Cheryl was still young, she wasn't affected by the move, but Darrell's late start in the second grade meant he was already behind. It would be extremely difficult to take him out of school and move again. Mary and I had our faith to turn to, so we sought answers through the power of prayer.

It helped when I learned about another person in a similar situation. Jim hired on as a supervisor, but he didn't fit in either. He seemed to take adversity in stride, and we became good friends. We both reported to work every day at the holding station and signed in. Much of the time we sat at a makeshift desk doing nothing except things that kept us from going stir crazy. Jim and I had a lot to learn about each other, and we had interesting stories to tell, but sharing stories got old. After a while, we both decided to sign in each day and then go home.

I learned that my travel and moving expenses would have to be repaid if I left my job before working three months. We couldn't afford that expense, but my conscience really bothered me. Sitting on my backside and doing nothing was not for me. Another engineer endured a similar situation by using his time to study and get a law degree. Since I wanted to work and be useful, studying for another degree didn't appeal at all. Looking for another job and facing the consequences seemed my only option.

Every day after signing in with NASA, I interviewed for jobs. There were several aircraft companies with branches in Huntsville that capitalized on the huge effort to put a man on the moon. Before long, I found a job at a branch of Lockheed Missiles and Space Company. My experience in aerodynamics helped me land the job. I explained I didn't want to end up with a dead-end position like I had experienced at Brown Engineering. The Lockheed personnel assured me that I would be challenged in the Research Park and would not work for a NASA Manager.

Now all I had to do was negotiate with my former bosses to get out of repaying my moving expenses. I felt I had a good case, since I had been misled about my supervising job. I decided to go first to the NASA manager hoping he would agree. That put the NASA manager in a difficult spot, since he knew if he did not tell me the truth, I would escalate my case. He agreed to say I had been misled when I told him I didn't need it in writing. Next, I met with the Vice President of Brown Engineering and told him my story. He said he could put me on the lay-off list and that would keep me from having to repay my moving expenses. I gladly agreed and was more than ready to go to my new job. Mary and I were greatly relieved that our prayers had been answered.

In April 1965 I began work with Lockheed in the Unsteady Aerodynamics Group—a new experience for me. Thus far, I had only worked with steady-state aerodynamics. All of us had to study hard to learn that part of aircraft engineering. Unsteady aerodynamics focused on time-dependent liquid or air flow movements and turned out to be a discipline that proved quite interesting. One day, I asked my group leader how he managed to advance in the field. His answer surprised me. He said, "You just have to be able to speak the language to manage the work."

His honest answer impressed me as he explained how he depended on the rest of us to learn the technical details. That made me work harder to learn more than just the language. This paid off when, after a year, I became the leader of the Unsteady Aerodynamics Group. Finally, I was a manager, and the engineers that worked for me were knowledgeable and experienced. I learned things from them that I have used throughout my career.

My work from 1965 to 1967, along with the work of many other Lockheed engineers, contributed to making the Saturn V rocket safe and ready to launch. We worked on two major problems in the design of the Saturn V. The huge rocket shuttered and shook during high winds. At first, we thought it would take a powerful wind to vibrate that large rocket. But we soon realized that the Saturn V had the same problems as a flagpole. A cross wind could seriously buffet a flagpole, since high velocity winds shed vortices that put alternating forces on the cylinder. We had to be sure that winds would not shake and topple the Saturn V and its three-man crew of astronauts who were sitting on top.

The other major concern involved the astronaut Launch Escape System (LES) that sat in the Apollo module on top of the Saturn V. A small rocket would ignite if the rest of the Saturn V failed during or after the launch. That small rocket would then pull the Apollo away from the vehicle, taking the astronauts to a safe altitude where their parachutes could deploy to bring them down safely. We were concerned that the LES could set up an oscillation that would cause the Saturn V to break up during launch. After conducting several high-speed wind tunnel tests, we determined oscillation caused by the module would not be a problem.

Twenty Six

Fun in Huntsville

Spending time outdoors and acquiring new athletic skills kept me refreshed and able to deal with my job-related stress. The Tennessee River that ran just south of Huntsville provided many places for recreation. Guntersville Lake, created by a dam on the river, was great for waterskiing, boating, and camping. I bought a used sixteen-foot runabout boat that the family used for fishing and water sports.

Mary and I found out that friends from our days at Mississippi State College (MSC) had moved to Huntsville. Some of my fellow aerospace graduates were working at NASA Marshall Space Flight Center. We were close friends with John and his wife Lacy while at college, and John and I were both military veterans. They had been our neighbors in the run-down Army barracks that had served as apartments for married students at MSC.

John and his young son were competitive water skiers and offered to teach me. My wet suit from my days in California came in handy and allowed me to waterski even in cold weather. While John patiently taught me how to ski, Mary and Lacy found plenty of ways to have fun. Just like old times.

I started with two skis on the Tennessee River, and at first was in the water more than on top of it. With John's help and patience, I mastered the technique and rode behind the boat with ease. Determined to learn more, I bought an AMF slalom ski called a Voit Barracuda. It was more like a bucking bronco. Since I understood scientific principle, I knew the hydrodynamics were wrong and that my weight needed to be further back

on the ski. When I moved both the front and the aft foot locations back one inch, it made a big difference and helped me master that barracuda. I still was no competitor, but I had a lot of fun. That ski is still mounted in the rafters of my workshop at home.

John and I spent a lot of time in our wet suits skiing the Tennessee River. People on boats and barges looked at us like we were crazy, but it was fun to be crazy. We loved to show off by jumping the high wake made by the barges. The only problem with cold weather skiing was putting our bare feet into the water. Waterskiing also became a family affair. Mary didn't ski much, but she drove the boat. I had a couple of wide skis that the children learned to ride.

East of Huntsville, Monte Sano rose about 1000 feet above the Tennessee River Valley. It wasn't as high as Palos Verdes in California but was high enough to get good views of the meandering Tennessee River. At night, the lights of Huntsville helped relieve some of our California homesickness. As much as I enjoyed driving to the top of Monte Sano, I wanted to get even higher—I needed to go flying.

The last time I had flown as pilot in command was in December 1958. George, my Lockheed coworker, was a current pilot. After much "hanger talk," he finally asked me to fly with him. I lit up like a child with a new toy. It took me a long two seconds to say, "Sure I'll go."

George said he would schedule a plane through the Lockheed Flying Club. Much to my delight, we flew the next weekend out of the Huntsville airport. The Piper Cherokee 180—a four place airplane with a low wing— was different from anything I had flown. A couple of others flew with us, but George put me in the copilot seat. After about thirty minutes, George turned toward a golf course and said, "You fly it and land it on the golf course."

Since it looked clear to me, I continued toward the golf course and started letting down. At about 500 feet, he took over. We both knew that we couldn't land on the golf course unless it was an emergency. After seven years of not flying, George said I did pretty well. "Why don't you start back flying and take more lessons?" he asked. Then he advised me to join the flying club so I could get lower rates.

Mary was never too excited about my hobby. With her diabetic condition and two young children still at home, she feared being left alone

should something happen to me. However, since she knew how important flying was to me, she reluctantly supported my flying lessons.

George helped me join the flying club and find an instructor. Soon I took my first lesson in a Piper Cherokee 140. I was apprehensive at first, but after a couple of flights with Grady the instructor, my confidence rose. After six hours of takeoffs and landings, slow flight stalls, and some night flying, Grady let me fly solo. Despite my nerves I summoned the courage to make the flight. With twenty-six hours of flying time and eleven more hours of training under my belt, I took my first solo cross-country flight to Birmingham and Tuscaloosa, Alabama and back to Huntsville.

The smog from the steel plants over Birmingham obscured my view, so I called the control tower for a vector to the airport. After a touch and go landing, I headed to Tuscaloosa. With no more problems, I returned to Huntsville quite pleased with my first solo flight. It took me a while to get over the thrill of flying cross country and come back down to earth. Like most pilots, flying was in my blood, and there was no way to flush it out. I had to fly.

My next trip took me to Memphis for a visit with my parents in Whitehaven, Tennessee. On a beautiful day, I flew over the Tennessee River, across Alabama, into Mississippi, and into Tennessee. Upon contacting the Memphis approach control, I was switched over to the Memphis airport tower and landed without incident.

The trip showed me how quickly I could fly relative to four hours behind the wheel, enabling me to have a longer visit with my parents. I spent the night, took off the next day for Huntsville, and in the process gained four more hours of round-trip cross-country flying. My training continued as I practiced stalls, short field take-off and landings, and more cross-country flying. I spent many hours with my instructor learning to fly with instruments so I would be safe in case of bad weather. On May 28, 1966, after sixty-one total hours of flight training, I received my private flying license.

That small plastic government-issued card was so much more than a license. My lifelong dream—that had begun when my friends and I sat in cockpits of scrapped planes and pretended to shoot down enemy aircraft—had been realized. No longer did I have to settle for waxing and taxiing planes for the Navy. Now I had the freedom to fly and soar on

silver wings as much as my budget would allow. Learning to fly planes other than trainers was the next step. In July 1966, I successfully checked out in a more powerful airplane. As I landed, there was no way of knowing it would be three long years before I would log more flying hours into my flight book.

My personal flying abruptly ended when Mary's Brother, Richard Gibson, was killed in a crop-dusting airplane. I got the word while on a trip to Lockheed Missiles and Space in Sunnyvale, California. My traveling partner took over my part of the trip and helped me arrange the flight home.

Crop dusting was the most dangerous job in aviation. Richard had been continuously crop dusting in Mississippi during the week of the accident. By Friday, he was tired, and his lungs were filled with fumes. On one more bypass, he flew too close to the ground, caught the wing, and crashed. Mary and I grieved over the loss of her brother. Richard and I had been close friends and had a lot in common with our love for aviation. The accident not only ended Richard's life, but it cut short my plans to continue flying lessons. Fear didn't keep me from getting back into the air, but my flying would have made Mary miserable. I loved her too much to do that.

Even though I didn't pilot a plane for three years, the desire never left me. I also knew my happiness at work depended on getting back into aviation engineering. Although the project to take men to the moon was exciting, that was not my passion. I was excited to learn that my former professor at Mississippi State, Dr. Joe Collins, had accepted a position as manager of the Aerodynamics Research Lab at Lockheed in Marietta, Georgia. I had worked for Dr. Collins and Dr. Raspet at Mississippi State while in college. I decided to contact Joe, hoping he would help me find a job in the field of aviation.

Mary and I discussed the pros and cons of moving to Georgia, and we both considered it a positive move. I sent Joe a friendly hand-written letter. That was probably not the best way to apply for a job, but it worked. Joe knew my background as a naval aircraft mechanic and that I had been a good student at Mississippi State. My experience as an aeronautical engineer in Advance Design at Douglas Aircraft was also a big plus. I later learned that practical experience benefits research work, and that's how I got the job.

Twenty Seven

The Air & Space Race

M y engineering career in aviation and outer space began between the years of 1950 and 1970. Great advancement in air and space travel occurred during that twenty-year period. Aircraft operating in our atmosphere gained airspeeds from two to three times the speed of sound. Space travel—just a dream in the early 1950s—became a reality by the 1960s.

Commercial passenger travel also reached its golden age. Turbo-propeller airliners and jet airliners dominated the skies. Eastern, United, TWA, and American Airlines competed to fly passengers from one end of the country to the other. Pan American dominated overseas travel.

The Cold War between the Soviet Union (U.S.S.R) and the United States of America fueled a competition to rule the skies. At the end of World War II, much of the military was depleted and the US Navy didn't even have enough funds to fuel their airplanes. When I was called to Navy active duty during the Korean War, I started seeing more advances in aviation. After Korea, the Cold War and atomic age provided a kick-start in the development of new military aircraft.

The first Lockheed C-130 Hercules went into service in 1956— the same year I graduated from college and began working for Douglas Aircraft. The four-engine turboprop military transport aircraft became the workhorse of military operations around the world. Since I couldn't see the future, I had no idea how important the C-130 would become in the advancement of my career. As I saw all the new developments

in commercial and military aircraft, I felt blessed to be a part of the aviation industry, and thankful that I had pursued my dream to work as an aeronautical engineer.

The adventure into the unknown and the excitement of outer space ignited the imaginations of people all over the world. Advances in space technology were occurring in both the Soviet Union and the United States. Building an engine that could launch a rocket into outer space was a huge challenge. There was great concern and fear the Soviets would overtake the US in accomplishing that feat.

On October 4, 1957, the Soviets launched the Sputnik satellite into low orbit. The U.S. was embarrassed to discover they were behind in the race to space. The development of a manned satellite flight received approval by Soviet leader, Khrushchev, in 1958. That same year President Eisenhower signed a bill establishing the National Aeronautics and Space Administration (NASA) which was responsible for the civilian space program as well as aeronautic and aerospace research. In 1958 the term aerospace was used for the first time to describe my field of engineering.

Yuri Gagarin in the Soviet Vostok 1 capsule made the world's first manned orbital spaceflight on April 12, 1961. At that time, I was busy finishing my master's degree in Aeronautical Engineering at the University of Southern California. One month later, I walked by Vice President Nixon to get my diploma. On May 25, 1961, President John F. Kennedy proposed to Congress, *"This nation should commit itself to achieving the goal, before this decade is out, of landing a man on the Moon and returning him safely to the Earth."*

The space race was on. Which country would win?

The greatest challenge was the survival of humans in space and the USA was playing catch up. Embarrassed again by the Soviets and the orbit by Gagarin, we forged ahead. NASA selected seven specialized test pilots to become physically and mentally fit astronauts. They were all considered to have the "right stuff." Using the single seat Mercury capsule, several flights were made into space, but only up and back down. On February 20, 1962, John Glenn made the first U.S. orbiting flight.

The original seven astronauts made several more Mercury flights, but it was not until the Gemini that we began to close the gap with the Soviets. Gemini allowed two astronauts to conduct space flight and extra-vehicular

activity or spacewalks. The first flight and orbits of the Gemini began with Grissom and Young on May 23, 1965. They made their contribution by proving they could maneuver the module vertically and horizontally. Then on June 3, 1965, James McDevitt controlling Gemini I piloted the module while Edward White made a successful spacewalk.

The Apollo module was built on all the successes of Mercury and Gemini with the goal of landing the first man on the moon. There were many adventures in each of the Apollo missions, but the greatest tragedy occurred while I was still in Huntsville. In January 1967 Virgil Grissom, Edward White, and Roger Chaffe died in the command module when it caught fire on the launch pad.

At the end of 1967 I left my job at Lockheed Missiles and Space Company in Huntsville, Alabama and moved to Lockheed Georgia, I stayed interested in the progress of the Saturn V and Apollo missions. The Apollo Mission 8 thrilled me the most. In December 1968, the rocket left the launch pad and headed for the moon. Two days later it arrived in its gravitational pull.

On Christmas Eve, astronauts Frank Borman, Jim Lovell, and Willian Anders orbited the moon ten times with each orbit taking two hours. They inspired the nation by reading to all the people on earth from the first chapter of Genesis. The country and the good earth needed to hear those encouraging words from outer space because the tragic assassinations of Martin Luther King, Jr. and Senator Robert Kennedy deeply affected the mood of the country. And the unpopular Vietnam War had led to demonstrations in the streets and the decision of President Lyndon Johnson to not seek reelection.

The greatest Apollo mission was Apollo 11. On July 21, 1969, Neil Armstrong put his foot on the moon and spoke these memorable words, "One small step for man, one giant leap for mankind." The astronauts that came home from that mission completed the challenge issued by President Kennedy. Not only did they walk on the moon, but they returned safely to earth.

It made me proud that I had contributed a small part to that effort. In spite of my love for aviation in inner space, working as a rocket scientist for outer space definitely had its benefits. Everything I learned prepared me for the next major step in my career and my new job at Lockheed Martin in Marietta, Georgia.

Twenty Eight

On to Georgia

By 1967, we had accumulated two wonderful children, a Siamese cat, and a lot of stuff. During our seventeen years of marriage, Mary and I had moved many times. We'd lived in five different states—sometimes twice—and in five different cities in California alone. The places we lived and the people we met had taught us many things. Wherever we were, we learned to use different phrases or idioms.

In the North if you didn't understand what someone said, you might say, "What?" In California you'd say, "Pardon?" We were excited to be moving to Georgia to learn the language of that state. We heard that saying "You Guys" wasn't acceptable and that we needed to say "Y'all" instead.

The former Bell Bomber Plant in Marietta, Georgia was home to the Lockheed-Martin Aeronautical Company. The thriving city of Marietta, north of Atlanta, struggled to accommodate its expanding population. Since we weren't familiar with the area, that move challenged the whole family.

Finding an apartment was difficult, because we needed to be close to my job, shopping, and decent schools. Our goal was to buy a house, but we rented in the interim and saved as much money as possible. We moved into an old WWII apartment complex that had been hastily built as public housing for employees of the Bell Bomber plant. At some point, the place had been remodeled, but it was neither modern nor spacious. The kids were cramped and playing outside wasn't safe. Our outdoor cat climbed

the walls and window blinds like a wild tiger. We knew finding a house with a yard had to happen soon.

Our realtor took us to look at many houses, but when she drove us by the Kennesaw Mountain National Battlefield Park, I knew we were headed in the right direction. The scenic drive impressed me when I saw beautiful houses surrounded by white fences and trees. When she showed us a new subdivision about five miles from the park, I was ready to buy any one of the unfinished houses on Hickory Crest Drive—sight unseen. Before long, we settled on a house with a big yard which gave the kids plenty of room to play. The animals in the neighborhood soon learned not to mess with our Siamese cat. We had to drive a distance for shopping, but that didn't last long because Marietta and Kennesaw were growing rapidly.

Kennesaw was home to many interesting historical sites connected to the Civil War. Earthworks and trenches surrounded our house. The famous train race of the war had started in downtown Kennesaw when a Confederate train was stolen by Union soldiers known as Andrews Raiders. Kennesaw Mountain became a major battlefield where the Confederates fought the Union trying to prevent General Sherman from making his famous and destructive march through Atlanta.

Not far behind our house was acreage that belonged to Wild Man, the local bigger-than- life Confederate. Wild Man—a white supremacist— owned a store in downtown Kennesaw where he sold Confederate and Klan memorabilia. His long hair and beard, along with two automatics— 45s in holsters on his hips—were his distinguishing characteristics. We were cautioned not to trespass onto his property.

After settling into our new home, I took a major step in my aeronautical engineering career. At first, I felt intimidated by the huge Lockheed Georgia complex, and I wondered where I would work in the immense facility. The plant at Dobbins Air Force Base had produced the famous Boeing B-29 during World War II. By the 1960s, Lockheed used the space to build the B-130 Hercules and the C-5 Galaxy. The bomber plant was located on the north side of the air base runway and covered several acres above and below ground. Most of the Lockheed personnel, including most of the engineers, worked in that building.

I had seen pictures of the Research Laboratory, where I hoped to be assigned, instead of being placed in a huge room with a noisy bunch

of engineers. That had been my fate when I had worked at Boeing as a college student and during my last two years at Douglas Aircraft. I had been spoiled by the nice new facility with individual cubicles at Lockheed Missiles and Space Company in Huntsville, Alabama.

When I reported to the personnel department on the north side of the airport, I was greatly relieved to be assigned to the research facility. The complex consisted of four buildings—administration, aerodynamics, structures, and electronics. The aerodynamics building was the largest and housed the engineering offices and a large laboratory. The laboratory contained a small wind tunnel, a smoke tunnel, a small water channel, an acoustics chamber, and a shop for building models. Wow was I impressed! If that wasn't enough, my two-man office had a window and a door. The icing on the cake was the nice size lake behind one of the buildings.

When I met with Dr. Joe Collins, we discussed old times. Then he introduced me to the other engineers and scientists as we toured the facilities. There was no delay in putting me to work since he already had a project lined up. Joe had recently received a United States patent for an innovation called span-wise blowing. My job was to learn as much about the concept as possible and then to exploit it by trying to obtain a research contract. We already had sponsorship from the Air Force for an Independent Research and Development investigation. We also hoped to be awarded a contract and some research monies.

I learned that span-wise blowing was the simple concept of blowing high pressure air over a wing from the side of the fuselage. In my experimental investigations, I found that it worked best if the wing had flow separation ahead of the jet. Without that flow separation, the wing lift might improve slightly but would cost more jet power than it was worth. Therefore, we began to exploit the configurations that had leading-edge flow separation, such as wings with a small leading-edge radius. We concluded that the vortices coming from the leading edge could be controlled with span-wise blowing. That improvement would add lift to the wing.

In the early years of aircraft design, any kind of vortex was considered a necessary evil because it caused drag and slowed down the airplane. But engineers were beginning to realize that vortices could benefit modern fighter aircraft. The thin-swept wings on those types of planes created leading-edge vortex flows that needed to be controlled in order for the

airplane to operate at high angles of attack. With the vortex controlled, the wing could get more lift with less drag due to flow separation. Span-wise blowing appeared to be the answer.

Working at Lockheed fulfilled me because I was once again working on airplanes and chasing whirlwinds. As a research scientist, I could think out of the box. Like our Siamese cat, I felt let out of my cage. I worked with a new level of engineers, many of whom had received their PHDs. With only my master's degree but lots of practical experience, I matched their expertise. We all gained by sharing our knowledge. My associates taught me new levels of higher mathematics. Scientists from various parts of the world—Great Britain, India, and Germany—became my friends. When opportunities arose, I shared my faith in Christ, and they were willing to listen.

In 1969, one of the managers in the research lab arranged for a small, twin-engine Beechcraft Model 18 to take us to the Air Force Research Laboratory at Wright-Patterson Air Force Base in Dayton, Ohio. I knew that plane since I had spent many hours flying in one as a safety observer and taxiing them while in the Navy. Six research scientists were selected to go to promote our research for potential contract assistance.

What a thrill to climb into that plane on such a beautiful day. As the only other pilot in the group, I sat near the cockpit so I could observe the actions of the crew. It was nostalgic to watch the pilot go through all the pre-flight routine like I had done for Navy pilots many years before. Soon we received clearance to taxi to the end of the long Air Force runway and take off for Dayton, Ohio.

The 450-mile flight took less than three hours. We had time to review our presentation and view the country below. We crossed the beautiful Tennessee River Valley that I had flown over while getting my pilot's license. From there on, it was all new to me. As we soared over Tennessee, we could see the Great Smoky Mountains in the distance. Then we flew over the Blue Grass country of Kentucky and the Ohio River before heading toward Dayton and Wright-Patterson Air Force Base. It was an uneventful, but enjoyable, flight.

In my career, I had made many contacts with Naval engineering personnel, and now I was excited to meet with my counterparts at the Air Force. Our early morning and afternoon meetings at the Air Force

gave us ample time for the return flight to Marietta. All of us hoped our efforts would lead to future contracts and help us with our Independent Research & Development (IRAD) work. I was pleased to have shared what I'd learned about span-wise blowing.

We were having a good time during our return flight. We began our approach to Dobbins Air Force Base in Marietta. As we entered the downwind leg of the approach, I could see the airport runway. Two exceptionally large airplanes ahead of us were getting ready to land—a propeller cargo airplane and a Lockheed C-5. We were far apart, so I didn't see any reason for concern. I was very wrong!

After both airplanes landed, we were still well separated on our final inbound leg. Then about twenty-five yards after we passed over the approach end of the runway and about 20 feet from the deck, the plane received a jolt. Our airplane rolled over to the right ninety degrees, and we almost landed upside down. Fortunately, we had an excellent pilot with aerobatic training who knew to hit the top rudder pedal. He leveled out the plane and used the long runway for a controlled landing. All of us onboard counted our blessings. I honestly believe our gracious Lord saved us so we could begin research that would save many lives in the future. As aeronautical engineers, we knew right away what had caused the drastic airplane roll. It was a trailing vortex or horizontal tornado from one or both big airplanes that had landed ahead of us. However, no one had any idea why that vortex lingered so long.

The next day at work, we had long discussions about what research needed to be done to keep the same thing from killing people in the future. Most of my fellow scientists said they would begin investigations on how to eliminate or reduce that vortex effect. I had already had some experience with vortex flows, so I went in a different direction. I wanted to learn how we could make those vortex flows work for us.

By that time, I had chased the whirlwind of life for almost 40 years, and the science of whirlwinds created by aircraft vortices became my passion. Vortices and the mechanisms that created them were complex entities and formed the foundation of flight for man-made aircraft and all flying creatures. I wanted to spend the rest of my career learning as much as possible about how to use that part of God's creation to benefit mankind.

My work—determining flying characteristics—made me more anxious to get back in the air. It took some effort to convince Mary that I needed to start flying again. She knew it was my life-long dream, so despite her fears after her brother's death, she finally agreed. The demands of life—as well as the expense of flying—kept me grounded more often than I liked, but finally I once again soared through the skies.

Twenty Nine

Family Adventures

Raising a family with school-age children presented many new problems and opportunities. A big concern was Mary's and Darrell's health. Mary's diabetes was hard to control, and when her insulin level rose too high, she got silly and passed out if she didn't get an immediate infusion of sugar. Most of the time, she knew her sugar levels were dropping, but other times she couldn't tell. I learned to depend on my faith and belief that the Lord would take care of her when I wasn't around.

Darrell had a short attention span and school became difficult for him. In California, he had done well with reading, writing, and spelling up through the second grade. He was even making progress in math. California had experimented with new math and gone back to the traditional way before he entered first grade. When we moved to Alabama and Georgia, schools were promoting the new math methods. That was confusing to Darrell, as well as to me. He had to stay back in the fourth grade, and from that point on, struggled in school.

When he turned thirteen, his life changed drastically. During a trip to the grocery store, he experienced a severe seizure. After many tests, he was diagnosed with epilepsy. We now knew the cause of his short attention span. With special drugs, Darrell could function, but he experienced a lot of side effects that were hard to manage. He really struggled to get through high school, but he did manage to graduate.

Despite those issues, our family had some fun times both on the water and in the air. Georgia's many lakes provided opportunities for fishing,

waterskiing, and swimming. Allatoona, the closest lake, was only thirty minutes away. Sometimes we ventured to Blue Ridge Lake about two hours from home. That beautiful deep lake, fed by the Toccoa River, had been formed by a large dam near the quaint town of Blue Ridge. The lush woods and hills provided good places to camp. Camping was fun for the kids and me, but Mary just tolerated it. On one of our trips, we learned that some large Pike had been seen in the lake. As we coasted into a cove, Cheryl hooked one of those big fish on her pole, and it started towing the boat. She held on as I grabbed the pole and wrestled with the fish until it broke the line.

Then we ventured into colder and deeper water to go waterskiing. Darrell and Cheryl had learned to waterski on two skis, but I liked the slalom. One day, Mary drove the boat at an extremely high speed with me on one ski. As she went into a sharp turn, I flew off and hit the water with my eyes wide open. My eyes burned and were so blurred, I couldn't see. It took me a few minutes to clear my vision. I never fell with my eyes open again.

Our next destination was to South Georgia and the Okefenokee Swamp. The National Wildlife Refuge covered nearly a half million acres. Many creatures resided there—bear, deer, bobcats, opossums, foxes, and raccoons. According to the park rangers, "Okefenokee Swamp Park instantly transports you into a prehistoric environment, populated by living dinosaurs or alligators, as well as unique species of carnivorous plants, rare birds and the opportunity to learn more about the ancient Okefenokee cultures."

All of that sounded exciting, so we reserved a cabin at Stephen Foster State Park on the banks of the Suwannee River—five hours from home. We settled in our cabin and prepared for our adventure. Early the next morning, we tried to arrange a tour of the swamp. A ranger told us, "You won't need a tour. The water is really low. You can guide the boat, and you won't get lost."

Encouraged by the ranger, we loaded up the large, flat-bottom rental boat. With our lunch and fishing gear safely stored, I cranked the engine. As we pulled away from the dock, we sang the lyrics of the Stephen Foster song, "Way Down Upon the Suwanee River."

We moved down the river and headed toward Billy's Lake and Billy's

Island. We learned the island had been named after a Seminole named Indian Billy, who was murdered on the island. It felt spooky to be in the middle of a lake with no one else around. We decided it was time to get our minds off our surroundings, so I rigged our cane fishing poles, and we dropped our lines into the water. Each pole was rigged with a colorful floating cork bobber that we hoped would attract fish.

Soon alligators bobbed up all around us. We were scared because our flat-bottom boat could have easily turned over. Mary hung on to her fishing pole as one of the alligators latched onto the red bobber and traveled with it. She yelled, "Charles! Charles! Charles!"

I grabbed the pole as the alligator towed us up the lake. Not wanting to lose the pole, I fumbled around in my fishing box, found my knife, and cut the line. With the boat motor running, we rode alongside that alligator. He crawled onto an island and started biting on the bobber like it was a good meal. That might have been Billy's Island, but we weren't going to hang around and find out. We turned around and headed back to the dock.

When I told the ranger, he explained that since the water level was low, alligators tended to move to deeper water and liked to hang around fishing boats hoping for a fish. I wish he'd told us that before we went on the trip.

Being around alligators was not my thing, but I still did something dumb. As we walked around the dock, I saw what appeared to be the tail of a small alligator. I reached down and grabbed the tail and asked Darrell if he wanted to see an alligator up close. He said, "No-ooo," but I continued to pull on that critter's tail. I soon found out it was not a little gator after all. It kept getting bigger all the time. I quickly let it go and that was the end of our alligator experiences.

When we weren't camping or chasing alligators, we liked to take long-distance flying trips. One weekend, we decided to fly to Memphis to see our families. I knew good visibility was vital for the trip. During the summertime in the South, a haze often hung in the air which limited long distance sight. An accurate weather report from flight services was essential. We planned to leave early in the morning to get ahead of any forming isolated thunderstorms, which often blew in during the afternoon.

With my flight plan in place, I scheduled a Cessna 172. It took longer than expected to get the family on board. The weather still looked good when we left Cobb County Airport and headed for Huntsville. As we

approached the Huntsville airport, visibility deteriorated. We decided to take a much-needed break and land until I could get a good weather report for the rest of the trip. The weather remained unpredictable, so we talked about renting a car to drive to Memphis but finally decided to fly back to Kennesaw. I knew then it was important for me to start instrument training.

The next flying trip was designed to be filled with fun adventures in South Georgia. A lot of planning went into that trip. We had to determine our destinations, check out the weather, and pack carefully, since the Cessna 172 had a small amount of storage and was weight limited. We didn't need heavy clothes, and we stowed items under our feet. At last, we were ready to fly.

Our first destination was Columbus, where we rented a car to see the sites. We settled into a hotel and then toured historic and notorious Phenix City, Alabama. During the 1940s and 50s, Phenix City had had a big problem with organized crime, prostitution, and gambling. A lot of customers probably came from Fort Benning, which was located nearby. A top-rated movie called "The Phenix City Story" was made about the murder of the Alabama Attorney General who had tried to rid the city of corruption. We were curious to see how the city had changed after its notorious past.

Our next stop was Albany and Valdosta, then on to the Georgia coast to see Jekyll Island and Savannah before heading north to Augusta, Athens, and back home. Reality hit the night before we were to fly on the next leg of the trip. Deteriorating weather and an overcast sky, with a 300-foot ceiling, kept us grounded. We extended the car rental and drove to scenic Providence Canyon State Park to see Georgia's Little Grand Canyon. We waited a couple more days for the clouds to lift, then finally left the plane in Columbus and drove to Callaway Gardens before heading back home. After several days, the weather cleared and a friend from the flying club flew me back to Columbus to retrieve the Cessna.

Our adventuresome vacation didn't turn out as expected, but it cleared my mind, and I was ready to go back to taming the whirlwind.

Thirty

The 1970s

The world was filled with excitement when the crew of Apollo 11 reached the Moon. This 1969 event was a fitting exclamation point to the turbulent Sixties. The country began moving in a new direction as the decade began. In November 1970, I reached the ripe old age of forty, which ushered in a new decade for me as well. I had reached the prime of my life—a time for me to evaluate what I had accomplished and what I had done to make a difference.

It wasn't as exciting as preparing for a moon landing, but my earlier research on span wise blowing (SWB) became mature enough for me to write a paper on the subject. That break-through concept gave a way to increase the lift for certain types of airplanes, especially fighter aircraft. I published the paper in the February 1969 issue of the American Institute of Aeronautics and Astronautics (AIAA). The distribution of that publication guaranteed that my scientific insights would be read and evaluated by institutions and companies worldwide. As a result, my paper was referenced in reports by scientists and engineers in the United States, France, Germany, and Russia.

My boss, Dr. Joe Collins, the inventor, and patent holder of this technology, also published a paper on the subject in 1970. When he presented his paper at the AIAA conference in Rome, Italy, more European countries learned about the SWB idea, giving it international recognition. In addition, the National Aeronautics and Space Administration (NASA) really promoted that concept. As a result, I hoped to get a contract for

Lockheed by visiting with NASA engineers at Langley Research Center in Virginia.

NASA wanted to hear about my research, but then duplicated my efforts in their own offices and laboratories. That frustrated me, but I had to accept it as a fact of life. I did benefit by making good friends and earning respect with my NASA contacts, which helped me at Lockheed. When my SWB research was noted in international papers and reports, it was a real ego booster. It eventually led me to write another AIAA paper, which I presented at the Georgia Institute of Technology.

After my presentation, several people talked with me, but old co-workers from my days at Douglas Aircraft made my day. I was excited to see Arty, with whom I shared my Christian faith. When Arty learned that I was presenting a paper, he came all the way from Chicago to see me. I believe the Lord showed me that my efforts to share the Gospel were not just for a moment—they were everlasting.

Two other attendees represented my former department manager Claude Arnold at Douglas Aircraft. Claude had accepted a management position at another large Aircraft Company and sent two of his marketing personnel to encourage me to come to San Diego to work for him. It was great to meet those two men and have dinner with them. It would have been an honor to work with Claude again, but I knew the business at his company was all about missiles and space. My mind had not changed since leaving Huntsville—airplanes and what made them fly was my passion. Much more still needed to be done on span-wise blowing (SWB).

My associates and I continued our research on SWB by conducting wind tunnel tests and exploring theoretical methods to extend the capabilities of concept. Using my knowledge about aircraft carrier operations, I realized that SWB could help improve the lift created by trailing edge flaps on attack and fighter-class naval aircraft. The Navy F8-U fighter was a prime candidate. I put together a proposal to submit to the Naval Air Systems Command (NASC.)

Lockheed's marketing engineer arranged for me to discuss my proposal with a high level NASC research manager in Washington, D.C. I was excited to talk about Navy aircraft again and it must have shown. The manager and I got along well, and the meeting resulted in a contract. The terms of the contract required Lockheed to build a small model of the

F8-U to test in its 30 x 40-inch research wind tunnel. It was fortunate that I had helped design and install a system in the wind tunnel that supplied the air needed for SWB and several other powered high lift concepts. We completed the contract in late 1971.

I wrote another AIAA paper about this SWB test and its results and delivered it at an AIAA conference in Los Angeles, CA in August 1972. I discovered later in my career that that paper, too, was often referenced in several institutes and countries around the world. I had the privilege of working on other Navy contracts during my years at Lockheed. Lockheed's major customer was the US Air Force, but my success in working on Navy contracts helped me stay employed.

The next Navy contract was with the Office of Naval Research (ONR.) It was ONR that came to us and not us to them. As the name implies, ONR's business was research. They were interested in getting into the evolving concepts for operations in the air, on the ocean, and under the water. The Lockheed Georgia Research Facility was ideal for such research. ONR wanted to develop a theoretical analysis of SWB and were willing to support the theory and related experimental efforts—quite a contrast to previous attempted NASA contacts.

I worked with two PHD capable and practical mathematicians. Dr. JG and Dr. RMS helped me with my rusty mathematics. I knew enough to supply them with the information required to develop a working, semi-empirical prediction for a SWB application. I learned a lot that helped me develop theoretical capabilities I needed in other projects.

While Doctors JG and RMS worked on the theory of vortex flow—which was being tamed by the span-wise blowing jet—I was learning much about jet flows. Jet flows are complex. Jets propel airplanes and entrain flow from outside of the jet. That is what controls the vortex generated in front of the SWB jet. We successfully completed the ONR contract and knew that what we had learned would be useful to us on future ONR contracts.

The Lockheed Research Laboratory consisted of organizations for at least three engineering disciplines— aerodynamics, structures, and electronics. That proved to be an efficient organization. I enjoyed seeing how the different disciplines worked together. Some of the engineers in

the Flight Sciences Division and the Research Division worked together on various projects throughout the year.

When Christmas rolled around each year, the Flight Sciences Division sponsored a Christmas party. Each employee drew another employee's name out of a basket. Each Secret Santa's goal was to provide a ridiculous gift to give to their recipient. My gift—at first very embarrassing—turned out to be the funniest gift at the party. Since I was a pilot and had worked with span-wise blowing, my highly creative Santa built a wooden box with a toilet seat mounted on top.

A short wing protruded from each side of the box with tubes pointing span-wise over each wing. That bunch of engineers immediately understood what generated the air to make that fake plane fly. We all laughed heartily at it. I'm still amused thinking about it today.

The Flight Sciences engineers were responsible for developing and maintaining the actual airplanes going into or already in production. If they got into a bind for engineering personnel, they pulled us out of research to work for them. Because of my practical experience at Douglas Aircraft, I helped Flight Sciences at least four times during my career at Lockheed. I didn't like being pulled away from research, but sure beat getting laid off when times were tough for the company. Many of my friends without practical experience were laid off.

My uncertain working conditions began around 1970. The C-5 Galaxy, designed and produced by Lockheed, served the U.S. Air Force starting in 1969. Cracks in the wings of many of the aircraft restricted its capability. That had to be corrected by Lockheed, which resulted in significant cost overruns. The first employees to be laid off came from the Research Department. Since I worked on Navy contracts, my name wasn't on a lay-off list. As a group leader, I had the unfortunate task of letting others go from the Research Department. For those still working in research, that was an ominous sign. With an uncertain future, I along with other engineers, started to think about possible alternative employment options. I hoped that SWB and working with the Flight Sciences Department would buy me enough time to decide what I wanted to do next.

I loved flying as pilot-in-command, so I seriously considered finding employment in the General Aviation industry, which encompasses all other types of aviation except commercial and military. I wanted to start my own

business one day but knew that meant I needed to know more about the business and finance fields. Ten years after completing my master's degree in Aeronautical Engineering, I decided to go back to school for a master's degree in Business Administration. Lockheed had an excellent scholarship program, so I knew cost would not be an issue. I decided to do what I had vowed I would never do again—raise a family, work full time, and go to night school.

It was a struggle for all of us. Mary and I had faced difficult decisions in the past regarding my career and she had always encouraged me to advance, but having children made it even harder. Darrell and Cheryl were having a hard time in middle school, and it fell on Mary to help them make passing grades. Despite many sacrifices and after three tough years at Georgia State University in downtown Atlanta, I graduated with my MBA in the spring of 1972. I had received a steady paycheck from Lockheed the whole time. Now I could think about other options for my future.

Thirty One

Facing Reality

L ockheed's Flight Sciences Division asked me to help on a proposal to design an airplane for the U.S. Air Force. It was unfortunate that Lockheed did not win that contract. The ultimate winner—the Fairchild Republic A-10 Thunderbolt II—known as the Warthog is still in service today.

When I returned to the Research Division, I resumed working on span-wise blowing and other high-lift research projects. I helped design a Laser Velocimeter—cutting-edge technology that helped aerodynamicists measure wind flow characteristics. This concept allowed us to study the details of vortex flow without placing an intrusive and interfering device in the tunnel itself. The information gained in these experiments helped me with my future applications of vortex phenomena.

My primary effort on SWB focused on vortex flow and the analysis of jet flows. Other powered-lift concepts, such as chord-wise blowing from a span-wise slot, also occupied my time. All this research was directed to high lift for short takeoff and landing (STOL) aircraft. In addition, vertical takeoff, and landing (VTOL) became a major interest for the military and commercial aviation industries. My previous experiences working with STOL and VTOL at Douglas Aircraft made this an exciting project for me.

I invested a lot of effort into these Lockheed projects, but my interests outside of work changed. My focus shifted to becoming a better pilot and taking my family on some exciting flying trips. In April 1973, I completed

my flight check on a Lockheed Flying Club Cessna 182. I graduated up from flying a medium powered plane to a high-powered cross-country airplane. When I gained confidence in flying the 182, I asked the family, "Do you want to go to the South Carolina beach?" Their exuberant "Yes" was all I needed to start planning the flight.

The 300-hundred-mile trip to Charleston, S.C. took two hours and ten minutes, as opposed to a seven-hour drive over two-lane country roads. We left early in the morning so we would have plenty of time to enjoy Charleston. I didn't tell the family my apprehension about landing at the Charleston Municipal Airport, which also was home to a Lockheed C-5 Galaxy base. I had already tangled with a C-5 vortex wake in our near-death experience at Dobbins Air Force Base in the Lockheed Beechcraft. I didn't want to do that again, so I planned to use my training for operating jointly in heavy traffic. If I saw that a C-5 had just landed, I would ask to circle the airport. Fortunately, the C-5s were quiet and the landing proved uneventful.

We rented a car, toured several historic sites in Charleston, and spent time an enjoyable time at Folly Beach. We planned our return flight for early afternoon on April 15th. My goal was to stop in two more cities on the way home to gain more cross-country experience toward my commercial pilot's license.

It didn't take long to realize that my flight plan and the air traffic controllers' flight plan didn't match. They lined me up for takeoff on the east-west runway in the direction of the Atlantic Ocean. I assumed flight control would tell me to turn back west as soon as I was airborne. After a mile in the air, I didn't hear a word, and it was only six miles to the ocean. I thought the tower wanted a lot of clearance for a C-5 take-off, so I kept going east out over the ocean. When we flew about six miles out to sea, I wondered if we were headed to the Bahamas. When I realized something was wrong, I called the tower to ask when they were going to send me back west. After a moment of silence, a smart-mouth controller gave me clearance to turn west, and then added, "And don't go all the way to Texas."

I did not know if he was joking or if it was his way of saying, "Don't you have enough sense to turn yourself around?" At a controlled airport, the pilot did not get to make that kind of decision. When we passed back

over dry land, we headed to Augusta and then Toccoa, GA. All of us relaxed as we circled over the North Georgia Mountains.

Our next flight that summer really tested my ability to get out of trouble. In July 1973, our friends flew with Mary and me to Jekyll Island. We couldn't wait to see the beauty of this barrier island off the east Georgia coast. The flight—350 miles in a Cessna 182—was enjoyable and uneventful. Since we only had three days for our trip, our scheduled return trip on July 7th to McCollum-Cobb County Airport came too quickly. The weather looked good as we boarded the plane a little before noon. On a typical hot July day, air rises creating vapor which leads to fog and rain. The weather report indicated that thunderstorms were bubbling up around Atlanta and low ceilings were headed in our direction.

By the time we flew over Dublin, the clear skies became hazy, so I climbed on top of the clouds. When I could no longer see land, it was decision time. I thought about making a 180 degree turn back to Dublin but called Flight Services in Macon instead. They connected me to approach control in Macon who asked my intentions. They advised me to vector to a clearing west of the Macon Airport. They said the ceiling at Macon was 1500 feet and after reaching the western clearing, I could descend and return under the ceiling to the airport. After landing safely in Macon, I went to Flight Services to check the weather for the rest of our trip.

Mary was usually very calm while I wrestled with making the right decisions about flying, and I could count on her to pray for safe travel. Our friends didn't look apprehensive either. Maybe it was blind faith, but everyone seemed willing to get back in the airplane for the flight home.

Flight Services told me to stay under the 1500-foot ceiling for the rest of trip. The skies were clear until our approach to the airport. To the north I could see dark skies. Flight services soon informed me that a thunderstorm had moved over McCollum Airport. My only option was to land at Peachtree-DeKalb. I called their tower frequency and received a quick clearance to land. Once the storm at McCollum had blown over, we flew the final lap of our trip and made it home safe and sound.

After 3 hours and 45 minutes of adrenaline-loaded flying time, I could take a deep breath. My passengers congratulated me on my wonderful job of getting us back home. I knew I had become a more seasoned pilot,

but I also knew I had come close to making two potentially fatal errors. The first was when I made a turn towards the clearing I saw to the east of Macon. I almost entered a sucker hole—a deceptive break in the clouds. Sucker holes can cause fatalities because you never know what to expect. That sucker hole closed before I got to it.

My other error occurred after I turned west to get on the other side of Macon. It looked like the clouds were dissipating and it was safe to drop down. In just a few seconds I saw a high hill directly in front of the plane. I immediately added power and climbed back to my previous altitude. The large clearing was not a sucker hole, but it acted like one. I received a lot of divine help on that trip, but I also realized the imperative of getting instrument rated. I knew I needed to learn a lot more about cross-country flying and how to avoid future mistakes.

From 1974 to 1976, I piloted family and friends on more cross-country trips. Many were day trips we liked to call $100 Hamburger Trips. Fly to Augusta or Waycross, eat a hamburger lunch at the airport, and fly home. Other trips took longer when we visited family in Memphis, Tennessee and Columbus, Mississippi. On one trip to Memphis, the weather closed in on us, so we landed in Muscle Shoals, Alabama, rented a car, and drove on to Memphis.

Thirty Two

My First Corporation

Flying a general aviation airplane thrilled and excited me, but I dreamed of starting a general aviation (GA) business. By the early 1970s, I thought the time had come to use my MBA and open a Fixed Base Operation (FBO) at a general aviation airport or find an airport management position.

An FBO provides airplane services such as fuel and maintenance, flight instruction, airplane storage and tie-downs, and sometimes sells planes. In 1972 major fuel suppliers provided financial help to set up FBO facilities, which included installing fuel tanks. My partners and I had to have their backing to move forward with an FBO.

After visiting airports with advertised management positions, I quickly learned that being a pilot and an aerospace engineer with an MBA did not give me the practical experience required to be an airport manager. My research about an FBO also led to a dead end. In 1973, the nation experienced a fuel crunch and prices skyrocketed. Major fuel suppliers no longer helped set up FBO facilities and existing ones were hurting for business. I had to face the reality that starting my own GA business needed to be put on the back burner.

In 1973, one of my close friends at First Baptist Church of Marietta told me about a breakthrough in the general aviation industry. Howard, who was an aviation enthusiast, heard about an innovative company in Long Branch, NJ that advertised a desktop flight simulator just for instrument flight training—the ATC-510 Personal Flight Simulator.

We thought the desk-top simulator would be perfect to provide instrument flight training for pilots who needed extra hours to become proficient. Extremely high fuel prices were limiting recreational flying and other modes of travel and commerce. The FAA agreed that time in a flight simulator, with an instructor provided valuable training for some of the many hours required to certify an instrument-rated pilot.

Howard and I believed that a flight training ground school would be a great business opportunity. Since any new business required a serious investment of time and money, we knew we needed help. Tom, a test pilot, and member of the Lockheed Flying Club, bought into our idea and contributed the cash infusion we needed. Other pilot friends in the flying club liked the idea of our school and encouraged us to move forward. My MBA, along with my expertise in accounting and marketing, made me confident the company would succeed.

We incorporated as Avair Inc. and named me President and Chief Financial Officer and Howard Vice President and Chief Marketing Officer. Tom became the Chief Pilot and Instructor.

The next step was to visit the simulator manufacturer located in New Jersey to negotiate a purchase of several ATC-510 simulators. Howard had a friend who was interested in flying us there in his high-performance Piper 180 airplane. This airplane had a cruising speed of approximately 150 knots per hour or 172 mph. At that speed it would take us about 5 hours to fly the 855 miles from Atlanta to the Newark vicinity, with one stop for refueling and rest.

The airplane was a four-place airplane and since the pilot had a friend going with him, only Howard and I could go. First, we had to find time to take a couple of days off from work. When the day for the trip arrived, we met at the Peachtree DeKalb Airport (PDK), made a flight plan, and checked the weather. A large high-pressure system existed off the coast, which could mean a tail wind and good flying all the way. We headed for the Linden, NJ airport, which was close to our destination in Long Branch.

Shortly after take-off, we realized the plane had a tail wind of approximately 70 to 75 mph. At that rate, our flying time would be only 3.5 hours and we wouldn't need a fuel stop. This meant the pilot must be alert before moving into an area that had a lot of air traffic. I don't believe our pilot contacted Air Traffic Control soon enough, since I saw a Twin

Beechcraft (B-18) come very close. I had already had a near fatal incident in a B-18. Colliding with one of those planes could end your life.

The plane made it to Linden, but I questioned the pilot's ability to get us safely back home. Since we left Atlanta early in the morning, we were able to meet our ATC-510 contacts and negotiate the purchase and shipping arrangements for the simulators early in the day. We left Linden soon after—and with God's help—made it to our planned refueling destination before heading home.

With the simulators on the way, a place was needed to conduct our business and train pilots. We rented a suite in an office building on New Spring Rd near Cumberland Mall, which was at the southern end of Cobb County and not far south of the McCollum-Cobb County Airport. The high cost of furnishing the office with desks and tables for the simulators proved to be more of an expense than we had expected, although it was typical with any new business.

The next important step was to hire an instrument-rated ground instructor. We were extremely fortunate to find a retired US Air Force pilot who had both ground and flight instrument instructor ratings. David had retired as a Full Colonel with over 10,000 flying hours and was an all-around good guy. Not only did he do a great job for Avair, but he helped me out personally.

David gave me flight instructions in a military T-34 trainer. When I had worked on the flight line in the Navy, I had flown in the back seat of several Navy SNJ trainers. Dave made it possible for me to sit in the front seat of a trainer that belonged to the Navy Flying Club and be trained like a military pilot. As a member of the Flying Club, Dave had access to this plane stationed at Dobbins Air Force Base. He not only helped me with my instrument training, but he worked very well with our ATC- 510 students. We paid him much less salary than he was worth.

We had everything we needed to get the business started except advertising and marketing. My MBA had taught me that this was essential to maintain a profitable business. The local television and radio stations gave us some free airtime to promote our business after we opened, but we couldn't afford paid advertising. Since our funds were limited, we mainly marketed the concept to our friends and associates interested in the aviation business. With all of us having full time jobs, except for Dave, the amount of time we could spend promoting the business was limited.

Avair also became the local distributor of the flight simulators and provided maintenance. One of our initial sales was to a group of African Americans who wanted to provide flight training to black students in high school and college. One of the managers at Lockheed already worked with some former Tuskegee pilots (Red Tail Aviators, World War II) to give flight training to young men. Their ground school was located at Fulton County Airport and our ATC-510 simulators were just what they needed for their Minority AA Aviators organization.

It was rewarding to work with some of the Tuskegee pilots. Most of them were still in their 50s and actively engaged with flying. I like to think that we helped, at least in a small way, to get organizations started like The TAI (Atlanta Chapter, Tuskegee Airmen, Inc.) which was incorporated in Atlanta in August 1976. Similar groups all over the US were dedicated to maintaining the traditions of the Tuskegee Airmen and preserving the legacy of the first generation of African American military aviators of the Second World War. Our company felt we were making an important contribution, and, at the same time, making our business more profitable.

To promote our company and provide a community service, we gave ground school training to a squadron of Aviation Boy Scouts. When the boys came to our office, they were assigned an ATC-510 simulator to operate. Since these simulators were designed to train existing pilots, we had to provide the Scouts basic pilot training as well. This time-consuming task cost us money needed for Dave's salary and rent expenses. We had to charge the Scouts a fee, which I did not want to do.

We did not want to exploit the parents, so with their permission, I took the boys on short flights at no charge. It helped me too since I needed to fly to stay current and proficient. I also worked with the Experimental Aviation Association (EAA). The EAA provided a program called "Young Eagles." The local EAA chapter set days when their pilots offered free flight time to Avair's Aviation Boy Scouts, who were encouraged to take advantage of this opportunity.

Despite our best efforts, our business did not grow fast enough to pay its bills. The promised advertising help from the manufacturer of the ATC-510 flight simulators had not materialized, and we did not have the money to find more customers. My partners and I brainstormed our next steps. Moving our office closer to a general aviation airport made better

sense than being close to a shopping mall. There were pros and cons to making a move. We knew we would face competition from other similar businesses at the airport and that we would have to employ a reliable full-time manager. There were four months remaining on our lease, so we limped along until we could find a better place.

During that interim period, we learned that ATC Flight Simulators had upgraded the ATC-510 to a newer version, the ATC-610. Along with several new bells and whistles, it looked more realistic. Enclosed on three sides, the operator felt like he was in an actual airplane with an authentic cockpit and instrument panel. With the upgrades, pilots could better practice instrument approaches to more airports.

The availability of the new simulators encouraged us to get serious about moving. Relocating to an airport would provide exposure to the right customers who could then be provided with the latest and greatest machines for their training. We knew we needed more investment money to buy the equipment. My task was to find a new investor so we could move forward with our plan. Howard and Tom started negotiations with Peachtree DeKalb Airport (PDK).

One of my aerodynamics associates at Lockheed agreed to invest in our operation. Ted, a member of the flying club, was like most aviators in that he pursued adventure and took on risk. With no family to support, he had money available to invest in our company. The rest of us had families and were hesitant to risk more of our savings. Having two children in high school who might want to go to college in a few years made me cautious. Mary's ongoing diabetic issues were expensive as well. However, I believed that everything would work out, since it was in God's hands.

Everything seemed to fall in place. We signed a three-year lease at PDK for a nice space that could attract potential customers. We also hired a full-time manager for the business. At first, I thought I would be set free from the numerous administrative tasks associated with the business, but reality set in. It did not take long to discover that new customers were few and far between. Our manager was not doing his job, and we had to fire him. In addition, we were stuck with a huge lease payment. I tried to pick up the slack and keep performing to expectations at Lockheed. It became too much for me, and I crashed physically and mentally.

Thirty Three

My Mid-life Crisis

When Mary and I agreed to start our business, we committed to making it work. Our strong faith kept us involved in our church, helped us share our faith with others, and helped us make wise financial decisions. We had no idea we were about to ride a three-year emotional roller coaster with many highs and lows. The turmoil of those three years took a great toll, but also led to a momentous life-changing event.

For most of my life, I had been able to overcome difficulties and remain strong. This time was different. My totally fatigued body and mind let me down. A heavy depression settled around my shoulders, and I informed the other investors they would have to handle the business. They were very understanding and took over my responsibilities. It should have helped, but it didn't. My family was in financial jeopardy, and I had let my business partners down.

Finding the money to pay my monthly portion of the lease was too much. The burden weighed me down and made me unable to function, so I cut myself off from almost everyone and became awfully hard to live with. My wife came to my rescue by encouraging me to look to God and discern his plan for this stage of my life. Bible studies, commentaries, and stories of missionaries who endured hard times spoke to my spirit. I wanted to discover how the godly faith of others helped them overcome their difficulties.

At Lockheed, I kept to myself while trying not to jeopardize my work. I was thankful to have a job that provided for my family. The Research

Department occupied an area that resembled a beautiful college campus. A lake and the surrounding trees kept me in touch with nature and in tune with God. During lunch, instead of going out to eat with the other engineers, I took my sack lunch and a commentary and sat under a tree and tried to enjoy the beauty of the lake and scenery. For weeks I read and prayed for God's direction. On Sunday at church, I continued to look for answers. The depression lingered, and nothing made me happy.

One Sunday after church, I entered the chapel and felt closer to God as I absorbed the atmosphere of that quiet, holy spot. The big Bible on the stand in front of the room caught my attention. It was open to Hebrews and the words of that chapter spoke to me.

> *"Therefore, since we are surrounded by such a great cloud of witnesses, let us throw off everything that hinders and the sin that so easily entangles. And let us run with perseverance the race marked out for us, fixing our eyes on Jesus, the pioneer and perfecter of faith. For the joy set before him he endured the cross, scorning its shame, and sat down at the right hand of the throne of God. Consider him who endured such opposition from sinners, so that you will not grow weary and lose heart. In your struggle against sin, you have not yet resisted to the point of shedding your blood.*

> *And have you completely forgotten this word of encouragement that addresses you as a father addresses his son? It says, "My son, do not make light of the Lord's discipline, and do not lose heart when he rebukes you, because the Lord disciplines the one he loves, and he chastens everyone he accepts as his son.*

> *Endure hardship as discipline; God is treating you as his children. For what children are not disciplined by their father? If you are not disciplined—and everyone undergoes discipline—then you are not legitimate, not true sons and daughters at all. Moreover, we have all had human fathers who disciplined us, and we respected them for it. How much more should we submit to the Father of spirits and live!*

144

They disciplined us for a little while as they thought best;
but God disciplines us for our good, in order that we may
share in his holiness. No discipline seems pleasant at the
time, but painful. Later on, however, it produces a harvest
of righteousness and peace for those who have been trained by
it." Hebrews 12:1-11 (NIV)

Those words from the Bible spoke directly to my spirit and lifted the fog of depression from my mind. The verses helped me realize God was with me regardless of my situation. As one of his children, he was using this difficult time to discipline me and bring me closer to him. I knew God would see me through. He showed me that the timing was not right for this type of business and that other opportunities were ahead.

During the next two weeks, I learned that Howard and Tom succeeded in releasing the company from the huge lease burden and sold some of the instrument trainers. In 1976 after three years of operation, Avair finally closed its doors. The many lessons I learned from that difficult experience helped me in future business endeavors and in my personal life. I realized that no valley was too deep or task too hard for God, and that if I walked close to him, he would see me through.

Thirty Four

My French Connection

At the end of 1976, my work on span-wise blowing (SWB) paid off. International aerospace engineers and managers began following my work and conducting their own studies. My research related to the application of SWB transonic flows attracted their attention. Previous applications of SWB were used for low speeds, whereas transonic flow occurred when approaching the speed of sound.

Lockheed Vice President of Engineering, Dr. Collins, believed that further studies in a hi-speed wind tunnel would benefit my research. Locating an available hi-speed wind tunnel took some time. The final decision initiated a joint effort between Lockheed and the ONERA wind tunnel in Modane, France located in the French Alps. For some time, the aerospace engineers and managers at the National d'Etudes et de Recherches Aérospatiales (ONERA), "National Studies of Aerospace Research" had been conducting their own research and following our work. Dr. Collins knew Dr. Quinton, the head of ONERA Fluid Mechanics.

Dan from the Aerodynamics Department and I were chosen to lead the effort. We made a good team since we had been friends for a long time and worked together as deacons at our church. Our task involved designing and building a wind tunnel model and coordinating our effort with our French counterparts. It helped that I had taken a night class on conversational French offered by Lockheed. Knowing some of the basics of the language made me confident I could communicate during our trip.

We decided that Mary would go with me on the trip, but making the

arrangements was a challenge. Having two teenagers, Darrell (19) and Cheryl (16), presented a dilemma. Darrell, who had recently graduated from high school, struggled with epilepsy and life in general. As a pretty and popular high-schooler, Cheryl had lots of girl and boy friends. We knew we needed a chaperone for them during the month we were in France. A college-age student agreed to assume that responsibility.

Our itinerary called for a flight from Atlanta to New York and on to Charles de Gaulle Airport in Paris. After three hours of restless sleep, we arrived in Paris the next morning and found our assigned hotel. Soon we received a call from Dr. Quinton at ONERA who said he would pick up us and take us on a walking tour of Paris. We grabbed some café au lait to wake us up and fortify us against the chilly and misty fall air. We knew better than to complain since we had as our personal tour guide a high-level executive from our collaborating company.

Dr. Quinton's first name sounded like Poisson—the French word for fish—so we nicknamed him PQ. As we toured the streets of Paris, he impressed us with his English skills and personality. PQ described in detail his participation in La Resistance during World War II. As we passed Sorbonne University, he pointed out bullet holes from the war in one of the buildings. At the Louvre, he introduced us to many of the exhibits. Leonardo da Vinci's Mona Lisa intrigued me with her smile and made me wonder who she was and what she was thinking.

The next day, we attended the Cathedral Notre-Dame de Paris. The mass celebrated La Toussaint de Jour (All Saints Day) which was a special day for French Catholics. The cathedral acoustics were poor, and the priest spoke in French as well as Latin, which we couldn't understand, but the impressive structure and service immersed us in French culture.

We said goodbye to Paris and on Monday boarded a high-speed train and headed toward Lyon and the French Alps. Three hours later we caught a slow, coal burning train and began the winding journey up into the mountains. We unloaded ourselves along with our luggage in Modane. We watched private automobiles with their passengers drive onto long, flat train cars for the journey through the Alps tunnel into Italy. For us, that trip had to wait for a later time.

A courier from the ONERA wind tunnel facility picked us up and took us to our hotel in a small village called Aussois (ou-swa.) Our rooms

in the Hotel Court Sejour were small, but nice. Since there were few guests in the hotel, we knew we could manage sharing the bathroom down the hall. The hotel restaurant served good meals for about eight US dollars a day. Aussois was a ski resort, but since it had received little snow, the ski season had not begun.

Another courier took us to work on Tuesday morning. The drive down from our high elevation (3500') in the Maurienne Valley in the Vanoise National Park acquainted us with beautiful scenery. The towering peaks of the Alps and the alpine houses on the sides of the mountains got our attention. The courier told us that most houses had a stable underneath for cows or sheep that gave the animals a warm place to stay and helped keep the house warm in winter.

Another interesting sight was a large metal elevated pipe on a frame high above the snow level. We passed under the yard-wide pipe several times as we drove down the mountain. We learned the pipe carried water from a reservoir several thousand feet down the mountainside to produce hydraulic power for the supersonic wind tunnel. When the wind tunnels were not operating, the hydraulic power produced electricity for the city of Modane.

The ONERA facility housed several wind tunnels. The test section of the largest supersonic tunnel was 24 feet, and the wind speed could exceed the speed of sound or Mach One. Dan and I were assigned to work in one of the smaller subsonic tunnels.

To make it easier for us to get to work, our French host said we would be assigned a Citroën. Instead of a beautiful Citroën DS, Avant Garde, we ended up with a Citroën 2CV with a two-cylinder engine and 12 horsepower. The car resembled a Volkswagen Beetle with sharp corners outside and almost no upholstery inside. The support springs were so weak that when someone sat in the back seat, the headlights pointed to the sky. An inside lever was necessary to adjust the direction of the lights. The weak springs allowed us to drive over some very rough roads. We had a lot of fun with this car and often drove into the countryside to meet some of the locals.

After two weeks of tests, the tunnel had to be shut down due to mechanical problems. We were excited about the shutdown because we wanted to explore more of our host country. In addition, Tucker and

Elaine—our good friends from church—were flying from Georgia to be our tour guides. Since Elaine worked for an airlines, they flew free all over the world. They rented a nice car, and we set out to explore the French countryside.

The first leg of our journey took us from Modane to Marseille on the Mediterranean Sea. Since we enjoyed sightseeing, the trip took two days to complete. We stopped in Avignon, an historic and interesting city. The Rhone River ran parallel to the road as we drove toward Pont Avignon, a famous medieval bridge that still stood on four Roman arches.

Our plans for the next day involved lunch in Marseille on the Mediterranean and travelling along the water's edge to Monte Carlo. Instead, we got lost in Marseille, and with my limited French found it difficult to get directions. We learned that French people really like foreigners to speak their language, but the shopkeepers were more interested in selling us something than in pointing us in the right direction. We finally found a good restaurant on the beach for lunch. The sea snails were tasty, but the other sea creatures in my salad were unidentifiable. However, the proprietors gave us good directions, and we were on our way.

Cannes, Nice, and Monte Carlo—the playgrounds of the rich and famous—beckoned to us. The beautiful beaches of the French Riviera lived up to their reputation. The high-rise condos and exclusive shops in Cannes and Nice invited us to come in and buy luxury goods, but we continued toward Monte Carlo.

Tucker and Elaine found a good, inexpensive hotel. Located on a narrow street just wide enough for one car, the small hotel's elevator barely accommodated two people with small bags. After a good night's sleep, we started a walking tour of the picturesque city. We passed a famous gambling casino we recognized from movies, but alas, no Hollywood stars. After cramming much scenery and history into one day, we headed to our next adventure.

We drove a different direction back to Modane so we could see more of the beautiful Alps. Our route took us through Turin, Italy where we saw destruction from World War II. Rusted railroad cars turned upside down littered the ground next to the tracks. It made us sad to recall the lives lost during the war. It also made us proud that the United States led the effort for the liberation of Europe.

With so much beauty all around, it was hard to stay sad long. The scenic smaller mountains and the snow-capped higher peaks of the Alps were breathtaking. The view made me think of the front range of the Rockies in Colorado. I think we saw about 500 miles of the Alps before we reached Susa where we drove onto a flatbed railroad car. After being securely anchored down, we began the final lap of our trip back to Modane. It felt strange to sit in our car as the train pulled us along the side of the mountain range and then into the long, dark tunnel through the mountain. We finally reached Modane and daylight. What a memorable trip. At that point, Tucker and Elaine left us to fly back to the USA, and Dan and I returned to work.

We made good progress in the repaired wind tunnel until I got sick from bad water. I stayed at the hotel near the bathroom while Mary left to find medicine. The medical facilities in Aussois were archaic, and the only place to get help was the Catholic infirmary. The black-haired locals stared at Mary's light brunet hair as she made to her way through town. The Catholic nuns gave her medicine containing charcoal, an old-fashioned remedy for intestinal upset. After I returned to work, Dan and I were unable to complete the required tests before our scheduled flight back home.

Lockheed management seemed pleased with our accomplishments but said we would need to return to France to finish the testing process. Due to scheduling problems at ONERA, it was June 1977 before we could again have access to the subsonic tunnel. Going to Paris and the beautiful Alps again in the warm month of June was an exciting opportunity. However, Mary wasn't happy because she couldn't go on the second trip.

We learned that during our first trip out of the country, our sixteen-year-old daughter had thrown a big party. At least thirty high schoolers descended on our house for a night of loud music and dancing. Neither Darrell nor the chaperone could control the raucous crowd. The neighbors called the police who calmed things down. Nobody was arrested, but we got an earful from the neighbors when we returned. Discipline was administered, but we knew we could not leave our teenagers home alone again.

Dan's wife accompanied us on our second trip to France. She nursed Dan when he got sick like I had on the first trip. When he recovered, we

had time to conduct successful wind tunnel tests as well as sightsee. This time, our destination was Mount Blanc, the highest peak in the Alps. At 15,000 feet this mountain towered over all the rest. We drove to Chamonix and rode 12,000 feet straight up in a scary cable car. At the top, we exited through an ice tunnel to get to solid ground.

Before we left France, I received a message from our Lockheed manager back home. He wanted me to travel to Munich, Germany to visit engineers at Messerschmitt-Bolkow-Blohm. The company wanted a briefing on the span-wise blowing concept. I had never traveled in Europe by myself, and I still had vivid memories of the Nazi atrocities in Germany during World War II. I finally convinced myself that in the thirty years since the end of the war, things had changed for the better.

My travel plans involved being driven by wind tunnel personnel in a deluxe Citroën to Geneva, Switzerland to board a flight to Munich. All went well until we reached the French-Swiss border. A guard that looked like a German soldier gave me orders in French. I couldn't understand his French, and my driver couldn't understand my English. We finally realized the guard wanted to inspect my suitcase. Later we heard that all vehicles were being stopped at the border because of a major robbery in Geneva. I passed the inspection and made my way to the airport and on to Munich. All went well with the meetings in Munich, and I was soon reunited with Dan in Modane. We completed our final tests and headed back to the good old USA.

Under Mary's supervision, our teenage children had caused no problems during my time in France. Even though neither Darrell nor Cheryl were academically inclined, they both managed to graduate from high school during the late 1970s. They still faced issues in determining what to do next with their lives, but at least their difficult teenage years were over. As a new decade loomed, Mary and I were looking forward to better days ahead.

Thirty Five

Studying Vortex Flow

My Lockheed research project on span-wise blowing reached a culmination with the successful wind tunnel tests we conducted in France. Dan, my project partner, and I were invited to present our findings in Lisbon, Portugal at the international American Institute of Aeronautics and Astronautics conference (AIAA). Since only one of us could go to Portugal, Dan and I agreed that Dan would present the paper, and my name would come first as one of the authors.

By the early 1980s, fan-jet engine development had accelerated and put a halt to the span-wise blowing concept. The original jet engine compressor created surplus air that could be siphoned for SWB. The newer fan-jet technology no longer produced surplus air that could easily be siphoned. It made me sad to see my concept put on the shelf, but in the field of research and development, there is always something new and interesting to work on.

Studies in the control of vortex flows had been conducted by several engineering organizations since the beginning of the 1970s. Vortex flow had always fascinated me, especially since my near-death experience with the strong trailing horizontal whirlwinds that came from a cargo plane when we landed in Marietta. But there was a significant difference between my work in vortex flow and most other engineering organizations. Most engineers wanted to eliminate the vortex generated by the sharp leading edge of the wings. I wanted to discover how to control the vortex and make it reduce drag.

All airplanes experience vortex flow during some part of their flight regime. Vortices coming from any spot on an airplane contribute to drag which slows down the plane and wastes fuel. Most commercial, military, and general aviation aircraft were designed to minimize vortex flow coming from the wing or tail leading edges. Some types of airplanes like the supersonic Concord benefitted from the generation of vortices. Lockheed wanted to figure out how to control vortices to benefit military aircraft, because the Air Force showed much interest. My interest and experience in that area put me right in the middle of that research.

The Lockheed Georgia Research Laboratory (LGRL) had several facilities for experimental investigations. I worked in a wind tunnel using a laser velocimeter to obtain forces, moments, and detail vortices. My work in smoke and water tunnels had taught me to interpret flow visualizations. An extensive theoretical analysis required much study and training in computer programing. Mathematical tools developed during my work on the Saturn V Apollo Moon Vehicle came in very handy. I had to analyze ground winds shedding vortices from the circular body of the Saturn V while on the launch pad. All this interesting research did not happen without interruption.

Three times my vortex flow research was interrupted when airplane design groups needed my help creating proposals for developing new airplanes. I asked myself the question, "Which comes first, the chicken or the egg?" If you don't build new airplanes to sell, you don't have money to do research; if you don't do research, you don't have clever ideas to design new airplanes. Fortunately for me, the managers of the design and the research organizations knew that I had experience in both. I had no choice but to follow the money and the greatest need, whether I liked it or not.

I packed up my personal belongings, engineering tools, and literature and moved to the Stability and Control Department (S&C.) This first move fit my interests and got me closer to the dynamic problems of flying. As a pilot, I learned a lot from my time in S&C and at the same time contributed my vortex flow expertise to the project.

Next, the manager put me to work on a proposal to modify—for commercial purposes— the well-known C-130 Hercules. The proposed design for the newly named L-400 featured a shorter wingspan and two engines instead of four. The commercial market required more strenuous

Federal Aviation Agency (FAA) certification than the military certification. That requirement created difficult problems for the designers and for me.

Extensive wind tunnel tests discovered a potentially dangerous flight condition. If the pilot induced a sideslip or yaw (rotation about the vertical axis) by pushing the rudder pedal too hard, the airplane would continue to rotate around the vertical axis until the airplane rolled over and entered an inverted dive. What a terrifying scenario that would have been.

After studying the problem, I visualized an aerodynamic fix using a vortex flow- producing shape. This triangular dorsal fin is commonly found on fish. Some airplanes sport dorsals that are small and rounded at the leading edge. My suggested dorsal was relatively large with a small leading-edge radius. The small radius was big enough not to cause a drag producing vortex until the yaw became high enough to create the vortex. The forming vortex created a large damping side force that prevented the yaw angle from getting too high. I presented this concept to the S&C manager, and after a bit of explanation, he agreed I could install and test my dorsal on the wind tunnel model. The tests proved it worked like a charm. The over-swing yaw was fixed with no commercial certification problem.

A few days later, I received a call to come to the manager's office. My first thought was, *what have I done now?* When I got to his office, there were several people there, including the chief engineer. *This must really be bad.* When I sat down, the manager said, "We have all decided you deserve a commendation for your solution to the over-swing yaw." Wow! What a relief and an honor. I never received another commendation while at Lockheed, but I found that the managers would now listen to my maverick ideas and sometimes try them.

It was not all work and no play during my time in the research lab. By the end of 1980, I had trained enough and learned enough to apply for my pilot instrument rating. I'd studied all the regulations, the use of the instrument approach plates and maps, and passed the written portion of the exam. Learning to interpret and follow air traffic control voice directions proved to be more difficult. My long exposure to loud aircraft engines and noisy wind tunnels had affected my hearing. With enough practice, I generally knew what the tower was going to say, so I managed to stumble through enough to apply for the instrument flight exam.

My flight instructor signed my logbook and approved my qualifications to take the exam. Next, I had to locate a FAA certified instrument flight examiner. My flying peers and instructor recommended an examiner in Berry Hill, Georgia–a small rural community southeast of Atlanta. I rented a Lockheed Flying Club airplane, and Mary and I flew down for the appointment. My nerves were on edge, but I soon relaxed when I met my examiner who wore denim overalls and acted like a good-old country boy.

"I'm Will Sutton, your flight examiner," he drawled. "Are you ready to go flying?" Then, he told Mary he would take good care of me and suggested she make herself at home in his office.

Since I could only rely on instruments to fly, I wore a hood, so I couldn't see outside of the plane. The only thing I could see was the instrument panel. Will told me we were heading to Macon, Georgia and that he would give me various tasks. My first task involved finding an intersection of two flight paths, and once we were there, to enter a standard holding pattern. Several maneuvers later, I was told to call Macon approach control to get clearance to make a specific standard instrument approach to Macon Airport.

During the approach, I thought I'd taken too much time before making a required turn. The Macon tower advised me I hadn't gone too far and was cleared to turn back toward the airport. After two more hours of stressful flying, Will said, "Let's go home."

Mary met us as we taxied to the tie down ramp. Mr. Sutton walked up to Mary and said, "Don't worry about flying with him. He will get you down safely."

Without another word, he wrote in my logbook. INSTRUMENT AIRPLANE CHECK RIDE, OK. Then he signed his name and added his FAA certification number. Praise the Lord! I'll always remember the date—December 29, 1980. What a great Christmas present and exciting New Year gift. I could already visualize many thrilling flying adventures during the decade of the 80s.

Thirty Six

Flying Far and Wide

Two days after getting my Instrument Pilot Rating, Mary and I took off from Cobb County Airport and headed for Memphis, Tennessee. I filed a flight plan under Instrument Flight Rules (IFR) and made the trip in 3.6 hours under the guidance of air traffic control. Our normal driving time for this trip took seven to eight hours, including stops for fuel and food. We spent New Year's Eve and Day with our parents and left Memphis on January 2, 1981. With a tailwind, we made the flight back home in 2.6 hours. For obvious reasons, I like the pilot adage, "May the wind always be at your back."

Flying IFR put me in a distinguished group of around 300,000 other pilots in the entire country. This certification rounded out my aviation career as an airman and aeronautical engineer. Getting a commercial pilot rating would be the icing on the cake. Many cross-country trips are required to receive this rating including a trip with three legs, which meant you must stop at three different airports.

Our seven-day flying trip vacation required careful planning and preparation. As Pilot in Command (PIC), I assumed responsibility for every detail of the trip. The most nerve-wracking and unknown part of the trip was the unpredictable weather. I kept reminding myself of the reason I worked so hard for my instrument rating, and FAA flight services would keep us informed about changing weather patterns.

Our first destination during the beautiful first week of September 1981 was Bluestone State Park in West Virginia. We checked out a Cessna

177RG Cherokee, which was the best cross-country airplane owned by the Lockheed Flying Club. The high-cruise speed airplane had a high wing without the normal wing strut and retractable landing gear.

I filed IFR with the traffic control at Cobb County Airport in Kennesaw, Georgia. After fueling the plane and loading our luggage, we took off for Charleston, West Virginia. Our route took us across the Blue Ridge Mountains to Knoxville, Tennessee. We soared over the foothills of the Appalachian Mountains as we crossed from Tennessee into Virginia. As we approached the West Virginia state line, we saw dense clouds directly ahead. *Do I fly right into that cloud bank, or do I contact air traffic control to direct me around?* The clouds didn't look like thunderstorms, so I decided to push ahead.

Confidence in my instrument rating almost got me into trouble. The altimeter read between 7,000 and 8,000 feet, and as I steered into the clouds, we were pushed up another 1,000 feet. I realized I had made a wrong decision but had no choice but to ride it out. The nearby mountains created an updraft I knew could be dangerous. I called air traffic control to vector me out. They gave me a westward heading, and we soon flew into clearer skies. Because I was way off course, I called the tower again for an updated flight plan into Charleston.

After a successful landing, I closed the flight plan, tied down the airplane, walked into the pilot's lounge, and collapsed. I had experienced the longest three hours of my life. My adrenaline rush kept me stressed for a while. Mary was totally non-stressed and oblivious to how close we had come to disaster. She was ready to start our vacation.

Our trip to the hotel near Bluestone State Park lasted another 2.5 hours. There were no clouds on the way and the updraft had disappeared. With beautiful weather on the horizon, we planned to spend five days exploring all that West Virginia had to offer.

The New River Gorge Bridge over a deep gorge boasted one of the best views in North America, behind Niagara Falls and the Grand Canyon. Daring folk's bungee jumped off that bridge, but I'd had enough adventure for a while. I wasn't ready to fly off a cliff tethered to a cord. After five fun-filled days of beautiful scenery, we headed back to Charleston so I could file my flight plan to Bowling Green, Kentucky.

I checked in with the Flight Service for weather predictions, and it

didn't look good. A dreary day with light rain was in the forecast, which would require a real test of my instrument rating. However, a decision to fly must be based on common sense and good judgment. With my limited experience, I understood I had to be cautious and only take measured risks.

After a good night's sleep, it was decision time. The weather report showed light rain and clouds all the way to Bowling Green. Clouds covered the normal cruise altitude all the way. To get on top of the clouds, I'd have to climb to 10,000 feet. The Flight Service personnel encouraged me to go, but I had to make the call. I prayed and then decided to file my IFR flight plan and go.

We flew into the bumpy clouds, but I was able to keep the airplane on the navigation beam. After climbing for a little less than ten minutes, we broke out on top. What an exhilarating experience for me—a newly rated IFR pilot. Suddenly, we were in the bright sunshine, and I knew my experience and God's help got us there. Still, it was comforting to know that someone on the ground could look at their radar and know exactly where we were.

After two hours of uneventful flying, flight control called with instructions to descend to 3,000 feet and prepare for the approach to Bowling Green. Soon we were back in the soupy clouds, totally dependent on-air traffic control. As I approached 3,000 feet, I could see the ground through little breaks in the clouds and the airport ahead. I began descending without reporting to ground control. My headphones crackled as he demanded, "What's your altitude?"

I realized my mistake when I let the plane drop to 2,800 feet, so I immediately climbed back to the 3,000-foot level. With the airport in view, I called the controller and cancelled instrument flight rules (IFR), and then contacted the tower at the Bowling Green airport. After almost three hours of flying, we finally received clearance to land. We had one night to unwind and get some rest before heading out on the third leg of our trip back to Kennesaw, Georgia.

I felt good about my flying accomplishments as a seasoned IFR pilot. I really could do what I had been trained to do. After touring Bowling Green, we went to a hotel, and I worked out a flight plan to take us into Cobb County Airport. My confidence was up and my apprehension down.

I knew when I got into that plane, my training would take over, and I could manage the flight.

The next day was Sunday and we knew it would take us about three hours to fly home. When morning came, we went to church to praise the Lord for being with us on the trip. Then, we grabbed a quick lunch and headed for the airport. The dreary weather persisted, but I felt confident it wouldn't be a problem. Once again, I filed an IFR flight plan, received a clearance from the tower, and climbed that plane above the clouds to 10,000 feet. About an hour into the flight, we saw what looked like a thunderstorm directly in our path. I knew we had to stay far away from those angry clouds. I depended on Atlanta approach control to vector us away from the storm, and soon they told me to descend to 3,000 feet. The dark billowing clouds were frightening as I waited for further instruction. When the controller called, he asked, "Are you getting any precipitation? I'm sorry, but I got you on the edge of a thunderstorm."

I started to respond, "No precipitation." Suddenly, we were under water, and I felt like I was navigating a submarine instead of a plane. I shouted, "We're getting it now."

"Turn to a heading of 095 and keep descending," the tower instructed.

Finally, we dropped below the clouds and headed directly to Cobb County Airport. I called the controller, thanked him, told him I could see the runway, and to cancel IFR. We made a good landing, taxied to the tie-down ramp, and sat in the plane a while praising God for a safe trip.

The successful completion of a complex cross-country trip for my commercial rating thrilled me. I had learned a lot more than how to navigate a three-legged trip. The next step in my IFR education would be to plan and safely execute an approach to an airport in real instrument weather. All my training in how to make instrument approaches needed to be put to the test.

That opportunity came the day after Christmas in 1986 when Mary and I decided to fly to Louisville, Mississippi to visit her sister's family. With the Flying Club's Cessna 172 RG gassed up and ready to go, we rose early to check the weather. Even though the weather in western Alabama looked questionable, we decided to take off and recheck the weather at the flight center in Anniston, Alabama. The weather service predicted some thin cloud coverage with tops at about 2000 feet above the surface—not

visual flying weather, but not bad for instrument flight. With clear skies and a full tank of fuel, I thought I could fly using instruments to the Columbus, Mississippi airport. I could always turn around and go back home if the ceiling below the clouds was not high enough to make a safe landing.

My apprehension was high as we approached the Columbus Airport. I kept reminding myself, *I can do this.* When I was handed off to the control tower, they told me the ceiling was 800 feet above the surface. Again, I reminded myself, *I can do this.* While just above the tops of the clouds, I lined up on the track to the instrument landing system outer marker. Then the controller advised me to descend into the clouds. As I stayed on the right track and descended on the glide slope, I saw glimpses of the ground through the clouds. It was tempting to drop below the glide slope and have airport visibility, but I knew that could be dangerous. Staying on the glide slope kept the plane above obstacles.

I stayed busy staying on the right track and the glide slope at the same time. The approach control called to tell me I was being handed off to the airport tower. Since I couldn't handle another task, I told him I was too busy and didn't call the tower until I was on the ground. I taxied to the Fixed Base Operator and shut down the engine. An employee rushed out to tell me that Flight Service wanted me to call them. *Was I in trouble?* I had forgotten to cancel my IFR plan, and the tower was holding a commercial airline until I canceled. The controller must have known he was dealing with a novice.

We called the family to let them know we had arrived safely. We rented a car at Columbus Airport and drove to Louisville. Everyone welcomed us and treated us like royalty. Mary's brothers and sisters were there, including Mary's brother Fred who was an executive commercial pilot and flight instructor. He told everyone not to expect us in that kind of weather. I proved to myself and everyone else that I had more training and sense of adventure than anyone thought. My nephew must have been impressed because he continued his flight training, and eventually became a flight instructor.

Thirty Seven

Go with the Flow

Returning to the Research Department at Lockheed meant I could resume my investigation of vortex flow with encouragement from management. My work benefitted from earlier research conducted by NASA engineer, Edward Polhamus. He explored the benefits of the leading-edge vortex in certain types of high-speed aircraft. In 1966, he discovered the lift force created by a wing with a leading-edge vortex is equivalent to the leading-edge thrust rotating up about 90 degrees or normal to the wing surface. When the air flow did not separate from the leading-edge of the wing, the force pointed forward in the direction of thrust.

Mr. Polhamus wrote an extended NASA report in 1986 entitled *"Vortex Lift Research: Early Contributions and some Current Challenges."* The Polhamus' leading-edge thrust concept helped me approximate a value for vortex lift but left me with unanswered questions as to how much the leading-edge thrust rotated. My research helped me answer those questions about the importance of leading-edge forces on all wings.

My earlier experience came from my work on the Saturn V Apollo moon launch rocket. Then I conducted theoretical and mathematical analyses of vortex flow ejecting from both sides of a circular cylinder. My master's level class at USC, where I learned those analytical tools, proved to be one of my most important classes. I struggled through the course and only made a C, but what I learned stuck with me. I still use those tools in the work I do today.

My research with Lockheed continued through the 1980s, allowing me to present several disclosures to Lockheed attorneys for patentable concepts. From these disclosures, another associate and I obtained a patent for airplane drag reduction. A second patent for improving airplane lift was also granted by Lockheed.

The complexity of my research required the development of new computer software. My Lockheed managers encouraged me to proceed. The software would be based on the mathematics I used to transform the flow around a cylinder with shedding vortices. Since I was particularly good with a slide rule, but just beginning to learn computer programming, they assigned a young engineer with computer coding experience to help me. George and I worked very well together on the challenging project. He didn't know much about vortex flow, and I was not a programmer. Despite our challenges, we developed successful preliminary software, which we presented as an AIAA report at a 1985 conference in Colorado Springs, Colorado. This report laid the groundwork for software that has continued to mature and is the basis for the software I use today.

My group leader, Johnnie Braden, liked our effort and told us, "I believe you have something there." This led to another collaborative effort with Johnnie on reducing the drag on the C-130 Hercules. Lockheed tried several concepts to reduce the afterbody drag. One was successful but led to structural problems. Johnnie and I were assigned to conduct further research.

We tested several concepts in a wind tunnel using a small model of the C-130. Nothing worked any better than the original Lockheed concept until we came up with a unique idea known as Terraced Channels. Terraced channels looked like crops growing on the side of a mountain. We cut a series of small channels along the side of the afterbody. They looked like a diamond-back rattlesnake moving itself over sand. These channels were cut so they trapped a small vortex moving like a tornado down the channel. They cut through the origin of the big vortex and entrained smooth air to the bottom and aft of the afterbody. It worked and reduced the aircraft drag significantly. Lockheed's patent attorneys liked it so well they secured a patent with Johnnie and me assigned as inventors, for which we received a nice bonus.

In 1984, NASA began testing an experimental Grumman X-29 airplane

with forward-swept wings. These wings seemed to have some aerodynamic advantages over the swept aft wing. Our research determined it created a problem when the wing stalled. I used my knowledge of both powered lift and vortex control to find a unique concept to avoid this stall problem. The result was higher lift, lower stall speed, and a safer airplane stall. A wind tunnel test proved it worked as expected. The Lockheed patent attorneys agreed it was unique and applied for a government patent. My name appeared as the inventor when the patent was issued on November 10, 1987, as *Passive Vortex Lift Control.*

Doing unorthodox research led to some pitfalls and benefits. My investigation of Passive Vortex Lift Control (PVLC) was conducted under an Air Force approved Independent Research and Development (IRAD) program. This meant the work was graded by both Lockheed management and the Air Force. I presented a report to a group of Lockheed personnel including the Vice President of Engineering. After my presentation and during the question-and-answer time, the Vice President said, "You have got to be kidding." I knew he was teasing me, but the other managers might have thought he meant it. Later my Department Manager told me they had given the project a high grade.

Lockheed's Chief Marketing Manager visited the Research Department to discuss future marketing of our innovations. During this discussion, he requested we send him ideas with potential for making a large profit for Lockheed. My office partner and I both had some proven innovations we thought would fit his request. In my case, I had a span-wise blowing concept that I thought was great.

The span-wise blowing concept had proven successful on a F4F Phantom jet. I suggested Lockheed submit a proposal to the Air Force to update all the Phantoms with span-wise blowing. I did as the marketing manager requested and sent my summary through what I thought were the appropriate channels. A few days later, my department manager told me to report to the chief engineer's office ASAP. He chewed me out up one side and down the other for submitting my summary to the marketing manager who liked the idea and had gone to the chief for approval. "Who do you think is going to pay for this," he barked.

"I don't know, but I thought it would have a high pay-off for Lockheed," I replied.

My normally soft-spoken department manager joined in, "Did you know Chuck had just been given a high commendation from the Vice President for his excellent IRAD work and a high Air Force grade?" The chief engineer realized he had been outranked but added, "Consider the proper protocol next time you have an idea."

My next wild idea came while working with aerodynamics engineers who were deeply involved in a study of a highly modified C-130. The plane had very high-lift trailing-edge flaps that created high lift for the wing. A major problem involved the horizontal tail, with downward flow from the wing causing a high angle of attack at the tail. With the engines at full power, the tail stalled, lost its lift, and the plane could not be controlled.

During some of my vortex-flow research investigations, I discovered a relatively small triangular shape surface could be added to the leading edge of a fighter type wing to increase the maximum lift of the wing. This device had a sharp leading edge on each side of the triangle that created vortices. These vortices continued over the wing to help prevent flow separation from the wing. After Lockheed patent attorneys created a patent disclosure for the concept, I was thrilled and jumped at the chance to fit the C-130 horizontal tail with our new device. Getting management approval would not be easy, since it involved an expensive wind tunnel test as well as labor for design, manufacturing, and installation.

I submitted the idea to the head of the Aerodynamics Department, knowing it would be a hard sell. Some of my past successes must have laid the groundwork because he approved it. Now he had to sell it to the Stability and Control (S&C) department manager and the chief engineer. He had a problem with the S&C department. They said it was their job and not aerodynamics. Despite their objections, my manager got the approval to proceed and immediately put me to work on the design.

My office partner and I began investigating the size and location of the leading-edge devices. My theoretical mathematics was in its beginning and not nearly as capable as it is today. I had a big problem with the size and required number of these devices.

One day my manager came by my desk and said, "You better make these things work. I have gone out on a limb for you."

I know today that just one small device would have worked, but then I proposed three relatively large devices to put on the horizontal tail. The

wind tunnel engineers, and the model shop began working to make it happen. They probably thought some crazy aerodynamicist had come up with this idea for a "Sawtooth Tail." The wind tunnel test proved my idea worked but also showed the devices were not practical because they would cause a lot of unwanted drag in cruise flight. They were never installed on an airplane.

My next assignment was complex and challenging. The Air Force was willing to spend a large sum of money for research to develop software to predict the aerodynamic characteristics of fighters at high angles of attack. Because of my knowledge of vortex flows, I was assigned to work on the contract. We were just getting started when Lockheed Georgia made the decision to relocate all engineering personnel to the Lockheed Burbank facility in California. We had two choices—stay in Georgia and be laid off or move to the West Coast.

Thirty Eight

Westward Ho

O ur children still depended on us, even though they could have managed their problems on their own. We thought it would be good for them to not have us around. With high school graduation behind them, both Cheryl and Darrell had moved out of the house. Cheryl dropped out of Kennesaw State College after one semester, and soon got a Mrs. Degree.

Darrell attended a Job Corps school in Albany, Georgia. Because of his limited attention span, Darrell had difficulty comprehending the material, but he did learn how to get along with all types of people. The counselors recommended he look for work in grocery stores, where he has been steadily employed for many years. He supports himself well, became a fine Christian, and makes friends wherever he goes.

Cheryl's marriage was short lived, but she gave birth in 1984 to our first grandson, Jesse James, who brought us immense joy. I really enjoyed spending time with Jesse, and through the years we became great buddies. One negative about moving was being away from our grandson for an extended length of time.

Our parents had died, so their well-being was no longer a concern. Mary managed her diabetes well, but issues with Diabetic Peripheral Neuropathy or painful nerve damage affected her quality of life. She could no longer drive, and her vision was deteriorating. We considered all these things as we contemplated a potential move. But with just two years before I would have enough service to qualify for retirement from Lockheed, I really had no choice. Mary and I had enjoyed living in California during

the early years of our marriage. We still had friends there even after living in Georgia for twenty-one years. All we had to do was pack up our house, arrange for a mover, and plan our route.

With Lockheed's generous moving allowance to cover our expenses, we loaded our car and headed for the Golden State. We lived six long months in California before our Georgia house sold. In the interim, we lived in a Hampton Inn until we could arrange for a permanent home. Our friends from Georgia—the Marietta West Team—were facing the same relocation issues.

Since Mary couldn't drive, we wanted to live by a shopping center with a grocery store. We bought a perfect condominium in the small city of Valencia. This pretty town close to Interstate 5 provided an ideal location for my daily commute to the Lockheed Burbank facility. The thirty-minute drive took me through a mountain pass in the Angeles National Forest. The distant mountain peaks—some as tall as 10,000 feet—were impressive when capped with snow. It thrilled me to be back in those majestic mountains.

My Marietta fellow engineers, and I began hiking and enjoying those mountains. Since I was still running about three miles every day, I needed to find a park with some dirt trails like the ones back home. Since Placenta Canyon State Park was only about ten miles from Valencia, I began to run the trail next to a creek that wound its way into a small canyon. The Park had historical significance. Some gold had been discovered there much earlier than the great gold rush near Sacramento. A gnarly oak tree that could have witnessed the gold discovery stood near the entrance to the park.

Lockheed Burbank worked under Navy regulations, and that made my work very enjoyable. The work environment was like the Research Department in Georgia where there was room for innovation. I immediately went to work on an Air Force contract. We had the task of developing software with the ability to predict the aerodynamic forces and stability of fighter aircraft at high angles of attack. My experience working on fighter aircraft with Douglas Aircraft, and analyzing vortex flows on the moon launch rockets prepared me well for this new challenge. The software I helped develop became known as HASC or High Angle of Attack–Stability & Control.

At the end of each busy week at work, I found time to pursue hands-on high angle of attack flying. Aerobatic flight training became my next big

adventure that was made possible by former Lockheed test pilot, Anthony W. "Tony" LeVier.

Tony was an air racer and test pilot for the Lockheed Corporation from 1940-1970. He was well known as the test pilot for the P-38 during World War II and testing other Lockheed jet aircraft like the P-80 Shooting Star and the F-104, an early supersonic airplane. Getting acquainted with Tony took me back to the days when, as a twelve-year-old, I played fighter pilot on a real P-38 in the field behind my house. At that time, I never imagined meeting the original test pilot. Not only did we become friends, but Tony also gave me a scholarship to take aerobatic flight training.

Tony and his associates were concerned about stall/spin flight training for private pilots. Since most general aviation pilots didn't experience spins during their flight training, Tony's group formed a safe flying foundation to resolve this problem. Tony was retired from Lockheed, but still had an office near where we worked. He liked to wander around our area and talk with the engineers so he could keep up with new developments. One day he asked us who'd had flight training. I immediately spoke up and said that I did. Then Tony inquired about my spin training. As the only pilot without that training, he set me up with a one-hour lesson at the Santa Paula Airport. In 1989, I began my aerobatic flight training. The first free hour piqued my interest, and I signed up for four more hours of rolls and spins.

The orange groves and flower farms lining the valley on the 34-mile drive on Highway 126 captured my attention as I drove to the Santa Paula Airport. On one of my drives, smoke from brushfires obstructed my view, and it took an extra two hours to detour south around the fires. Most days, the views were spectacular, both from the highway and from the air.

I learned aerobatics in an American Champion Super Decathlon—a very well-built airplane for that kind of flying. The instructor taught me loops, rolls, wingovers, two-turn spins and recoveries, victory rolls, one-half rolls, and inverted flight.

During my final hour, I tried hammerhead stalls—a maneuver where you fly straight ahead, add maximum continuous power, then pull up 90 degrees. Once the airplane stalled, I used the rudder to head down toward the surface, pulled out, and flew straight and level again. Upon successfully performing all those maneuvers, my instructor suggested we return to the airport. After we landed, he had to sit to recover from motion sickness.

During my Navy days, I had flown in the back seat of SNJ airplanes, so the flight didn't bother me. I loved aerobatic flying and would do again today if given the right airplane and the right instructor.

In September 1988, I joined a flying club that operated out of the main Burbank airport. It was challenging to share airspace with commercial aircraft that used that airport. My small plane was dwarfed by the large wide-body jets that carried passengers to cities across the US. It was there I learned how to avoid vortex wakes from those heavy airplanes. I had a lot of experience in a Cessna 172 and Cessna 182 but wanted to learn how to fly a low-wing, PA-28-236 Piper Dakota.

Flying out of Burbank in the Piper Dakota to Santa Catalina Island gave me a lesson in flight navigation. After take-off, I flew over the San Fernando Valley, the Santa Monica Mountains, and into the congested Los Angeles air traffic.

Flying to Santa Catalina required us to find the corridor for general aviation aircraft that provided visual flight (VFR) over the LAX airport. Under normal circumstances, that would have been a scenic trip, with the Pacific Ocean directly to the south and west of the Los Angeles area. But my instructor wanted us to pick up a friend of his at the Hawthorne Airport. That airport was just a short distance northeast of LAX. I had to concentrate on making radio contact and dropping out of the corridor before landing at the Hawthorne airport. It was good practice, but I stayed occupied and couldn't enjoy the sights.

We climbed back up to the flight corridor altitude and turned directly south to Santa Catalina Island. The next obstacle was landing at the Santa Catalina airport, with its unique runway that sloped upward and ended at a steep cliff. Both characteristics made it difficult to make the right approach. An electronic glide slope and airport traffic control helped us make a safe landing and take-off for our return flight. Making it back to Burbank without incident greatly increased my flying confidence.

Flying out of Burbank in a Cessna 182 for a night instrument practice flight presented new challenges, but that flight provided the kind of training I needed to become a better pilot. All my flying adventures also helped me become a better engineer, because seeds were planted in my mind for creating innovative ideas to mitigate loss of control in flight and save fuel. Now, I had to turn my dreams into reality.

Thirty Nine

California Living

The innovation I worked on at Lockheed Burbank was a further development of the HASSC software. Working with younger engineers from Lockheed as well as sub-contracting companies challenged me. We traveled to the University of Kansas for wind tunnel tests and to a small company near the Los Angeles airport for flow-visualization tests in a water-flow tunnel.

Lockheed Missile and Space Company (LMSC) in Sunnyvale, CA supported our project. Lars Ericsson, a well-known missile and space engineer who I had worked with in Huntsville, had expertise in aeroelastic engineering. He helped solve a problem commonly found on fighter aircraft called "Nose Slice," an unexpected maneuver that happens when a fighter gets to a high angle of attack. The slim, circular body and sharp nose of fighter aircraft made the jet take an uncontrolled rotation to either the right or left. Vortex formation on the circular nose was like what I studied while working on the Saturn launch rocket for the moon mission. The main difference was that the dynamic motion of the airplane created asymmetric vortices, which produced a side force causing the airplane to rotate.

Several concepts for solving that problem were evaluated. Sub-contractor Nielsen Engineering & Research (NEAR) investigated the rest of the airplane fuselage forces. My group had the difficult responsibility of analyzing the wings and tail control surfaces. I also presented the AIAA report that George and I had written in 1985 about vortex lift

aerodynamics. That convinced the project manager to have my group proceed with developing the methods of the report to analyze and predict the high, angle-of-attack aerodynamics of the project.

Charlie—one of the young engineers on my team—had served in the Marines. He had earned his BS in Aerospace Engineering while serving on the San Diego Police Force. His strong work ethic and expert computer skills made him quite valuable to the project. He interacted well with Tim the project's Technical Monitor from the Air Force Research Laboratory. Tim liked the progress we were making on the project and encouraged us to continue.

The software that was created by Lars Ericsson and my group of aerodynamicists had to be merged into one major software to create HASC. The merging also incorporated Lockheed software called VORLAX and the Dixon software known as VORLIF. This complex process took longer than expected and was still not completed when I retired from Lockheed.

During my off time, Mary and I enjoyed exploring and dining with our Marietta West friends. We liked to go to various movie set locations around southern California. All types of films were made in that area. *Duel*—the scary movie about the semi-truck chasing Dennis Weaver in a car through the mountainous roads of the Angeles National Forest—was filmed close to where we lived. Several movies about test pilots flying out of Edwards Air Force Base or the airport at Mojave, California made it to the silver screen.

Movie sets of old western towns dotted the landscape. The town of Saugus was about five miles from where we lived, and we often went there to eat at a 100-year-old restaurant that resembled a saloon. We heard a story about a family that ate there, and during their meal a roach crawled along their table. The man of the family went to the owner and told him they were not going to pay for their food. The owner pulled out a 45-caliber revolver, laid it on the counter, and said, "You will pay." They paid and fled.

I was serving as program organizer of my local AIAA when we received a special invitation to attend an historical event at Edwards Air Force Base. Through some of our work at Lockheed, we had close contact with a high-level NASA manager at the Base. He arranged for our section to be admitted to the VIP viewing area to watch the landing of the Columbia

Space Shuttle on August 13, 1989. It was the first flight of a space shuttle since the heart-breaking explosion of the Challenger in1986.

When the shuttle reached 55,000 feet above the surface, we all jumped at the sound of an explosive sonic boom. At that point, the shuttle became a glider with no power. It circled over the airport and glided all the way to the landing, close to where we stood. What a thrill it was to watch it land at a speed of about 200 miles per hour, being slowed only by a drag chute.

I recalled memories of my involvement in the initial design stages and operation of the Shuttle. Lockheed had sent me to Houston, Texas to share my idea for improving the landing capability of the Shuttle. I met with Claude, my former manager at Douglas Aircraft, to explain my span-wise blowing concept. He explained that the Shuttle could not stand the extra weight that my concept would create.

At another time Lockheed proposed that the C-5 Galaxy be used as the transport vehicle for the Shuttle to be flown from the landing site back to the launch site. I helped run a water channel test to show how the Shuttle could be released from the top of the C-5 and glide to the launch site. In the end, NASA decided to use the Boeing 747 instead of the C-5.

After that successful program managing the shuttle event, I continued working for our section of the AIAA. That volunteer effort proved to be helpful in my career. My section leaders made a proposal to the National AIAA to make me an Associate Fellow. It was a real honor to receive that title.

Our third time in California was full of good and bad events. Even though we didn't worry about our adult children, Mary's health problems became more acute. Because of her severe back pain, she took regular doses of a morphine-based drug. One Sunday after church while we were enjoying lunch with our Marietta West friends, Mary suddenly started having severe stomach cramps. At the emergency room, the doctor diagnosed a hole in her stomach caused by the morphine. "She will need to be admitted for a couple of weeks," the doctor said.

In addition, her diabetes was causing her eyesight to deteriorate. Her ophthalmologist referred her to a retina specialist who recommended a risky procedure to reattach the retina. After much prayer, we concluded she would lose her sight without the procedure, so we decided to proceed

with the surgery. The successful surgery gave her better vision for a few more years.

We saw our children when we traveled back to Georgia for Christmas. On one such occasion, we attended Darrell's wedding. Cheryl and her five-year-old son Jesse traveled to California to visit us. I enjoyed spoiling him like a good grandfather and building lifelong bonds. We took them to the famous spots in Hollywood. Cheryl wanted to go to a theater where a famous male singing group was appearing in person. We didn't have tickets, but Cheryl insisted we go to the theater. She was thrilled when she saw the singers get into their limousine after the performance.

With all the good times we were having and my challenging—but enjoyable work—our time in California flew by. My retirement from Lockheed was rapidly approaching, but there were other things to do first. At the end of 1989, I had completed another report on vortex flow that could be presented at a major AIAA conference in Seattle, Washington. Mary and I seized that opportunity to take a vacation after my presentation. We looked forward to going back to Seattle where we had lived while I worked as a co-op at Boeing during my college days.

We stayed in downtown Seattle near the hotel for the AIAA conference for three days and planned at our own expense to move to a cheaper hotel. Our plans changed when we made a lucky discovery. It was dark when Mary and I walked to our hotel after the conference. The dim streetlights didn't help, so we felt unnerved when we saw no one on the street. As we walked, I spotted a man's billfold on the sidewalk. We looked to see who might have dropped it, but with no one else in sight, I put the wallet in my pocket. We didn't want to linger, so we quickly made our way to the hotel.

We recognized the expensive name brand on the billfold and looked for identification. No ID, just $100 bills. We continued to count until it totaled $900. With no identification, we couldn't return the money to its owner. We thought about taking it to the police, but what would they do with it? Something told us it was not the right thing to do. We considered that since we found it in a creepy area, it might have been dropped during an exchange of drugs and money. With no other options, we decided our find was providential, so we extended our vacation for several more days so we could see more beautiful sights in Washington State.

We travelled north toward Canada where we caught a ferry to Victoria

Island, British Columbia. In the little town of Port Gamble, we checked into an ancient bed and breakfast. The décor in our room included a galvanized metal wash tub that hung on the wall. A garden hose attached to the water faucet in the sink was used to fill it up. Neither of us wanted to bathe in that tub, so after a good breakfast the next morning we drove to Port Angeles to catch the ferry. Our ferry trip showcased beautiful scenes of the snow-topped Olympia Mountains behind us and the beckoning islands before us.

The sweet smell of flowers greeted us as we toured the city. Hanging flower baskets hung from every streetlamp. We were wowed by the floral displays in the spectacular Butchart Gardens. Then we toured a replica of Anne Hathaway's house that was decorated in the style of the Shakespearian era. Anne Hathaway, the wife of William Shakespeare, was a devoted spouse and mother to their three children.

Thanks to a careless drug dealer, we had a wonderful vacation in Victoria. As we boarded the ferry and drove back to Seattle, we talked about our adventure. Our free vacation came to an end when we boarded our plane and headed back to Los Angeles.

Fourty

Time to Retire

My 25th anniversary as a Lockheed employee was fast approaching. That meant at age 59, I could retire with a life-long pension. While considering my options, Lockheed announced a deal to speed up the retirement of long-term employees. I qualified for the deal, which meant I would have an income to support us for the foreseeable future. The retirement offers also meant Mary would have good health insurance if something happened to me. That was important to our peace of mind.

I retired on December 29, 1989, but not before my engineering peers and some managers gave me a going away party. Many of my co-workers showed up to celebrate my departure and gave me some great gifts. My most cherished possession is a 30 x 20 cartoon painting that depicts my twenty-four years at Lockheed. The graphics department created the painting that was signed by everyone in attendance. A light blue sky frames the background of the United States with an enlarged California showcasing the Burbank facility. Flying over the Burbank facility is a highly oversized picture of me flying an old biplane. On the side of the plane is "Dixon Flying Service." It depicts me with a small body and a big head like a cartoon character saying, "I'm just a good ole' Georgia boy in a strange land."

On the east coast of the US, an enlarged building shows the Lockheed Georgia building and a large rocket recognizing my time working on the Saturn V moon launch rocket with the words, "Chuck's an Engineer's Engineer." To the right of the rocket is a cartoon Lockheed C-130 that

says, "He's an Aviator Extraordinaire! A Tamer of the Wild Vortex." One of my friend's comments reads, "Best wishes for your retirement—all two weeks of it."

I enjoyed doing nothing my first two weeks at home because I didn't expect my sabbatical to last long. There were discussions at Lockheed about me coming back as a consultant. I had been one of the prime developers of the software for the High Angle of Attack Air Force contract, and there was still much more to be done on that contract. My associates had urged me to take advantage of the good retirement package offered by Lockheed, since I could come back as a consultant to complete the job. When the consultant work didn't materialize right away, boredom set in.

There was not much for me to do around our little condo. I was restless, and since Mary was not used to having me around, I was getting on her nerves. We used some of our extra time to become more involved in our church. We also planned sightseeing trips back to some of the places in California we had enjoyed visiting.

Our first return visit was to the mountainous resort village at Big Bear Lake. The scenic 130-mile drive took us to Palmdale at the edge of the Mojave Desert. In the distance we could see a snow-capped mountain range. I recognized Mt. Baldy and Mount San Gorgonio—two 10,000 ft. peaks that stood above the rest. Our ride took us into a canyon between those two mountains. Then we wound our way up San Gorgonia to Big Bear Lake Village.

We enjoyed our little cabin and a relaxing week in the fresh mountain air. The time together gave us time to think about the future. What were we going to do for the rest of lives? We talked at length about our hopes and dreams. Since the consulting work had not panned out as expected, we discussed moving back to Georgia to be around our children and grandchild.

After our relaxing week, we returned to Santa Clarita to plan our next steps. Much to my surprise, the decision was made for us when Lockheed decided to close its Burbank facility and send every employee back to Georgia. If I were going to find a consulting job, it would be back in Georgia.

The major thing we had to do was sell our condominium. Our real estate agent quickly found a buyer, but we had to accept a second mortgage.

We knew we were taking a chance but felt better when the real estate agent said that she would handle all money transfers.

A moving company shipped our furniture and personal items to Georgia. I had to pay for all our moving expenses since I was no longer a Lockheed employee. Mary's diabetic neuropathy prevented her from riding with me to Georgia. The only solution was for her to fly ahead to her family in Tennessee.

It was a sad day for me as I started that long, lonely drive to Memphis. Leaving the California lifestyle behind was bittersweet. Since I only planned to drive around five hours each day, I knew it would take me several days to complete the trip. I headed toward Palmdale like we had done when we visited Big Bear Village. Between Santa Clarita and Palmdale, I went by Aqua Dulce (Sweet Water), California for the last time. Aqua Dulce had a small airport which I used to fly to from Burbank to get that "$100 hamburger" at the airport café. The cost of renting the plane and fuel made it an expensive but delicious burger.

I continued my trip down memory lane when my route took me from Palmdale to Victorville past the San Andreas Fault. The fault formed the tectonic boundary between the Pacific Plate and the North American Plate. It ran north and south through California for about 750 miles. Many have joked, "If those plates separate, some of California will be in the Pacific Ocean." As I traveled through Victorville, my thoughts went back to a sad memory. That was where the Navy F6F fighter plane I had serviced as a plane captain had crashed.

There were many memorable places that Mary and I had driven through on our trips back and forth to California. Most of those trips were made before I-40 was built. In earlier days, we traveled on Route 66 with all its interesting sites.

By the time I got to Arizona, a thunderstorm was moving from west to east. I drove each day in good weather then caught up with the storm when I stopped for supper. All night while I slept, the storm traveled. When I got up in the morning, I drove under clear skies until time for supper, when I would catch up with the storm again. That happened all the way to Memphis. It seemed I was not alone. God was refreshing the air and leading me to my destination. I made it to Memphis as clear-headed as anyone could be after driving 2,000 miles.

After a joyous reunion with Mary and visiting with our families, we drove another eight hours to Georgia. Even though we had previously lived there, it was going to be different this time. Since I would no longer have a job waiting for me at Lockheed, I was uncertain and anxious about my future.

We hoped we could find another place to live in Kennesaw—our home before moving to California. I wanted to be near Kennesaw Mountain and its great running and hiking trails. Mary, however, wanted to find a condo close to a shopping area where she could walk to stores like she had done in California.

We decided to lease an apartment for six months while we searched for a condo. We found one in East Marietta close to the Chattahoochee River and Johnson Ferry Road. The road got its name from the ferry that used to take Cobb County residents to Atlanta before the bridge was built. There was a nice park near the river with a reasonably good hiking and running trail. I could get my running done on the trail, but the trail did not measure up to the Kennesaw Mountain trails. On top of that too many dogs used the trails as their potty.

There was still no word from Lockheed about consultant work, so I decided to do something entirely different. I believed God had developed my talent and called me to work with a mission aviation organization, Jungle Aviation and Radio Service (JAARS.) After finding out they would be glad to have us help, we packed up and headed for Waxhaw, North Carolina. JAARS provided us a temporary place to live. Then we completed an orientation and met the people with whom we would be working.

JAARS, a subsidiary of Wycliffe Bible Translators USA, functioned as an interdenominational, nonprofit organization with a stated goal to "See a Bible translation program in progress in every language still needing one by 2025." Mary and I felt the need to share in God's work and wanted to help JAARS personnel accomplish that task.

Mary worked with some ladies helping to do the paperwork required for translating the Bible. My job in the hanger was to help Jeff, who was working to make significant modifications of a short take-off and landing (STOL) aircraft called the "Helio Courier." The airplane was

a very efficient STOL airplane, but JAARS wanted to reduce its fuel consumption.

Jeff wanted to use fiberglass molding to streamline the nose of the airplane. As an aerodynamics engineer, I knew what should be done, but it was too late to suggest changes. Since I always enjoyed working with my hands, I began to help him do it his way.

My contribution was to suggest that he modify the part of the airplane called the dorsal. The dorsal is a triangular surface attached to the front of the vertical fin. It had a large leading-edge radius that I thought should have been smaller. I explained that that modification would make the big fin have a better directional-stability, and the dorsal would have less drag. I did not get to stay around long enough to see how all the modifications worked.

For various reasons, Mary and I decided we needed to return home. I still hoped to go back to work with Lockheed, and Mary was not happy with what she had been doing. She said the work was boring, and she was having a hard time fitting in with the ladies. I don't know if it was her fault or if the group was a clique.

Sometimes even Christians get satisfied with the people already around them and don't want to include others. That was not what Jesus taught us. He said, "Love your neighbor as you love yourself." Jesus taught us that this commandment defines all the rest of the Ten Commandments.

Jeff certainly practiced that commandment. Jeff and I stayed in touch with each other after I left. He told me that the modification of the dorsal did indeed reduce the drag of the Helio Courier.

As satisfying as it was to get my hands on an airplane at JAARS, I wanted a paying job. We were doing well enough on retirement pay and our savings, but I could see those funds would not last the rest of our lives. It was obvious that Lockheed was dragging its feet on a contract job, so it was time for me to search for employment.

The last time I had looked for a job was 25 years earlier. That was when I was unhappy with the job I had in Huntsville, Alabama. At that time, all I had to do was walk down the street to Lockheed Missiles and Space. After working so many years with Lockheed, I was "like a fish out of water." *What was I going to do?* I was willing to look at all kinds of work.

I learned that a nearby Catholic church was offering night classes on

how to write resumes and find jobs. I enrolled in the program, updated my resume, and contacted several companies. I even contacted the IRS who asked for an extensive background check. Since I had passed background checks and gotten government clearances while working on military aircraft, I did not want to spend my time doing that again. Other contacts I made indicated that I was either too old or had too much education.

One letter that contained a job offer remained unopened. I found it in some of my papers twenty years later when I was cleaning out for a move to a new house. It was an offer for a teaching position at the University of Kansas. As you will see in the rest of my story, God had a different future in mind for me.

Fourty One

A New Direction

The job search instructor at the Catholic church recommended I read a book called *What Color is Your Parachute*. That book encouraged readers to look for work in their area of expertise and enjoyment. After reading the book, I realized I needed to remain in the field of aviation. The best way for me to do that was to try to start my own business again. As I was gearing up to move in that direction, Lockheed called me back to help finish the contract I had been working on at the time of my retirement.

The time had come to find a new home in Georgia. Not far from our apartment, we found a condominium complex called the Villas at Park Air. The name appealed to me because Park Air was a small airport I had visited in the past. Mary was quite pleased since she could walk to a nearby shopping center. With the help of a real estate agent, we soon signed a contract on a condominium. We moved in and started to make improvements.

Our real estate agent had deceived us and had never told us about the poor condo management. Instead, she had told us the community was quiet; but the opposite was the reality. With little insulation in our walls, we heard noisy traffic day and night. At night we heard and felt a small sonic boom as each truck passed our bedroom. As soon as we got to sleep, another truck would roar past.

Then we found termites in the walls and learned that the condo management paid little attention to maintenance. We told the real-estate agent we had been misled. "Conned" would have described it better, but we

restrained ourselves. The agent did not care. For her it was a contract with no way out. The only other option was to take the real-estate company to court. In addition, we were not getting timely payments from the second mortgage we had taken in California. Mary's physical condition was not good, and I was really struggling to maintain my equilibrium.

Mary and I were cared for by God's grace and our faith. However, we did not know what to do until an idea came to us. We called to schedule a visit with the previous owners of the condo to discuss with them the problems we had encountered and the sorry treatment by the real estate agent. They agreed to let us out of the contract. It helped that we had made some major improvements to their condo.

The real-estate agent didn't agree and claimed we still owed her a commission. We agreed to pay her commission and charge nothing for the improvements we had made. That settled the matter.

That major bump in the road cost us $10,000. We could have fought it in court based on the termite problem, but it would have cost us attorney fees plus mental and physical distress. By November 1990, we were free of the condo. We had learned a valuable lesson, and we were able to move on.

We wasted no time finding another apartment closer to the Lockheed plant. I was happy to be closer to Kennesaw Mountain National Park. After every day's work at Lockheed, I changed into my running clothes and made a three-mile run in the park. On one of those runs an amazing thing happened. Larry, a good Christian friend, and I were running together up one of the hills in the park. Near the top of the hill a young couple was running down the hill towards us. As we got closer, I thought I recognized someone. The couple stopped close to us and the man surprised me by saying, "Hi Chuck."

He re-introduced himself to me as Brian and asked if I remembered when I had shared my Christian faith with him. Before I could respond, he said with great joy, "I am a Christian now. I found Jesus Christ the way you explained him to me."

I then remembered that two years before I had moved to California, he and I had been working late at the Lockheed plant in Georgia. I saw the chance to go to his desk to share my faith again with him. I said, "As you know I have been sharing my belief about Jesus with you. I want to give you this little book of John's Gospel. It will tell you all about Jesus."

He reluctantly took the book and laid it on his desk. Before we had further contact, I moved to California.

Brian might have read that little book, or perhaps he had met another Christian who encouraged him to study the Bible. Maybe it was the young lady with him at the park. My friend Larry spoke fluently with her in Spanish while I talked with Brian. He learned she was a Christian, too. It could be she had the joy of praying with Brian when he accepted Christ. No matter who led him to Christ, I was thrilled to have planted the seed.

Mary's life and mine was full of both good and not so good news. Soon I rejoined the Lockheed Georgia Employees' Flying Club and became active in the local chapter of the Experimental Aircraft Association (EAA.) As part of EAA, I flew for the Young Eagles project. Also, I flew some for "Angel Flight" an organization that manages trips to take patients to doctor's appointments in distant cities. Flying for the Young Eagles organization was my favorite thing to do. Children and youth, ages eight to fifteen, signed up for a free hour-long trip on a four-place airplane. The goal was to stimulate their interest in the field of aviation.

The not so good news was that Mary's health was deteriorating. Her life-long battle with diabetes had caused her retina to detach. Before leaving California, she had retinal detachment surgery in one of her eyes. The surgeon had resisted going as far as needed to save her eye, so the problem was getting worse. Our research in Georgia led us to the Emory Eye Clinic and to a doctor who was considered best eye surgeon in the world. Unless he went all the way, he realized she would completely lose sight in that eye. On top of that, she had poor vision in the other eye. As my dad used to say, "She was blind in one eye and couldn't see out of the other one."

The surgeon was able to save her eye so she could see to get around. However, she could still claim to be legally blind since her vision in the left eye was 20/200. We were thrilled that Mary had received the miracle of extended sight. Now we could plan the next phase of our future.

We started looking for a ranch house to buy since Mary had difficulties with stairs. Only two-story homes were available, so we decided to build a house. We searched to find two acres in the Kennesaw area. It was disappointing that no one wanted to sell two acres. Landowners were

holding out to make huge profits by selling more acreage to developers for subdivisions.

We were not sure where to turn. That is when it occurred to us that we had not turned our plans over to God and trusted Him to provide. One weekend afternoon, Mary and I drove to our old neighborhood. We hoped to see some of our former neighbors and maybe learn about available property. We saw Ed working in his front yard. He was a member of our church at Marietta First Baptist, and I remembered that he was a housing contractor. After a great reunion, I asked if he knew of any available property. Much to my surprise Ed responded, "Yes, I have a friend who has about eight acres of land and wants to build on it, but he says he has to sell some of it before he can afford to build."

After we saw the beautiful, forested lot and met the owner, we knew that God had answered our prayers. The results of that meeting worked more miracles than any of us realized. We learned the landowner and his wife had been praying for a buyer. We both contracted with Ed to build our houses. The housing market had been so bad, Ed had also been praying for work. What a glorious God! He brought all of us together to answer our prayers.

Fourty Two

Building Our House

The house plan we chose, with everything on one level, was just what Mary needed. Since the property sloped, I decided to add a daylight basement that could be used for a workshop and boat storage. On many days during the next year, we entertained ourselves by driving to the building site, pulling out our lawn chairs, and watching the construction process. Finally, in March 1992, we moved in.

Much to my delight, I had room to spread out and enjoy the beauty all around. We had lived in cramped quarters with a yard of scrubby trees for too long in California. Now I had a beautiful yard filled with tall trees and flower beds for digging and planting. Mary was pleased with the house, but there was one drawback. She couldn't walk to the stores like she did in California. She was still able to drive short distances but worried she would lose her sight again and be stuck up in the woods. Mary did everything she could do to keep her diabetes under control. She always ate properly and exercised every day on her stationary bike that we set up on the screened-in back porch. Even though she did the best she could, her insulin would get out of sync.

Mary vetoed my offer to find someone to be with her or check up on her every day. One day while walking to the neighbor's house, she had an insulin reaction. She didn't know where she was, so she sat down on the side of the road. Another neighbor saw her and took her into their house. When the EMTs arrived, they noticed her medical alert bracelet explaining her diabetes. After giving her sugar, she recovered quickly.

I felt bad that I couldn't be with her all the time, but I was still consulting at Lockheed. It was almost like old times reporting to work at Lockheed, except that time I was not an employee but a contract engineer. I had to punch a time clock in the morning and at the end of the day, but it was annoying since my previous category of engineering didn't require me to clock in every day. When the contract ran out, I was called back as a consultant on the same project. It was a better arrangement for Lockheed, since they didn't have to pay a contracting company, and I made a better salary as a consultant. When we finished the contract, we published the final report in October 1992.

After completing the HASC Code (High Angle of Attack Stability & Control) contract, Mary and I enjoyed some real retirement time and made up for lost time with our grandson Jesse. He was born in 1983, but we missed most of his growing up years while we were in California. Jesse and Mary loved to joke and laugh, and he really lifted her spirits. I stayed busy putting things back together that he loved to take apart, like his bicycle. He was fascinated by how everything worked. I wondered if he would grow up to be an engineer like me.

As much as I enjoyed my early retirement, I loved working on new aviation projects even more. Since retirement pay did not provide enough money to continue flying or participate in any other fun activities that Mary and I enjoyed, I looked for more consulting work.

Filing a DBA (Doing Business AS) registration with the State of Georgia was my next step. I began doing business as Consulting Aviation Services, which gave my efforts more credibility and enabled me to set up a business banking account and create business cards.

The success of the work I had done on the HASC Code opened a new opportunity for me. The US Air Force was interested in further developing that software. I had some ideas about how to extend the capabilities of the code. However, I knew it would require some wind tunnel testing. My neighbor John, from whom we had bought our land, owned a manufacturing business. We decided to submit a proposal to the Air Force with me doing the aeronautical work and John's company manufacturing the parts.

I travelled to Wright Patterson Air Force Base in Dayton, Ohio to meet with Tim, the Air Force Technical Monitor. Tim and I had

worked together on my previous efforts at Lockheed, and he showed great interest in my suggested improvements to the HASC Code. Over a million dollars had been put into the code development, but further upgrades were welcome.

Tim had to decide how he was going to get the Air Force funds needed to proceed. We learned that that kind of research had to be approved by the Air Force Office of Scientific Research (AFOSR) and the funding could only be given to a recognized research organization.

Tim really wanted to help me to get the project done, so he proposed I work through Georgia Tech. The AFOSR had a project that fit the category of research, and Bill found the required funds to get the contract started. That worked fine for me, but I felt bad for John, since Georgia Tech would be doing the manufacturing. John was a good Christian man, and he graciously said, "He was glad to have helped."

Once the paperwork was completed, I went to work on the two-year effort. The dynamics of vortex flow had not been included in the original HASC Code. Adding vortex breakdown and buffet required complex wind tunnel tests and software code writing. The last time I worked in those areas had been thirty years earlier during my time in Huntsville studying the Saturn V moon rocket. Times and methods had changed, and I struggled to get up to speed. We also made some changes to improve the steady state aerodynamics. The work was exciting, and important improvements were made to the HASC Code. Working with Georgia Tech personnel, especially the students, was an enjoyable experience.

Even though the work at Georgia Tech was not complete, I started writing an AIAA (American Association of Aerodynamics & Astronautics) paper to present in Phoenix, Arizona in August 1994. The work had reached a good milestone that I was eager to share with my fellow aerodynamicists. Going to Arizona would be a welcome break for Mary and me.

AIAA had selected a classy place in Phoenix for the meeting. They were able to secure good rates because fewer people traveled to Phoenix in August because of the intense heat. Daytime temperatures of over 100 degrees made it unbearable outside. My presentation went well, but we were anxious to get back east of the Mississippi.

Mary enjoyed the trip and seemed happy to be back in Georgia, but during the fall she experienced a chronic depression. Since she could no longer drive, she stayed at home by herself while I worked at Georgia Tech. It was hard to get friends and family to come for a visit or to take her places. Everyone had their own lives to live.

Fourty Three

End of an Era

On Thursday night, December 22, 1994, Mary and I had gone to bed. After a trip to the bathroom around 3:00 a.m., I was getting back into bed when I heard the strangest sigh. WOOSH! It was like all the air was leaving Mary's body. I immediately picked her up and put her on the floor to start CPR. She did not respond, and I feared it was the end.

I called 911. The EMTs continued CPR as they loaded her into the ambulance. A Cobb County policeman arrived and took me to the hospital behind the ambulance. I called my children, our pastor, and friends. Soon after we arrived at the hospital, the doctor came out and gave us the sad news. Mary's death could not have occurred at a worse time, December 22—almost Christmas.

Both sides of our families were busy planning for the holidays, but I had to share the news with them so that I could make plans for the funeral. My children and friends were a big help. Everyone was upset, especially Darrell and his wife Delcina since Mary died on their wedding anniversary. Now every time their anniversary came, they would be reminded of that difficult time.

I asked Darrell recently what he remembered about the funeral, and after twenty-five years he said, "Our anniversary." He also remembered that Mary's older brother had a tough time. I had been in deep grief and hadn't paid attention to anyone else's problems.

The service was held in the chapel at Mays Ward-Dobbins Funeral Home on December 28, giving family members from Louisiana and

Tennessee time to travel to Georgia after Christmas and return home before New Year's Day. We buried her at Cheatham Hill Memorial Park in Marietta. I chose a verse from Proverbs 31:29 to engrave on her headstone that described Mary perfectly.

"Many wives and mothers have done well,
but you excel them all."

Not long after the funeral, God confirmed the truth of the selected verse. I received a sympathy card from a lady in Iowa that had been an old friend of Mary's. She had not seen or talked with Mary for a long time, but somehow had gotten word of Mary's death and the date it occurred. She told me that about the time of Mary's death, she'd had a dream and saw Mary singing with a host of angels in heaven. Knowing that gave me great comfort.

Mary and I had forty-four years of joys and challenges, but our love had remained strong through it all. When Mary was thirteen, she had overheard a doctor say she probably would not live past thirty. Because of her careful attention to her health, she lived until age sixty-one.

I knew Mary was no longer suffering and had a joyful home in heaven. I also knew I would see her again someday. Even though I grieved her passing for several months, God helped me move on with my life.

My work provided a diversion from my grief, giving me someplace to go and people to be around. When my mind stayed busy, I didn't dwell on the past. However, I knew my life didn't need to be all work, so I eventually sought out fun things to do.

In January1995 a widowed friend invited me to go with him and his brother to Salt Lake City for a skiing trip. As a bonus, he was a ski instructor. The highlight of the week was a night skiing adventure at Park City, Utah.

Coming home to face a lonely house was harder than I had expected. Miss Kitty the cat came to live with me when my daughter, Cheryl, said she couldn't keep her anymore. That cat gave me a lot of companionship and comfort when she purred on my lap.

My work with Georgia Tech continued through June 1995, with the report being published in October 1995. The popularity of the HASC

Code and the work I completed continued to grow. The software generated from that contract became of interest to NASA, located at Langley Airforce Base, and to Lockheed in Fort Worth Texas. They wanted to make some additions to the HASC source code. Since I had been responsible for the development of a major part of the code, they wanted me to make the upgrades. I was asked to be a consultant for them, and they agreed that I could do it in Georgia. Cost and technical proposals were presented in March 1995, and I began work in May. That work continued until September 1995.

To keep my mind occupied during my off hours, I came up with the idea of taking my eleven-year-old grandson Jesse on a long trip out West. Cheryl was reluctant to let him go, but Jesse and I talked her into it. I had made that trip many times, so I knew what was in store. For me, it would bring back many fond memories of the cross-country trips Mary and I had made. My daughter's father-in-law loaned us his pop-up camper—just what we needed. We could explore areas where no lodging was available and save a lot of money for other fun things.

Beginning in Kennesaw, Georgia, we planned to go first to Holly Springs, Mississippi to visit my brother-in-law, Fred. Then we would go through Whitehaven and Memphis, Tennessee and through Arkansas to Oklahoma City. There we would pick up Interstate 40 that paralleled along the famous Route 66. From there we would go through Amarillo, Texas, then New Mexico and the Grand Canyon in Arizona. Several national parks in Utah were on our itinerary, along with a visit to Salt Lake City. Our final western destination was to be Yellowstone National Park, before heading back home to Georgia.

Once school was out, Jesse was free to travel. We visited all our destinations except Salt Lake City and Yellowstone National Park. We had been on the road almost three weeks and were having a ball, but Cheryl could not stand to have Jesse away from her any longer. So, we decided to head back home, taking with us a lifetime of memories and bonding experiences that still are strong today.

Fourty Four

The Dating Scene

As I concluded the Air Force contract, I started something new that I had not done in 45 years—dating. When my daughter Cheryl suggested I needed to start dating. I said, "Who, me, I am 65 years old. Who would want to date me?"

She said, "You're still a good-looking man. Go to a singles meeting."

The word got out, and before I could find a singles group, I began getting set up by well-meaning friends. Two of those dates turned out to be duds. There was one lady I dated that appealed to me, and apparently, I appealed to her for a while. Let us just call her Jan. We only dated for about two months.

I learned about a training course for small businesses that would teach me how to win a Small Business Innovative Research (SBIR) government contract. Since I was finished with all my Lockheed contracts, I thought I should take advantage of the opportunity. The course was offered in Salt Lake City, which was ideal for me. I had met a nice lady in Salt Lake City when I went there for skiing earlier in the year. She managed the condominium where we had stayed the previous January. I hadn't learned much about her except that she was very friendly, and she was a Baptist. Being a Baptist in Mormon country was very impressive to me. I thought that if I ever wanted to start dating again, she was the type for me. I knew her name and that she was a Baptist, so to find her I just had to find the Baptist church. With two good reasons to go to Salt Lake City, I flew to Utah.

The SBIR training was successful and led to a new contract. I also learned how to be out-going with the ladies who attended the meeting.

To continue my Salt Lake adventure, I found the Baptist Church where my lady friend would be on Sunday. At the church, I asked someone if she knew my friend. She said, "Yes, she is sitting down front with her husband." That really burst my bubble! Oh well, Salt Lake City was too far away for courting anyway.

Back in Georgia, I dated Jan a few more times, but then found another outlet for meeting women—the Marietta United Methodist Singles Organization. The church provided a place for older singles to meet every Monday night for Bible studies, educational presentations, and dancing. As noted earlier, I was raised in a dancing family. Dancing for me was a way to use music to express your joy, just like David did in the Bible. I did not know a lot of fancy dancing steps, but I had music in my soul. I was taught to follow the music and let the steps come automatically. If my partner followed me, we could enjoy dancing.

One time I had a dancing partner that knew me very well. She was a flight instructor who worked at the McCollum airport. When we were dancing together, she was trying to do steps she knew, instead of following me. She said, "Chuck, what are you doing?" I said, "I'm doing what my feet tell me to do. You are not teaching a student pilot, just follow me."

Most of the ladies liked my dancing, and I began dating one. It wasn't long before we were going out for dinner and movies together. I was getting the hang of the dating business.

During my dating experience, I started teaching a singles class in my church. I assumed I was qualified, because I now had some experience, and it was good to share the experiences of others. Almost all the members were divorced. They seemed to need more attention than those whose spouses had passed on. It was a joyful experience to teach others that with all the difficulties in life, God was there to help. In my search for companionship, my class members were a big help. I eventually discovered it was not a good idea to reach out for female companionship in my church.

In 1985, I'd had a bad hernia in the lower abdominal area that involved major surgery and a long recovery. Now at the end of 1995, I was facing it again. This time, I qualified for laparoscopy. That innovation was a miracle to me. I was in the hospital for less than a week and free to do whatever I wanted after a week or two.

Jan visited me while I was in the hospital and invited me to her

Christmas party. She also told me her family was going to Steamboat Springs, Colorado for skiing in January, and she invited me to join them. Since I liked to ski, I was excited. Joining them meant I would fly out there by myself and get my own lodging, but I would know somebody there. That was good enough for me. It was hard for me to realize that I would have hernia surgery and then go skiing in two or three weeks.

Was the trip a success? The skiing was fun, but the comradery was not. I met her sons and daughters, and they all went to the difficult ski trails that I could not handle. On top of that, there was a lot of bickering going on between Jan and her family. Jan was not the person I thought she was, and I felt only tolerated. I was not too happy in the airplane going home either. My loneliness was not helped when I sat by a fellow who was heading east to get married.

God's timing is always perfect, but it wasn't matching mine. I had to learn that lesson and teach it to my singles class. There was a younger married couple helping me with the class, and they had been divorced like much of the rest of the members. They were more familiar with that part of being single than I was. I sensed that because of the differences between my years of experience in teaching and my age, there was a minor conflict between us, but nothing serious.

I thought maybe there was some concern about me going to the Monday night singles' meeting and dancing. There was a divorced lady that joined our class, and she was appealing to me. I approached her, she expressed interest, and we had several dates. However, undesirable gossip led me to believe that trying to find a companion in the church was probably not the thing to do. I decided to stick to the Marietta Singles.

I heard about another singles group that met in Tucker, Georgia. There I met a genuinely nice lady who enjoyed dancing with me, and she became a good friend. Let's call her Beth. Beth was from Gainesville, Georgia and was a member of a Methodist church in Gainesville. She invited me to come with her to a church party in Gainesville. To get invited to a church party was a plus for me. Not only that, but she was a widow too. I knew I would not know anyone else at the party, but what could I lose besides several miles of interstate travel. That turned out well, and we began dating a lot. In fact, I began thinking Beth may be the one that God had chosen for me. The big question I had was, why did God choose one so far away?

Fourty Five

A Match Made in Heaven

While dating Beth, something still led me to the Marietta singles' meeting every Monday. Now I know it was God. One Monday night I gave a ride to a lady friend. It wasn't a date, and we danced with whomever we wanted. As the DJ played another song, I looked across the floor and saw a lady going through the motions of dancing by herself. I walked over and asked her if she would like to dance. She said yes, and we danced a bit, but the song was over before we could talk. We went back to her table and sat down to get acquainted. When a new song started, another fellow came over to ask her to dance before I did. I found myself sitting there like a bump on a pickle waiting for her to come back to the table.

Then we had a long slow dance together. Something told me to ask her what church she attended. She said, "Smyrna First Baptist Church, and I teach singles in Sunday School." I told her I was a Baptist too and taught singles. We were off to a good start, especially after we learned that both our spouses had died.

We continued to dance with others, but before the evening was over, I saw my new friend heading my way. She had already given me her telephone number. "Will you call me Wednesday," she said.

"I sure will," I replied. Her name was Frieda, and the day was March 4, 1996. When Frieda and I reminisce about our first meeting, we think of the Rodgers & Hammerstein song written for *South Pacific*, "Some

Enchanted Evening." We were both strangers who met across a crowded room, who knew we would see each another again.

Our next date was on March 13, 1996, at the Olive Garden restaurant. For three hours we talked about our backgrounds and interests and ignored the hints from the wait staff that we needed to leave. I learned that Frieda was a Yankee from about as far north in New York State as you can go without being in Canada. I was raised a southerner, but I had lived much of my life as far northwest in this country as you can get, not counting Alaska. Despite these differences, there was something magnetic about our personalities that brought us together. As in physics, opposites attract.

We discussed our Christian backgrounds at length. I hadn't dated anyone so far that I felt comfortable with while discussing that subject. It was also interesting to me that Frieda was a graduate of the New Orleans Baptist Seminary.

I told her I was looking for a companion that would become my wife—and was not looking for a one-night stand. I had made that comment to almost all the ladies I had dated, and it didn't go over well with some of them. Most had been divorced and were afraid to even think about remarriage. Just being a friend and having a date was all they wanted. After making that comment to Frieda, I did not hear any apprehension. She told me later she was in shock and didn't know what to say. I thought we might have another date soon if she agreed.

A few days later, I called her and asked if she would like to go to a real nice place for lunch. I had chosen a unique restaurant across the street from the entrance to Kennesaw Mountain National Battlefield Park. The restaurant was a winery—and not knowing her thoughts about a winery—I added they had really good food. She said she would be glad to meet me there.

The restaurant was a romantic place in a beautiful setting—landscaped like a park with trees all around. It was a place we would not forget. In other words, it was the kind of place to impress your date, and it worked! In fact, we enjoyed being together so much that after lunch we took a casual walk in the park around the base of Kennesaw Mountain. I didn't know what she thought about hiking, so I chose an easy trail that I often ran on.

When we got on the south side of the mountain, there was a small path that led up to a picturesque location. Huge rocks with round domes

peeked out of the side of the mountain trail. We found an inviting place to sit. I asked her if she knew it was called the "Kissing Rock." *God made me do it.* She said, "No I didn't." Then, I added," I guess we shouldn't let it go to waste." We had our first kiss, and the day was just getting started.

As we walked to the park exit, I asked her if she would like to go flying. She thought I meant at some other time. Before she could change her mind, I said, "When we get out of the park, I'll call the scheduling office and see if an airplane is available." Frieda had never flown in a small private airplane. It was a good thing a plane was available, or she might have backed out.

We proceeded to the airport and went out to the flying club's Cessna 172. I secured her into the plane seat and then conducted the standard preflight check. All checked out, so I cranked the engine, and we were cleared to taxi to the point of take-off. To make it a pleasant and scenic flight, we went up to the north Georgia mountains. Flying conditions were perfect, and I had no problem in making it a smooth flight. After two hours, we returned to the airport and made a good landing.

Frieda appeared to have enjoyed the flight, or maybe she was only glad to get back on the ground. We were both enjoying our time together, or we would not have asked each other, "What's next?" The day and our date still were not over. Dinner was next on the schedule, and then a movie. It was getting late and time to go home. Did we kiss goodnight? Yes! We both had had a great day we would never forget.

I understand, that when Frieda got home, her youngest son was waiting for her. He had called numerous times and was worried about her. Payback might be the word that fits the situation. Now he knew how she had felt after sitting up late and waiting for him to get home after being with his girlfriend. After he settled down, Frieda had the joy of telling him about our day. His comment was, "Is he after your money?"

We dated frequently the rest of March and into April. We also went to both of our churches and to the classes we taught. Frieda was welcomed in the class I was teaching. In fact, they agreed that she should come with us to our annual retreat in Toccoa in the North Georgia Mountains. That turned out to be an event God used to direct our future. While sitting in the swing on the cabin porch, we agreed we were in love. I felt God had given me several relationships that had not been right for me so I would

recognize the right one when it came along. Frieda and I had not been together long, but we knew that the love we had found was God's choice.

With that settled, we both had an important confession for the other. The next afternoon of the retreat, we hiked to Toccoa Falls with another couple. Frieda and I went off on a separate trail to sit and talk. I was about to tell her something she should know before we continued our relationship. She said she had something profoundly serious to tell me first. She was worried, and I understood why after she told me. "I have a serious liver disease that will require a liver transplant."

I thought about that for a moment. All I knew was that I was very attracted to her, and I should not let her illness be an obstacle. Finally, I spoke up and said, "You do have good insurance, don't you?" I guess I just wanted to know if there were any more issues I needed to know about.

Charles and Frieda at Taccoa Falls Georgia

We both laughed. Then I said, "Let me tell you about myself. I am 65 years old and older than you." I didn't look my age and was as healthy and active as most men ten years younger. We both agreed we could overcome both of our situations with God's help.

I still had a problem to solve—my relationship with Beth in Gainesville, Georgia. We had dated and become close friends, and at one time I had wondered if she was the one for me. Beth had even bought a pretty dress for my four-year-old granddaughter. I owed her an explanation and believed a face-to-face contact with Beth was necessary. I told Frieda I was going to see Beth for the last time. That made her apprehensive, so I promised to call her as soon as I got home. Beth and I parted friends and she wished me well with my new relationship.

Fourty Six

A New Future

After only three weeks from the time Frieda and I met, I proposed marriage. She immediately accepted, and we began to plan our future together. There was one requirement which was hard for me. Since Frieda was allergic to cats and most dogs, Miss Kitty had to go. My cat had been very comforting to me for more than a year since Mary's passing.

I agreed but didn't know how to handle that problem. Soon I got the answer. I had become good friends with the man who provided pest control at my house. One day while he was doing his job, I told him I was getting married and my concern about Miss Kitty. He said, "I have a cat that needs a friend, and we would enjoy having her." *WOW, it looks like both Miss Kitty and I found new mates.*

There was another meaningful experience going on during all our not so long courtship. After my trip to Salt Lake City to learn how to write and win a SBIR contract from the Air Force, I started writing a proposal. I had been successful with the small contracts from Georgia Tech and Lockheed Fort Worth to improve the HASC software. Therefore, I thought more modifications of the HASC software would be a winner. At that time, the HASC software had worked only on fighter aircraft. My proposal to the Air Force would be to extend the software to work on general aviation and commercial airplanes.

There are fundamental differences in the wing shapes for those aircraft. I won the proposal for the contract and received notice from the Air Force during our courtship. I like to tell people, "I won two proposals

almost at the same time. One was the Air Force SBIR contract, and the other was Frieda."

Then came the joy of telling our friends and families about our plans. Many were concerned we were rushing things, but it wasn't like Frieda and I were teenagers. We'd both had experiences with long marriages and hard knocks, and we believed that God had answered our prayers for a special partner. We decided Frieda would sell her house and move into mine after our marriage.

We wanted a meaningful wedding ceremony. Our first marriages had been simple affairs, so we decided we wanted the best we could afford the second time around. Frieda wanted a typical June wedding. To complete the circle, we picked "The Winery" for the rehearsal dinner.

On June 8, 1996—three months after we met—Frieda and I were married and began a new and adventurous life together. Neither she nor I had been able to afford an elaborate honeymoon for our first marriages. We had both spent our first honeymoons in the Tennessee mountains. This time was different. We took a three-part honeymoon ending with a cruise to Bermuda.

We began with three nights at a nice hotel at Stone Mountain Park near Atlanta. We were there only one night when we got a call from Frieda's real estate agent. She had a buyer for her house. We never thought she would get a sale that quickly.

The 1996 Summer Olympics were being held in Atlanta and the buyer wanted to get moved in before the festivities. It was great that it happened so fast, but we had to take care of business before continuing our honeymoon. We met with the agent to sign papers. There would be time before the closing for us to get back from our honeymoon We knew the move would be a huge task during the summer heat, but it was a great relief to have the sale done. Maybe that was God's way of saying, "Have a blessed honeymoon. Your marriage is my will."

We flew to New York City for the next phase of our trip. We spent two days touring the highlights of the Big Apple. Both of us had been to New York City before, but it still was an adventure. We took the subway out to the harbor to catch the ferry to the Statue of Liberty and Ellis Island. We rode to the top of the Empire State Building and toured the shops in Times Square. After walking back to our big closet hotel room, we noted some

activity on a street near us. It was a movie production set starring George Clooney in an action film. The next day we took a hair-raising taxi ride to the Port of New York to board our cruise ship.

We boarded the Norwegian cruise ship at about 5 p.m. in the evening. We had a great meal and settled down in our cabin as the ship made its way out to sea. We were ready to have a fantastic honeymoon.

Neither one of us had ever traveled on a luxury cruise ship like that one. During my Navy days, I'd had a wild cruise on an aircraft carrier—a ship as big or bigger than this cruise ship—but Frieda had never been on a cruise of any type. She was about to experience the effect of rough seas like I had when going through a typhoon in the Pacific.

We weren't in a hurricane, but the sea was rough. Frieda got sick and stayed that way until we arrived in Bermuda. I had licked the motion sickness problem a few years earlier, so on this trip I did a lot of running to the infirmary and snack counters to get something she could hold down. Nothing helped except the dry land of Bermuda.

The next day she was well enough to start touring the port city of Hamilton. At lunch we found a nice beach cove for a picnic. I convinced Frieda to go snorkeling with me in the ocean. She had never been snorkeling, so I had fun teaching her. It's never easy the first time, but she gave it a good try, and I was proud of her.

That day I made the mistake of leaving my contact lenses in my eyes. After floating on the surface and watching a fish below, I dove down to it. I never saw my contacts again. I guess I gave them to the fish.

We wanted to tour more of the island but had no means to travel, until we spotted a Moped Scooter rental store near the ship dock. We rented a two-seater and after a little orientation, we were off. To make things more exciting, all vehicles drove on the left side of the road in that British Territory. That was a new experience for both of us.

I admit that driving on the left side was difficult at first. The biggest problem was making a right turn. You had to make your brain turn upside down. We didn't have turn signals, so I had to use hand signals, and that meant I had to steer with one hand. We saw many beautiful sights on the island, so it was worth the risk.

As we boarded our ship, we saw an ambulance pull up that offloaded a

passenger in a full body cast. We learned later that he had been in a Moped accident. We were thankful to be back on the ship with all bones intact.

Frieda readily agreed that I was the more adventurous person, but she would be willing to try as much as she could. After all, she had gone flying with me. We enjoyed the rest of the time in Bermuda before sailing back to New York City. As soon as we set sail, Frieda turned pale and green again.

We were advised that a straight sail back to New York would not be possible because of a hurricane in the Atlantic. The seas were even rougher than before, and Frieda couldn't even get off the bed without getting violently ill. I was as glad to finally see the Statue of Liberty as I had been many years before when I had been on the aircraft carrier Ranger and saw the Golden Gate Bridge. On that trip the ship had been pushed by a Pacific typhoon, and I had been sick for days.

Flying home to Atlanta was uneventful, but busy days were ahead. We closed on Frieda's house and the moving process began. I also had packing to do in what would become our home. I wanted it to feel like it was Frieda's home and not just a place to live.

There were several memories of Mary I had to store in the attic. That was difficult, but I loved Frieda and realized I had started a new life. I felt sure Mary would have wanted me to move on with my life. God was taking care of her now.

It was now time for me to help God take care of Frieda. I believed he had great plans and adventures ahead for us. We had a new business to run and health problems to overcome. My motto was "Onward and Upward."

Fourty Seven

Consulting Aviation Services

E ver since my Lockheed retirement, I had been doing business as Consulting Aviation Services. I had provided significant improvements to the High Angle of Attack (HASC) software that helped me get a contract from the Air Force. It was obtained as a Small Business Independent Research (SBIR) contract. An SBIR contract was designed to help small businesses get started. I decided it was time to incorporate to protect us from liability. Consulting Aviation Services, Inc. (CAS) was launched in April 1996.

Engineering help and additional financing were required to get the company up and running. I brought in two Lockheed retirees that I had known for years as business partners. They provided some finances, but mostly engineering expertise.

Under that contract, we produced significant improvements in the HASC software needed for the design of new airplanes and modifications of older airplanes. Because of our changes, the name of the software was changed from HASC to Consulting Aviation Services Stability & Control (CASSC).

Prior to this contract only fighter airplanes with very thin wing airfoils could be analyzed and improved. HASC worked to understand and control the leading-edge vortex that forms at high angles of attack (AOA) of fighter aircraft. AOA is the angle between the longitudinal axis of the airplane and the wind relative to the airplane. Except for level flight, it's not the angle between the longitudinal axis and the ground. HASC was exactly

accurate in predicting the maximum AOA. That is the angle of attack where the airplane lift reaches its maximum and the airplane stalls and plummets out of the sky.

Unless you had an airplane with a controllable stall and a well-trained pilot, you didn't want to be in it. The Federal Aviation Administration (FAA) regulations were designed to assure this level of safety was obtained. However, stall problems did occur. CAS remained dedicated to creating concepts that made stalls controllable and capable of saving lives.

The upgraded CASSC software predicted the stall and the post-stall characteristics of almost all conventional types of airplanes accurately. The initial proof of the quality of the new software was provided by an accurate prediction of the stall characteristics on an airplane tested in a large wind tunnel. We completed the Air Force Contract, and a report was provided to the Air Force in January of 1997.

Soon after the Air Force report, we wrote another report for an AIAA Symposium to be presented in San Jose, California. We didn't know it at the time, but the software we created under that contract would become the foundation of CAS for many years to come. That contract was the first completed government contract for CAS, and it called for a celebration!

Mississippi State University (MSU) was sponsoring an alumni trip to Austria. Frieda and I said, "Why not go? We may never have the chance again."

We packed up and traveled to Europe in February 1997. We had gotten married in June 1996 and were already going to Europe. Frieda had never been to Europe, and I bet she thought, "I must have married the right man." Life had not been easy for her before she married me, and she had not traveled like I had. It was good that she was adventurous, because I expected we would be traveling a lot more. After all, we were in the aviation business.

The trip began with a flight on Lufthansa to Munich, Germany. One of the first things we learned was that in Germany the city is called München. Twenty years prior, I had traveled alone on a business trip to München. Now I was with some of my fellow alumni from MSU. The tour guides took good care of our itinerary, allowing us to see many more of the sights of München than I had seen before. They also told us that no Nazis were allowed in the city.

It was surprising to see grass covered mounds in the center of the city. Our tour guide said those memorial mounds were filled with rubble from the World War II bombing by the Allies. They served to remind the Germans of their history under the Nazis.

Our next destination was Salzburg, Austria where the movie, *The Sound of Music* was filmed. Salzburg was the birthplace of Mozart, and his lively music filled the air in and around the interesting Mozart Museum. An amazing 11[th]-century castle—Festung Hohensalzburg—overlooked *Salzburg* from a hill on the outskirts of the city. After we toured the castle, we climbed to the top to see a magnificent and expansive view of the Alps. Our guides pointed out several spots where the movie had been filmed.

We really wanted to see inside the Abbey where Maria served as a nun. Somehow word had gotten to the nuns that a group from Mississippi was visiting Salzburg. One of the nuns was from Mississippi, and she wanted us to visit. The Abbey was extremely strict about having strangers inside just like in the days when Maria was there. However, they agreed to allow two from our group to come. I don't remember why Frieda and I were selected, but we were. The Nun who requested the visitors was quite pleased to see us and greeted us warmly. We weren't allowed to see much of the Abbey, but we were glad to be there.

We saw many of the scenic areas from the movie where the Von Trapp family performed. One was the gazebo where the Captain and Maria fell in love while singing *Something Good* and where Liesl sang *I Am Sixteen Going on Seventeen*. Another movie site was the reflective lake in front of the Von Trapp family palace. We also toured the cathedral on the outskirts of Salzburg where Maria married Captain von Trapp.

After leaving Salzburg we headed for the Alps. Taking a horse- drawn sleigh ride high into the mountains was an unforgettable experience. On that freezing cold February day, we snuggled up and had a lot of fun. I wanted to ski in the Alps, but the snow levels were unusually low that year. Only expert skiers could manage the higher, riskier slopes, and I was at best an intermediate skier.

Ice crystals clung to the trees of the beautiful city of Vienna, which overlooked the Danube River. One of the scenic buildings we saw was the Kunsthistorisches Museum. At one time it had been a famous palace, but now housed some of the most famous paintings in the world in its

galleries. We didn't get to go in, but we enjoyed the Museum grounds and gardens which were manicured to perfection. Another unique place was the Austria Imperial Treasury, which displayed the imperial jewelry. A third magnificent building was the Hoflburg Palace, the center of government.

One more story will summarize the joy we had on that trip. A couple from our group had a great reason for being on the trip. The husband was a World War II member of the USA Occupation Forces. He happened to be stationed near Salzburg and had been involved in finding entertainers from Austria who would be willing to perform for our troops. That is where he met his wife. They married in Austria, and he took her to the USA. To the best of my knowledge, they had not been back to Austria until the time of our trip in 1997. We all celebrated with them.

Fourty Eight

Busy and Traumatic Days

Our next event took place in June 1997 at the AIAA symposium in San Jose, California. There I presented an AIAA report to publicize the CASSC software. Subsequent discussions of flight and simulator tests showed that CASSC gave accurate stall characteristics on a small twin-engine airplane, a single-engine airplane, and a Boeing 737-800 airliner.

Freida's liver problems made traveling difficult. That was mainly due to all the medicines she had to take. However, she was a determined lady who was not going to let that be an issue. She had never been to California and wanted to see it all. I was determined to take her to the best sites all around San Francisco. She did well until she was driving on the curvy roads through Napa Valley. Her medicine put her into a daze, she drifted off to sleep, and the car went out of control. I grabbed the steering wheel before we went into a ditch. Our nerves were shot, but after some rest, I took control of the car and drove the rest of the trip.

That same summer we volunteered to go on a Builders for Christ trip. That trip took us to Sparks, Nevada—a suburb of Reno—to help construct a church. We wondered why we should build a church in the middle of a gambling town. We learned that many Sparks' citizens believed in God, and they needed a church building in which to reach and teach people about Christ.

Our lodging was in the former officers' quarters at Stead Air Force Base. The base was decommissioned in 1966 and turned over to the public. That rang a bell with me, because I knew it was now Stead Airport home

of the annual Reno Air Races. The air races were not going on while we were there. I hoped to someday see the races, but at that time we had more important work to accomplish.

Building a church with the Builders of Christ was tough and strenuous work. The group was filled with folks who were a joy to be around. Our days started early. Frieda, along with some other cooks, got up early to fix breakfast for about thirty-five people so they could get to work by 7:00 a.m.

After our workdays we met for worship at the church building site. There was no roof—only open frames, roof studs, and ceiling joists. We sang uplifting songs and prayed. On Wednesday night, a young man from the Caribbean got up to sing. As his voice rang out, a colorful bird landed on a roof stud right in front of him and began to sing with him. After the young man stopped singing, the bird sat there a while then flew away. I believe it sat there long enough to tell us that God was pleased with what we were doing.

We went to the casinos in Reno a few times. Some folks did some minor gambling with the one-arm bandits, but the main reason we went to the casinos was to get wonderful meals at exceptionally low prices. On our last day, we did some sight-seeing at an old Western town and visited the house used in the TV series Bonanza.

Back home in Georgia, Frieda started having serious problems with her health. Water began collecting in her lungs and abdomen. She went to a lung doctor to go through a painful treatment for removing the fluid. This doctor gave us a fright by telling us she might have cancer. We knew that an abnormal accumulation of fluid in the abdomen, called ascites, could be caused by advanced cirrhosis of the liver.

We made a follow-up appointment with the Emory transplant doctors. They immediately diagnosed her problem as ascites caused by her deteriorating liver, and they set her up for more extensive tests. At the beginning of 1998, Frieda's name was placed on the national liver transplant donor list. We began praying in earnest for the miracle of a donated organ. It was a hard prayer because it meant someone else would die before she could get a liver.

Despite our difficulties, we were able to joke about Frieda's liver problems. There was a stigma associated with having cirrhosis of the

liver. A lot of people thought it was caused by drinking alcohol. That had nothing to do with Frieda's malady. She told people she had Baptist Cirrhosis, since Baptists at that time abstained from drinking alcohol. She made the doctors laugh when she said she had PBC or Primary Biliary (Baptist) Cirrhosis.

Even though Frieda was on the liver transplant list, the doctors said it would be quite a while before she would get a liver. The effects of the ascites caused other parts of her body to deteriorate, and it was recommended that she have abdominal surgery. In February 1998 she had successful surgery, but the recovery period was tough and painful.

When I was not driving Frieda to doctors' appointments across Atlanta, I was preparing a CAS proposal for Lockheed Marietta. My company had been working with Lockheed on propeller analysis for wind tunnel tests of the C-130J airplane. Earlier in my career at Lockheed, I had made some vertical tail improvements for a proposed L400—a two engine C-130. Since the tail was the same as the C-130J, and I now had the CASSC software, I proposed a much better design for the C-130J tail.

As soon as I finished the proposal, I made an appointment to meet with the Lockheed project manager and some other engineers. On May 11, 1998, in the middle of my presentation, a Lockheed secretary broke into the discussion to tell me, "Your wife is heading to the hospital to get a new liver." The Lockheed crew pushed me out the door and escorted me through the building and parking lot to go to her.

It had only been five months since Frieda had been listed for transplant, and we were shocked that she was called so soon. After a mad dash through the rush hour traffic on the Atlanta interstates, she was admitted to Emory Hospital and tested again to make sure the donor liver would be a good match.

It was many hours before I got to see her in ICU recovery. She looked like a porcupine with so many tubes coming out of her body. I rejoiced that she had a new liver and a new life. Frieda recovered well from the surgery, but it took many visits back and forth to Emory for checkups to tweak her anti-rejection medicines. Those were not fun trips but were necessary for at least a year.

I got the Lockheed contract, successfully finished the work, and wrote

a report called "C-130J Dorsal/Vertical Stall Analysis." Despite a terribly busy and traumatic year, I delivered the report on September 8, 1998.

When life settled down, I got back into the pilot's seat to do some purposeful flying. The work of two organizations appealed to my desire to use my flying ability to serve other people. Angel Flight raised funds to pay for flights of medically disabled persons. Potential donors were given complimentary flights to encourage them to fund future Angel Flight missions. In September 1998 Frieda and I flew from McCollum Airport to Peachtree/DeKalb Airport (PDK) to pick up potential Angel Flight donors. Before I started the engine, I always said a prayer. I told my passengers, "I'm not afraid. I'm just thanking God for the opportunity to fly."

Frieda stayed at the airport while I took three passengers up over Atlanta and Stone Mountain then back to PDK for a landing. That first flight worked out perfectly when the control tower directed me in on the planned route. While landing my second flight, I lost contact with the control tower. All I could do was make a 180 degree turn and start the landing again. I flew to the far end of the airport and radioed the tower. After circling the airport several more times, the tower gave me permission to land. I am sure my passengers wondered when we were going to land, and so did I.

Another type of flying I enjoyed was with the Experimental Aircraft Association (EAA). Most of the local EAA chapters participated in a program called "Young Eagles." That program was designed to give children between the ages of 8 and 17 an opportunity to experience flight in a general aviation aircraft while educating them about flying. The program was offered free of charge with costs being covered by the volunteers. I was one of those volunteers serving through the local EAA chapter 268. I flew Young Eagles at the end of 1998 and into 1999.

I used most of my other airtime for maintaining instrument flying proficiency. Frieda and I took a trip to Greenville, South Carolina in the flying club's Cessna 172 RG. We spent most of the day visiting some of Frieda's friends. Before we left Greenville, I discovered an engine problem during the run-up checkout. Mechanics at the airport repaired the engine so we could fly back home.

My company work for Consulting Aviation Services (CAS) kept me

busy in 1999. To earn income for CAS, we served as administrators for short-term contract engineers who worked as consultants at Lockheed. Most of those engineers were retirees who had been called back to Lockheed to work on various projects. We used the overhead income to begin the complicated and expensive task of filing a patent application.

During my employment at Lockheed, I had worked on an innovation that mounted on the leading-edge of wings to delay flow separation and stall on a portion of the wing. The triangular shaped device was designed with airfoils to create stable vortexes on each side of the device. Those vortices delayed stall on a portion of the wing behind it. Controlling stall was much desired because it could prevent airplanes from crashing.

I wanted to patent that unique device, but there was a problem. I had made a disclosure to the Lockheed patent office, and that made it Lockheed's property. Lockheed, however, had not applied to get a patent for the several years it had been in their possession. I hoped they would release it to me.

Some of Lockheed's patent lawyers remembered me, since I had made several patent disclosures, which had resulted in at least two patents for Lockheed. I wrote letters and made several calls to the patent department asking for release of that disclosure. It was released with only one condition— if Lockheed used the device on their airplanes, I could not charge them for royalties. That was not a problem, since the best candidates for the device were not built by Lockheed.

Patent lawyers were expensive, and a lot of effort was required by my company to provide them with the information they needed. That was a huge risk of time and money, but it proved to a wise risk. The patent application called Vortex Control Eaglets was filed to the United States Patent and Trademark Office in 1999. That effort prepared the way for a real future for our company. The decade of the 1990s came to an end with the groundwork laid for an exciting 21st century.

Fourty Nine

A New Millennium

Y2K phobia—the fear of computers going crazy—dominated the headlines as 1999 ended. Computer systems were designed to work with the binary numbering system, or a two-digit code. When written in the late 20th century, each year was represented by two digits—for example 65 and not 1965. With the dawn of the 21st century, a four-digit code year became a necessity—for example 2000 and not 00. A software fix provided hope that computers would not crash. People faced great uncertainty and stockpiled food, water, and other survival necessities in case stores could not open. No crash happened, and the dawn of a new millennium came in peacefully.

In 2000 I became the Young Eagles' coordinator for EAA chapter 268. Not only did I fly the children, but I also made all the arrangements for getting groups of children involved. I also had to enlist enough volunteer pilots for the day of flight. In addition, I had to continue my regular flying to stay proficient with my instrument rating. Of the two, flying for the Young Eagles was more fun. At the end of my term of service, I received the 2000 Chapter Service Award signed by the President of the Experimental Aviation Association.

*For dedicated service within your Chapter, this award is
presented in recognition of your service and assistance to foster
the growth of sport aviation through Chapter activities.*

The year 2000 also ushered in some stressful challenges. Frieda's oldest sister, Jan Whaley, died in January. She and her husband Curt lived in

Pensacola, Florida. Frieda had left Webster, New York after graduating from high school to live with Jan and Curt in Atlanta, Georgia.

Jan was buried in the National Cemetery at the Naval Air Station in Pensacola. She qualified for that location since Curt had served as a naval aviator during the Korean War. Curt and I had become good friends since we had so much in common. I had kept the type of planes in good flying condition that he had flown during the war. We were both private pilots as well. I had tried to be a subtle witness to Curt regarding my Christian faith. Much later in our lives, I learned that my witness had had some part in Curt trusting Jesus Christ.

Two years to the day after Frieda's transplant on May 12, 2000, she began to reject her new liver. We were surprised and scared since she'd had no problems since the surgery. During the four days she spent in the hospital, the doctors got the rejection under control and adjusted her immune suppressant medication. After several weeks she adjusted to the new meds, and we were able to go on another adventure.

We had already booked a July 2000 Alaskan Inside Passage Cruise— the first cruise we had booked since our trip to Bermuda. Frieda had stocked up on every seasick remedy she could find. We were told that the Inside Passage trip would have much less rough water, so we decided to take the risk.

The Inside Passage route followed the 500-mile-long panhandle of Alaska. The panhandle hosted much beauty and action. The route included many expeditions, intriguing towns, native Alaskan villages, and adventures. One of the most impressive sights was watching the whales' breach. A whale breached when it reached high speed just under the water, leapt high out of the water, rolled over on its back, and came down slapping its tail on the water. On both sides of the ship, we saw bears, eagles, and other wild animals in the raw wilderness. Numerous waterfalls splashed their way down the mountains and added to unforgettable memories of our trip.

Our ship stopped at the native village of Haines. After hiking along a stream where we saw giant Sockeye salmon making their way up the river, we reached our picnic destination. Fresh barbeque salmon topped the menu along with steak for those who did not like fish. Frieda had never eaten barbeque salmon and said she would order steak. Once I convinced her to try the salmon, she could not get enough. We have never been able to duplicate that delicious feast.

More adventures awaited us in Skagway, Alaska. Frieda was not up to a hike, but I joined a group to hike up the White Pass, an historic part of the Klondike gold rush trail. I loved getting out in the Alaskan wilderness. Our lady tour guide kept encouraging us to make noise so that bears would not bother us. As we walked along the path, she told us about the plants, trees, and wildlife of the area. We didn't have time to even think about bears before we reached a river where we boarded canoes to make our way down river to Skagway.

Along the way our guide pointed out the remains of old log buildings that had been used as rest points on the White Pass trail. In Skagway we learned about the wild west days of the gold rush. Nobody wanted to cross paths with desperado Soapy Smith. There were many other dangerous people like him in Skagway, but that had not stopped the adventurous people who passed through there on their way to the gold fields. We could have learned much more about the gold rush days, but the ship signaled its horn to call us to board.

Our ship's next destination was Glacier Bay and the Grand Pacific Glacier—accessible only by boat, airplane, or helicopter. As we traveled through the bay, we were impressed by the mountains, waterfalls, and colorful flowers. I hoped the ship's helmsman would keep a close eye on the blue ice flows surrounding our ship.

The boat parked in front of the giant glacier so we could enjoy the view of the seals sleeping on those ice flows. We wanted to see calving action on the glacier and were not disappointed. Calving is the process where great chunks of ice fall from the glacier into the bay.

We soon heard a great roar as a monstrous chunk of ice fell from the glacier. A huge wake rose in the water, and our ship experienced a roller coaster ride on the waves.

More excursions awaited us in Juneau, the capital of Alaska—a small and pretty city. Frieda and I decided to go on two different tours. Her tour took her whale watching on a high-speed catamaran boat. She decided to risk her tendency to get seasick on a boat that would skim over the waves and not rock and roll in the water. The fast and extremely smooth ride stopped when it spotted the whales so that tourists could photograph the whales breaching. After her great adventure, she was glad to return to dry land.

My tour literally took me off the water and into the air on a float plane. In all my years of flying, I had never taken off on a float plane. Back in my Navy days, I had flown on a Navy Consolidated PBY Catalina amphibious aircraft. It had floats and wheels, but we had taken off from an airport.

The Alaskan bush country airplane, a de Haviland Beaver, was a very rugged and powerful airplane. Bush pilots wanted to fly a truck with wings, and that was what they got. That airplane had the load carrying ability and range they wanted, and I had always wanted to fly in one.

I had helped design airplanes with STOL (short take-off and landing). The STOL Beaver airplane also had a power plant I liked. The Pratt & Whitney R985 engine powered the World War II trainers that I worked on during the Korean War. When I taxied them, I could feel those powerful engines.

As I boarded the plane with the other tourists, I told the pilot I also flew and would like to sit in the co-pilot's seat. He immediately agreed. After getting a safety briefing and all the required clearances, we taxied down the bay. That big engine with its three-bladed propeller moved us on the water. At first the high drag of the water made the engines work hard to get the floats "on the step" (the speed at which floats are just skimming the top of the water.)

Free at last! We flew through a light rain, but to the pilot, that was a common event. Despite the overcast skies, a spectacular view awaited us. We could see several other bays and lakes at lower altitudes, but ahead and all around us were snowcapped mountains.

Soon we saw the huge glacier where it dumped its ice into the bay. As we flew over the glacier with mountains on both sides, I didn't worry about being trapped in the valley; there was plenty of space to turn around. The immense size and power of the glacier reminded me of God's great power in creating such a beautiful world. The glacier had large cracks in it, but I had faith in that airplane.

Flying back to Juneau and floating to a landing near the big cruise ship was exhilarating. I met up with Frieda and we shared our exciting adventures as we headed back to the ship. After so many adventures, we were ready to sail back to Seattle for an appointment with a company that expressed interest in CAS technology.

Fifty

Unexpected Events

Research conducted by my company gave me data that provided significant proof of concept for our unique CASSC software. Our software data lined up closely with NASA's full-scale wind tunnel test data on a Cessna 210 general aviation airplane. With proof of its accuracy, we wanted to use CASSC to examine how well our innovation called Vortex Control Eaglets would work on a Cessna 172.

The patent on our Eaglets would soon be issued, and we needed proof on a well-known airplane for marketing purposes. The purpose of the Eaglets on the wing leading edge ahead of the aileron was to delay the stall, which kept the airplane under control. A stall would cause the airplane to roll in the opposite direction from where you wanted it to go, and that could cause it to go into a spin. We hoped our innovation would control the stall and save lives. Having this capability—and hoping to get it into the market—was the reason we stayed in Seattle after our Alaska cruise.

I had an appointment with the CEO and owner of Boundary Layer Research located in Everett, Washington. When Frieda first heard the name, she thought I had spoken French and said *Boundelair*. A boundary layer is a complex aerodynamic term, which simply means the thin layer of air or a fluid that flows near the surface of a solid object like a wing. It could be difficult to control, and that was how our VC Eaglets could help. I hoped to get the attention of the CEO on either CASSC software, VC Eaglets, or maybe both.

We left the cruise ship and found our hotel in Seattle. We then had

a great meal of Alaskan halibut. After a good night's sleep, we rented a car and headed for Everett. We gave ourselves plenty of time to enjoy the sights along the way. It was a clear day, and we had a magnificent view of snow-capped Mount Rainier.

My meeting turned out to be quite surprising because the CEO expressed little interested in either the software or the Eaglets. He had something else in mind that turned out to be a life-changing event for my company. He had a copy of a US patent laying on his desk, and he asked me to look at it. It was one of the patents I had worked on at Lockheed. Johnny Braden and I had applied for that patent in 1984, and Lockheed had obtained it in 1988. Johnny and I were listed as inventors, even though it was assigned to Lockheed.

The patent was for devices to reduce the after-body drag of the Lockheed C-130. Several prior innovations had been tested and had failed. One had been structurally unfit. The patented concept required a series of vortices created along the side of the after-body, running at an angle from top down and aft on the fuselage to under the bottom of the fuselage. Those vortices were created with grooves in the fuselage. That was not practical to manufacture and very difficult to install.

However, there was a stroke of genius in the concept. For the first time, I became aware of the concept of multiple longitudinal vortices running from the forward part of the fuselage to the aft end. Working together like a gaggle of geese in flight, each vortex created significant drag reduction for the one behind it.

That is what the CEO of Boundary Layer Research could see. The CEO asked me if I thought I could come up with a more practical method to create those vortices, and if I could, he would support me in developing the concept. I believed we could replace the grooves with Finlets—devices shaped like fish fins—on the outside of the fuselage. The CEO shared his vision with me because he had seen my innovative nature in CASSC and VC Eaglets.

The result of my visit to Everett was not what I thought it would be, but it turned out to be the future cornerstone of my company. Leaving the beauty of Alaska and Washington was hard to do but going home to Georgia had great appeal. Now we had a new project to add to our tasks at CAS.

As a person who had recently retired from Lockheed, I loved staying busy and always thought God's purpose for me was to serve others through aviation. I believed my innovations would help me fulfill that purpose. VC Eaglets would save lives, and the new project—Vortex Control Finlets—would improve airplane performance and provide jobs.

Frieda's help was invaluable. She not only served as a great administrator for CAS, but she also encouraged me to reach for the sky. She oversaw the business of providing our consultant services. That service provided consulting engineers for temporary projects at Lockheed. Many were retired engineers from Lockheed.

Our collaboration was good business for Lockheed and CAS. Frieda took care of contracts, accounting, payroll, and taxes. Those contract funds provided monies for CAS so we could work on other projects. Frieda had a sign on the wall by her desk that asked the consulting engineers, "Would you like to talk to the man in charge or the woman who knows what's going on?" She did what I didn't want to do.

By the end of 2000, our CASSC software was working so well we considered it to be a product we could sell. To create interest in the aviation industry, I wrote a paper that I hoped to present to an AIAA conference in Anaheim, California in June 2001. Writing papers was a difficult and time-consuming task, but I pushed forward and submitted my paper to the conference ahead of the deadline.

In my spare time, I enjoyed flying for pleasure and to give pleasure to others. Before Christmas, our church held a silent auction for missions. I offered to provide an hour-long flight around the North Georgia area. Church members would bid various amounts of money, and the top bidder would win that flight. On December 28, I took the winners, a mother and her two home-schooled daughters, to the local airport. They were all excited about flying.

I secured a Cessna 182 RG (Retractable Landing Gear) from our flying club for the flight. That type of airplane was perfect and had the power and space needed. The airplane was relatively fast in cruise (160 mph), so we could go a long distance in the time we had.

We left the Cobb County airport and flew round trip up to the North Georgia mountains. On the way back to the airport, the mother asked me if I had seen the airplane that had flown close to us. I had to admit I had

not seen it, but I knew I should have. Since there were still fall colors on the trees, I wondered if the airplane had blended in with the colors. I also thought I might have sight problems. The flight ended well, but I decided to see my eye doctor. He diagnosed me with cataracts in both eyes. I was grounded from flying until I could schedule cataract surgery.

It was a disappointing ending for 2000 and not a good beginning for 2001. *Would I ever again be pilot in command?* At age seventy, I stayed busy at work and needed more airtime to stay proficient. But it was encouraging to hear about octogenarians that were still flying.

A recent commentary by Lisa Turner in the January 2020 issue of Sport Aviation magazine says it all for me: ". . . *Airplanes represent our creative drive and are a link to both our physical and spiritual connections with the earth and the heavens.*"

Fifty One

A Year of Change

Instead of flying, I channeled my airplane passion into my innovations. My CAS partner and I began working to make my ideas for Vortex Control Finlets into a patentable concept.

The goal with Finlets was to eliminate a rogue vortex at the side edges near the flat bottom of the C-130 afterbody. I used my CASSC software to model the rogue vortex. Running only a flat-bottom model—with and without the rogue vortex—produced an approximation of the drag in each scenario. We made an educated guess for how much drag could be eliminated with Finlets. However, we knew that Finlets could be placed on a C-130 easier and cheaper than the previous fix of afterbody grooves.

After much analysis and design work, we came up with a design ready to submit to a patent attorney. We invested a great deal of time and money during 2001 before the attorney applied for a United States Patent.

In the interim we negotiated with Boundary Layer Research Corporation (BLR) for potential development of Finlets on the C-130. BLR personnel were serious about getting Finlets into the market. They used their influence and contacts to find financial backing, to get a US Air Force contract, and to meet with an Israeli representative here in the United States.

CAS met with retirees from Lockheed who expressed interest in our concept. They had all had experience with the afterbody drag of the C-130, and they knew how difficult and expensive the project would be.

One of the retirees had been my department manager for a short time at Lockheed, and I felt honored that he wanted to be involved.

Much of my time was spent preparing a paper to present at the AIAA conference in Anaheim, California on the value of the CASSC software. No other software could predict the aerodynamic characteristics of an airplane as well as CASSC. In June 2001 Frieda and I flew to Anaheim for both business and pleasure. My presentation at the conference went well with much interest shown by the attendees.

Our vacation officially began with a trip to Huntington Beach, my former home. Frieda was excited to make her first trip to Southern California, and I was excited to introduce Frieda to some of my great California friends. We also toured Los Angeles and Torrance before heading down the coast to see the world-famous San Diego Zoo in Balboa Park.

The zoo had a large wooded natural habitat set aside for all kinds of live birds. The stuffed bird display showed interesting details about each part of the bird. A predator bird with its wings spread out caught my attention. On each wing was a triangular-shaped feather extending from the leading edge. That feather was called an "Alula", and its shape was just like the shape of our patented VC Eaglet. We learned that the bird extended that device to control its landing—identical to the purpose of the Eaglet.

I realized God had created that concept first and had passed the idea on to me—at least I wanted to think so. I studied predatory birds after that trip and learned a lot about them. A group of scientists in South Korea also studied that phenomenon and discovered that the Alula wing created vortices just like our Eaglets.

Coronado Island was a beautiful place to visit. It had perfect temperatures and a nice breeze coming off the Pacific. The pink Hotel Del Coronado on the island impressed us. Since we were so close to the Mexican border, we went to Tijuana, just to say we had been there. Not at all impressed by the sleezy shops and unsanitary conditions in Tijuana, we cut our visit short and headed back to LA where we caught our plane to Atlanta.

Back at home I received a surprising call from the purchasing department at Lockheed California. They wanted to buy four copies of our CASSC software. We already had training manuals ready to deliver.

That purchase greatly boosted our morale. Our trip to the West Coast turned out to be very profitable after all. In addition, we sold a copy of the software to BLR.

Other surprises were in store for 2001. On Labor Day weekend, we were glad to see Frieda's niece, Sandy DuVall, and her husband at church. After the service, Sandy asked, "Do you still have passports, and do you want to go to France this coming Thursday?"

"Yes, but why such short notice?"

Sandy, a French teacher, had organized a group tour to France for the parents of her former students. One couple had dropped out because of health issues and wanted to sell their spots on the tour at a discount. We bought plane tickets and frantically packed our bags.

Curt Whaley, Sandy's father, was also going on the trip. Curt and I shared a love of flying and similar experiences in the Naval Air Force. As a former Eastern Airlines captain, he was able to get us invited into the cockpit on our overnight flight to Frankfurt, Germany. On that clear night, we saw an expansive view of the galaxy. We did not know that after this trip, guests would be forbidden to enter cockpits.

We boarded a bus in Frankfurt the next morning and headed to the Alsace-Lorraine area of France. That was the major wine growing section of France and was Trés Magnifique Campagna (very beautiful countryside). We were not wine connoisseurs since Frieda had to avoid it altogether because of her liver transplant.

We enjoyed the scenery but remembered the history of the area. We drove through the Argon Forest where fierce battles had taken place in World War I. In addition, the Battle of the Bulge in WWII had occurred to the north. I remembered seeing newsreels of those battles as a 13-year-old boy. The tour group went from tasting wine to tasting mustard when we visited Dijon, a lovely small city.

Our next stop was a more sobering experience. We toured a German concentration and extermination camp. Natzweiler-Struthof was the only concentration camp built by the Nazis on French territory. At that time, the Alsace-Lorraine territory had been annexed as part of the Third Reich. It was gruesome to see the German experimental medical rooms, the cremation furnaces, and marks on the walls made by the prisoners. Since World War II, I had seen many pictures of the atrocities of the

concentration camps, but to be standing in one stirred my soul. Frieda and I were glad we went, but also glad to be moving on.

Our next major destination was Strasbourg where we would begin a cruise on the Rhine River. On the bus trip to Strasbourg, we stopped for a lunch break and noticed a cluster of people around a black and white television mounted on the wall. As we got closer, we saw an airplane hitting a skyscraper. It looked like an old King Kong movie. Sandy was able to understand the commentator enough to know the airplane had hit one of the World Trade Towers in Manhattan. The date was Tuesday, September 11, 2001.

At first, we thought the plane crash was an accident. I remembered that at the end of World War II, a North American B-25 accidently crashed into the Empire State Building. Not speaking or understanding French handicapped our understanding of the news broadcasts. Later in the tour, we picked up the BBC broadcasts and English written newspapers and learned the horrific details of the terrorist attack.

When we arrived in Strasbourg, we were reminded once again of WWII. We crossed a large plaza and remembered pictures we had seen of thousands of German soldiers with swastikas saluting Adolph Hitler. Our somber mood must have showed because a French lady came up to us and said, "We are very sorry such a horrible event occurred in America." Others crossed their arms over their hearts in a show of solidarity.

Once we boarded the cruise ship in Strasbourg, we learned that all international flights had been shut down, and nobody knew when airports would reopen. An al-Qaeda terrorist group had not only attacked the twin towers but had hijacked and crashed two other planes—one at the Pentagon in Washington and one in a field in Pennsylvania. We were stuck in France, and our return to the USA was in jeopardy.

As we traveled north on the Rhine River, we saw France on our left side and Germany on our right. As the river meandered further into Germany, ancient structures and castles appeared on the hillsides. One evening after dark, the boat parked with many others on the river. Live fireworks cascaded down the castles and burst in the sky overhead. We were at the right place at the right time to enjoy that annual event.

Mainz, Germany, located on the Rhine river where the Main River joins the Rhine, captured our interest. The printing press that printed the

original English language Guttenberg Bible was in Mainz. The printing machine was the first to use mass-produced movable metal type. Books that had previously been hand copied had become much more available after 1440 AD and had helped bring Europe out of the Dark Ages and into the Protestant Reformation.

In Cologne, Germany, we toured the impressive Cathedral of Cologne. We were surprised to see bullet holes in the cathedral walls from the Allied bombing of World War II.

The next day we boarded our bus for Frankfurt, Germany. We learned that the flights to the USA had just reopened, and we could fly from Frankfurt to Atlanta as planned. Hallelujah! We could go back home.

The overwhelming security at the Frankfurt airport—with military guards dressed in full battle gear carrying AK-47 rifles—sobered us. Our tour guide told us not to speak or smile as we entered security and to do everything we were told without question. All passengers were thoroughly searched including an older lady in our group with a heart monitor. The security personnel made her go into a private room and completely strip down.

Our nerves were shot by the time we found our seats on the Lufthansa jumbo jet and took off. What a relief to be in the air heading for home. Seven hours later, the pilot told us we were in USA airspace! All the passengers started singing "God Bless America." We were happy to land on American soil. I felt like I did when my Lockheed associates and I had landed safely after being tossed about by the wake of the huge C-5 airplane.

As 2001 ended, CAS was granted the patent we had applied for in 1999. That patent was for the life-saving concept we called "Vortex Control Eaglets." It was issued on November 20, 2001, with its official name, "Method and Apparatus for Generating a Stable Leading-Edge-Lifting-Vortex Controller."

We ended the year on a high note and looked forward to what God had in store for us and for our company in 2002.

Fifty Two

Western Adventures

Frieda and I decided to take an extended western vacation in 2002. Ever since I had traveled with my eleven-year-old grandson, Jesse, to the National parks, I had wanted to go back. Since Frieda had never been, we planned a three-week trip in our Dodge van packed with camping gear.

Jesse and I had roamed the west in 1995 with a pop-up camper that we used every night. Frieda had serious doubts about camping, but since she wanted to make this trip, she agreed to give it a try. That was just one of Frieda's characteristics that made me love her—she was willing to be adventurous like I was. I had learned over the years that you had to take calculated risks, or you wouldn't enjoy much in life.

Somehow, we managed to get every camping gadget in the back of the van—a lot more than a good camper would have brought. I had once managed to spend at least a week camping with only a 25 lb. bag on my back, but for this trip I had a novice to consider who enjoyed her creature comforts. My goal was to set up camp near the Grand Canyon. There we would have an unobstructed view of the galaxies and be close to some of the National Parks in Utah.

We finally left Georgia in early May and headed toward Memphis, Tennessee, just north of my hometown of Whitehaven. Neither of us realized we were truly heading west until we crossed the Mississippi River and reached Interstate 40 in West Memphis, Arkansas. The flat Mississippi delta stretched before us until we arrived in Little Rock. We then drove

through the hills and valleys of the Ozark Mountains and spent the night in Fort Smith, Arkansas.

The drive to Oklahoma City was long, flat, and boring with little changing landscape along the way. Things got more interesting when we reached the celebrated "Route 66", often called the "Mother Road."

That road from Chicago, Illinois to Santa Monica, California had been an acclaimed route for about a century. I had traveled the "Mother Road" many times in the 1950s and 1960s. There was no Interstate 40 back then, and it was much slower traveling than in 2002. To get the adventure and the nostalgia of Route 66, we got off the Interstate and rode on the old highway. Our Route 66 road trip involved much more than tourist attractions and sights. It was a personal journey of discovery.

There were many historical man-made and natural sites along the route. We left the Interstate before Amarillo, Texas and saw old Cadillac automobiles stacked with their noses buried in the sand at an angle of 50 to 60 degrees. No one knew why or how they were put there.

We found our hotel in Amarillo and enjoyed a restful night's sleep. We gradually gained altitude going from 1000 feet in Georgia to 3600 feet in Amarillo. The dry, dusty, windy conditions gave Frieda sinus issues. As we approached Albuquerque, New Mexico at 5000 feet, I knew we needed to climb slowly and drink plenty of water to avoid getting sick.

I had been through Albuquerque many times, and it always seemed an enigma to me. During my Navy days, I had flown over the city in a R4D plane into very bumpy air at 12,000 feet. When I drove from California back to Tennessee in my younger years, getting through Albuquerque had been a relief because of its high mountains and curvy roads.

We circled the roads around Albuquerque trying to find our reserved hotel room. With no GPS, we had to rely on maps and gas station directions to help us find our way. A long day on the road and rising altitude exhausted us and made us testy. After dark, we finally found our hotel and collapsed. Frieda woke up with an excruciating altitude headache the next morning. After breakfast, strong coffee, and pain pills, she felt good enough to continue toward Santa Fe, New Mexico.

We climbed an additional 2000 feet to get to Santa Fe. The city was once part of Mexico, and Spanish architecture and culture still dominated. I knew Santa Fe served as the gateway to Los Alamos National Laboratory

(LANL). Its mission during World War II had been to house the top-secret Manhattan Project and the design and development of nuclear weapons. I had heard so much about that place, I had to at least drive by it. Frieda still felt queasy, so we then headed back to Albuquerque for another good night's sleep.

Our trip through the wild west continued the next day as we drove through New Mexico and headed toward Arizona. I had promised Frieda a stop in Gallup, New Mexico-—the heart of Navajo country. Gallup's numerous jewelry stores were filled with beautiful Native American creations. After only making a dent in the number of jewelry stores, I drug Frieda away. I wanted to put my credit card back in my wallet and "head 'em up and move 'em out".

Our next big adventure awaited us at the Grand Canyon, but other stops along the way could not be missed. The Painted Desert and the Petrified Forest had to be experienced because they defied description. As we rode along I-40, we saw petrified tree stumps and flat lenticular clouds in the blue sky that reminded us we were in the desert.

The beauty of the Painted Desert depends on what season you happen to be there. Other times when I had visited, the colors had been light-red, pink, and tan. However, sometimes greens and blues were visible. The wind blowing against the rocks and sand hills made smooth cone shapes with plateaus on top. We could imagine giant dinosaurs stomping across the immense landscape.

We passed through a portion of the Hopi Indian Reservation as we drove I-40 to Flagstaff. We detoured to see the Meteor Crater that was created about 50,000 years ago when a rogue meteor or asteroid managed to get through the atmosphere and impact the Southwest.

After a long day of driving and sightseeing, we made it to Flagstaff. We spent the night there before driving sixty miles north to the Grand Canyon. That would-be Frieda's first time to see that natural wonder.

I planned to set up our first camp near the Canyon, but Frieda still had problems with the altitude and her asthma. We found a small hotel, and after a good night's sleep, she felt better. The next day we toured the rim of the Canyon and saw the inspiring beauty of God's creation. While taking a rest, we had a close encounter with a California Condor—one of the largest birds on Earth.

As we looked over the ridge, we spotted two Condors in their nest. We had learned the Condors were an endangered species. With a wingspan of up to twelve feet and a weight of over thirty ponds, they had been known to soar miles without flapping their wings. We took pictures and watched the birds in their nest for a while before resuming our walk on the ridge. Suddenly, one of the birds took flight and soared about six feet over us. What an awesome sight. The only thing that could have stirred me more would have been a one-mile hike to the base of the Canyon, but then I would have had to climb back up.

The next day Frieda was still having sinus problems and did not feel like hiking. She told me to go on, and that she would be alright. I enjoyed God's magnificent creation and felt his presence as I hiked along the ridge. My ears perked up when I heard singing ahead of me. As I got closer, I saw two young men who appeared to be foreign visitors. They were singing "How Great Thou Art" in broken English. I caught up with them and started singing too. We knew nothing about each other, but we were all together in the Spirit. We smiled, waved goodbye, and went our separate ways. What a great way to end our visit to the Grand Canyon.

Fifty Three

National Parks

We drove to the north side of the Grand Canyon then around Lake Powell and across the Glen Canyon Dam. That was the same way my grandson, Jesse, and I had gone in 1995. My plan was to find a campground by the lake.

Things had really changed in the seven years since Jesse and I visited. It was surprising and disappointing to see the bare ground of Lake Powell. A three-year drought had dropped the lake water level over 100 feet and moved the shoreline a mile back from the highway. We found a place to spend the night after the rapidly dropping temperatures prevented us from camping.

Another expansive canyon awaited us at Zion National Park. The views were amazing, especially Checkerboard Mesa. The mountain had been eroded by the wind into squares that made it look like a giant checkerboard. Chillier winds meant we still would not be camping.

As we made our way to Bryce Canyon, we found a cluster of tiny cottages, each with about 100 square feet of floor space—room for a bed, a toilet, and a small kitchenet. Bryce Canyon's chiseled red rock formations called hoodoos were a sight to see. Created by wind and water erosion over thousands of years, the geological structures resembled exquisite works of art.

More beautiful scenery surrounded us as we headed north to Salt Lake City. I had traveled to Salt Lake City several times for business and skiing. The trip with Frieda topped them all. Everywhere we looked,

we saw evidence of the city's Mormon history. The Mormon Tabernacle dominated the skyline, and its choir was well known for its beautiful music. When we crossed at a stop light, we heard seagulls singing. Mormons credit the seagulls with saving the early pioneers by eating the infestation of katydids that tried to decimate their crops.

We toured the State Capital building and learned that the marble for the building had come from Georgia. Just a few months before our visit, Park City, Utah had been the home of the 2002 Winter Olympics. We rode to the top of the ski jump slopes and the bobsled ride and marveled at the death-defying nerve it took to leap off those platforms.

Yellowstone Park beckoned us, so we hit the road again. After seeing Pocatello, Idaho Falls and acres of potato fields, we drove into Wyoming and found the Park entrance. We entered a huge plateau called a caldera, where volcanic eruptions had occurred millions of years before. At 8,000 feet elevation, Yellowstone Lake was frozen over. Hot spots like the Old Faithful Geyser and bubbling lava pots attracted Bison in search of heat and vegetation. After spending the night in the Old Faithfull Inn, we headed south toward Jackson Hole and the Grand Tetons.

The ranches and cattle farms of Jackson Hole had magnificent views of the Grand Teton Mountain Range. We hiked around Jackson Hole Lake and visited the boutique shops on Main Street. The time had come to move on and head southeast. We had already been to many states on this wild west trip, and there were more to go before the Mississippi River.

We drove through Wyoming, Nebraska, and Kansas. At St. Louis, Missouri, the Mississippi River had overflowed its banks, and we were unable to go up into the Arch. Since we were anxious to get back home, we headed south toward Memphis and the tall green trees of the south. Frieda's dry eyes and headaches improved greatly in the humid air. We arrived in Georgia without camping once. I was disappointed, but Frieda was thrilled.

Getting home meant getting back to CAS business and more sales trips. We had sold two copies of our CASSC software to AFRL (Air Force Research Laboratory). Training their engineers to use the software was part of the sale. In July 2002, Arnold—one of my employees—and I rented a car and headed to Ohio.

We stopped at Cumberland River Falls in the Daniel Boone National

Forest. That diversion broke up the trip and helped us experience the natural beauty around us. Next, we visited the University of Cincinnati to try to sell my software to their Engineering School. We made some good contacts, but no sales.

At Wright Patterson Air Force Base in Dayton, Ohio, we taught a class of engineers how to use the CASSC code. We must have done a good job because they recommended us as a sub-contractor for other Air Force projects. That helped us stay in business at CAS for several months.

Our business of providing contract engineers for Lockheed was going well. Frieda and her niece, Sandy DuVall, managed the administrative end of the business. We had hired Sandy not long after we made the trip to France. She proved to be a godsend for our business.

Our patent attorney advised us that our Finlets patent application was official. Nobody could copy our innovation before we received the official patent. Our growing business offered a bright future for the company, its employees, and its partners.

In October Arnold proposed an exciting trip for himself and me to visit his brother's lodge in Whitefish, Montana. It sounded like my kind of trip—hiking, fishing, and camping. I bought a new backpack that I filled and sent ahead to Montana.

Whitefish bordered Glacier National Park with its inspiring mountain peaks, waterfalls, rushing streams, and glaciers. The fantastic view on the flight from Atlanta to Missoula, Montana stirred me. The small plane that took us from Kalispell flew over beautiful Flathead Lake. Gorgeous scenery surrounded us on the drive through the mountain forest to the lodge.

The rustic lodge exceeded my expectations in size and beauty. We each settled into our rooms and then started planning our Glacier Park adventures. After our long arduous trip, we travelers needed a good night's rest before we could take advantage of all that nature offered.

At Glacier Park the next day we learned the rules and regulations for hiking and camping in the park. Our course instructed us concerning what to do if we met up with a grizzly bear. We were told to make noise, pay attention to our surroundings, hike in a group, keep pets on a leash, and hike only on marked trails and during the daytime. We encountered no bears on our short hike.

After our hike, we went to find a steak house. I ordered a prime rib then realized the waiter had not asked me how I wanted it cooked. When the waiter returned to the table, I complained, "You did not ask how to cook my steak."

"Oh! We don't ask that," he replied. "You'll get what the chef wants you to have."

I was stunned. "Boy, this is a tough place," I said to Arnold.

A few minutes later the chef came out and told us his steaks tasted best the way he cooked them. He said he wanted us to get the best flavor of the meat. After enjoying an exceptional meal, we went back to the lodge, well fed and ready to go camping the next day.

It dropped below freezing at night in the mountains. The other fellows were younger than me and better able to handle the cold. I hoped to acclimate, but in the meantime, I decided to go fishing in the nearby lake. The owner of the lodge was not going camping either, so he told me to take the ATV to the lake and to throw back any fish I caught that were under two feet long.

Every time I threw my line in the water, I caught a white trout. Most of them were small, and I threw them back. I finally caught two fish measuring 17-18 inches. Even though I could not keep the fish, my fishing in Montana was a success.

We spent the rest of our time hiking through Glacier National Park. Despite my older age, I out hiked most of them. My great trip came to an end, and I was ready to leave the refreshing mountain air and head for the joys and challenges of home.

While we were away, my other two partners in CAS had decided that our contracting business with Lockheed could be improved. They proposed bringing in two of their Lockheed friends as equal partners, without my agreement, and with no investment of capital. Neither Frieda nor I were happy about this, but we were outnumbered. They no longer had the same goal for the business as I did. Since two of them were currently working in the Lockheed Aerodynamics Department, they wanted to convince the managers to give more business to CAS. I wanted to focus my company on developing my patent ideas for vortex control. I felt that they had taken over the business. As 2002 wound down, I decided to deal with that problem after the first of the year.

Fifty Four

Trouble on the Horizon

The new year began with trouble on the horizon. It became obvious that my other partners did not share my vision for the company. They were enjoying the monetary benefits of our consultant contracting business and their Lockheed retirement. Finding new consultants for Lockheed comprised their contribution to the company.

Sandy, Frieda, and I took care of all the administrative paperwork and payroll for that effort. CASSC provided income for our company, but the partners showed no interest in my software product. They did not have the dream of CAS becoming a great business like I did.

When I received my master's degree in business administration, I was inspired by a dream to create a top-notch aviation company, and I was willing to take risks to make it happen. We would have to spend money to seriously market my software and patented inventions which meant hiring engineers to help me with my designs. I needed help that would not say "Yes, but" and always have some excuse for not agreeing.

Other changes Frieda, Sandy, and I wanted to make really caused the bubble to burst. The extremely small office we rented across from McCollum Airport no longer worked for us. With the need for new employees came the need for more space. In addition, our landlord stayed in hot water with the City of Kennesaw Fire Marshal and would not make the required upgrades unless we paid for them. So, we started looking for office space in a good location that would give our business more credibility.

Since Frieda and I wanted to buy the office condo without CAS money, we decided not to tell our other partners about our plans. Frieda and Sandy found a two-level suite that would meet our current and future needs. It had a finished upstairs and an unfinished basement with about 2,200 square feet. The location off Interstate 75 could easily be reached by potential customers.

The second problem involved my salary. I worked at least four days a week, and the other partners hardly showed up at all. I felt I deserved to be paid for my efforts. When I explained the two issues at the monthly partner meeting, emotions ran high. They vetoed moving to a larger space, paying more rent, and increasing my pay. I had brought two partners in to help me develop my business five years earlier, and now I had four partners who stood in the way of moving the business forward. They were not interested in marketing my patents or seeking any sources of revenue other than being a job shop for Lockheed consultants.

Since CAS could accomplish nothing under those circumstances, I knew something drastic had to be done. After much prayer, Frieda and I decided we would buy out the other partners. We did not have the funds to spare, but we believed if we borrowed the money, I could bring in enough business to pay off the loan. The Bible verse from Philippians 4:13, "I can do all things through Christ who strengthens me," gave me the courage to write a forceful letter explaining my plan.

My letter—which Frieda helped me write—surprised everyone when I presented it at the next partner meeting. None of them thought I had the nerve or funds to challenge them. My quiet personality, however, had been riled, and my determination to buy them out was not something they had considered. Risking everything, we borrowed the needed money from a family member. We drew up legal documents, paid the partners off, and reclaimed their company stock. Free at last!

We were not naïve and knew there would be many bumps in the road ahead. Two other engineers that believed in me enough to work for a small hourly wage moved with us to the new office space. I had hired Arnold to be my marketing engineer and Roger, a brilliant engineer and mathematician with a PHD who had worked with me in the research department at Lockheed. Both engineers had seen some tough times, and

needed a paycheck, and I needed their help. I believed God had put us together because we needed each other.

Since we still had the consultant business with Lockheed, we were doing reasonably well. Then, our former partners decided to start their own job shop company and convinced some of our consultants to work with them instead of CAS. That hurt us financially, but gradually we enlisted other consultants from other Lockheed departments.

Before the end of 2003, we received a call from a new aviation company in Georgia that needed some aeronautical engineering help. Their project required both engineering help and French speaking capabilities. Sandy was fluent in French, and we qualified in aviation. The company had purchased discarded French jet trainers and wanted to convert them to general aviation aircraft for private pilots and small companies needing four-seat jet capabilities. They had already modified one airplane, and it looked appealing. That effort lasted about a year and kept us afloat.

My good reputation with the technical leaders at the Air Force Research Lab (AFRL) led to recommendations that CAS become a sub-contractor on two other Air Force projects. We helped with the design of an Unmanned Aerial Vehicle (UAV) using my CASSC software to provide the flying characteristics. The aircraft was powered and controlled by a jet blowing from a slot that opened near the leading edge of the wing. To make that work with CASSC, we needed a theoretical method to predict the two-dimensional aerodynamic characteristics of an airfoil with slot jet blowing over the upper surface. Georgia Tech was experimenting with that method.

Their method used the early stages of Computational Fluid Dynamics (CFD). The results compared to experimental data needed to be stronger, so Roger and I requested a clearance from AFRL to develop a new theory. When we presented the final report to them, their technical personnel were clearly pleased. That effort increased our creditability and enabled us to get more contracts later.

In December 2003, Frieda and I attended the Centennial of Powered Flight to celebrate the Wright Brothers first flight at Kitty Hawk, North Carolina. The rainy weather put a damper on some of the activities, but we enjoyed being part of history.

I helped organize a surprise 60th birthday party for Frieda on February

8, 2004. I told her we were going to a new French restaurant, but instead we went to Sandy's community clubhouse where about 50 of her friends and family were gathered to celebrate the Big 6-0.

On April 6, 2004, Patent # US 6,715,717 B2 "Method and Apparatus for Introducing Controlled Vortices to Reduce Afterbody Drag" was issued to CAS. That was the official name of what we eventually called Vortex Control Finlets.

To market the Finlets, we flew to the West Coast to visit Aviation Partners Boeing, Inc. (APB) and James Raisbeck Engineering at the old Boeing Airport in Seattle, Washington. APB was well established in developing and selling winglets to Boeing and airlines and too busy to get involved with another project. We did, however, lay the groundwork for future efforts. Raisbeck was very gracious, but all he would say was, "It is a good idea." I believe we were competing with one of his concepts.

I visited again with the CEO of Boundary Layer Research Inc. in Everett, Washington, but the company was experiencing financial troubles. I realized much more work would be required before we could move forward with Finlets.

In November 2004, Frieda and I took a vacation to see my grandson, Jesse, and his family in Hawaii. His first tour of military duty had assigned him to Hickam Air Force Base in Honolulu for three years. During our two-week trip, we spent time with our family and saw the sights. Our tour of the Pearl Harbor Memorial stirred our souls. After a few days on Waikiki Beach, we flew to Maui for a traditional luau. We also went parasailing and took a cruise on a submarine. Both islands were exotic and beautiful.

In July 2005 Frieda and I joined a group tour to the Canadian Rockies. We flew to Calgary in Alberta, Canada to start the trip. Our bus drove us to Banff National Park where we saw one captivating mountain scene after another. Next, we headed to the Columbia Icefield in Jasper National Park. We got off the bus and boarded a large red icefield vehicle with giant snow tires. We drove onto the glacier and stopped on a large solid expanse. Then we got out and walked across the bone-chilling, cold ice.

I had seen videos of the glass canopy train trip from Calgary to Vancouver where the mountains are visible from all sides. We boarded the

train and headed for Vancouver. It was an overnight trip and a different experience trying to sleep on a stop and go noisy train.

We left the mountains behind us and headed for the great Pacific Ocean where we toured the picturesque gardens of Vancouver and ate halibut and salmon at every meal.

Fifty Five

Eaglets to the Rescue

It was time to stop spending money and get back to earning it. By the end of 2005, we were able to pay off the loan we used to buy out our partners two years earlier. However, we knew we still had much more work to do.

In 2006 I spent a lot of time trying to find a company interested in supporting us in the development of the VC Eaglet concept. Through prayer, God led me to the right person. My contact with the Civil Air Patrol gave me the name and phone number of the Director and Owner of a research and test company in Mojave, California. I started our phone conversation by telling him about the life-saving capability of the VC Eaglets. That got his attention because he had recently lost two test pilots who entered a dangerous stall and could not get out of it. The result was they had crashed and both pilots had died. He immediately saw that VC Eaglets might have saved their lives. I told Robert, the director, that saving lives was the reason I invented Eaglets.

When I told Robert that I received my Aeronautical Engineering Degree from Mississippi State University (MSU), we became close friends. He had served as Director of the Aero Physics Department at MSU after I graduated. I worked in the Aero Physics Department when I was a Junior and Senior at MSU. We were going to work well together.

We hoped to get a Small Business Independent Research (SBIR) contract from NASA to get funds to design the VC Eaglets for a small, two-seat, twin engine airplane. NASA recognized my CASSC software since I had worked with them earlier and had already proved I could

predict the Aerodynamic Characteristics quite accurately. But they said there was not enough research to contribute to get an SBIR.

Much to my joy, Robert agreed to pay for the flight test if I would create the design with my software and manufacture the VC Eaglets. That was the break I had been looking for. CAS and the Robert's company became partners.

The first thing I needed to settle was getting another company to manufacture the VC Eaglets from composite material—commonly called fiberglass. I had another friend in the business who needed the manufacturing job and gave me a price I could afford. Robert rounded up all the aircraft design information I needed to get CASSC working. We were going to do something abnormal, and that was go direct from software design to flight test without doing a wind tunnel test first.

By the end of 2006, we had all the information we needed to begin the design with CASSC. Before the end of January 2007, we had completed the design work and the VC Eaglet fabrication, and we headed for Mojave, California. By the end of week, the VC Eaglets were installed. In February 2007, all the flight tests were completed. Flight tests analysis proved our predicted results to be correct.

Some examples of the results are given below:

1. Flow separation indicated with tufts showed the same span-wise progression as predicted by CASSC.
2. Based on the recorded data, the angle of attack, initiation of stall, and fully developed stall agreed with CASSC.
3. Elimination of aileron reversal by the Eaglets was demonstrated. As predicted by CASSC, aileron effectiveness was extremely low in the fully stalled condition, but no aileron reversal occurred even with full aileron deflection.
4. The improved roll damping predicted by CASSC was illustrated by the video results, and the pilot's comment substantiated it.

Small Twin Airplane with Life Saving Vortex Control Eaglets

As the test pilot, Robert was incredibly happy with the results. If VC Eaglets had been on the twin engine airplane, it would not have crashed, and lives would have been saved! I was extremely happy and praising God for making all that happen. To get those results published, Robert and I wrote a paper for the AIAA conference in 2008. It was titled "Software to Flight Test – Innovation for Taming the Stall." Robert also wrote a paper to present at a test pilots' conference.

Robert was so pleased with the results, he decided to put VC Eaglets on his single engine Bonanza. I was glad to design and fabricate the Eaglets for the Bonanza because that give me a great introduction to the General Aviation (private owner aircraft) industry. By the middle of 2008, Eaglets on the Bonanza had been tested, and the results were as good as those for the twin engine airplane. With Eaglets, the Bonanza could not be made to spin, which is a dangerous flight condition. The Bonanza with Eaglets worked so well Robert got a contract to train FAA test pilots the correct way to control unusual flight conditions.

My innovation credibility was blossoming. It was not often an aeronautical engineer got his ideas installed, working on an airplane, and got credit for doing it. Now the hard work began.

I had heard many times, "You can build a better mouse trap, but the real work is just beginning. You have to get it into the market." The Georgia Centers of Innovation Aviation heard of my device, and they assigned a representative of their organization to work with me on the marketing. They also invited me to compete for the Georgia *"Outstanding Aerospace Innovation of 2007."* This required getting endorsements from others aware of my innovative ability. Frieda sent out letters to solicit recommendations.

One of the most rewarding endorsements, was the Air Force Research Laboratory (AFRL) at Wright Patterson Air Force Base, Dayton, Ohio. We received an official AFRL letter. A summary of the letter is presented in the following comments:

- They recommended Consulting Aviation Services (CAS) for the Ben T. Epps Aerospace Innovation Trophy - Trophy for Invention.
- They noted CAS was highly deserving of this honor.
- CAS was also noted to have a proven track record of innovation within the aerospace community.
- Our patented VC Eaglet devices were particularly noted. In addition to general aviation aircraft, several USAF aircraft could benefit from VC Eaglets, such as the C12, C-27 and C-130.
- They noted that VC Eaglets are not just vortex generators. They improve control characteristics when the wing is at or near stall.
- They were designed using the software package CASSC (also developed by CAS). We have used this software for several years for many applications and have found it to be very accurate and reliable.
- Out of control situations resulting from flight near or at wing stall are a major source of accidents in the general aviation community.
- CAS has proven the effectiveness of VC Eaglets in flight.

Much to our surprise at CAS, we won the trophy. "Georgia *Outstanding Aerospace Innovation of 2007"* was presented to us on October 20, 2007, at a formal black-tie awards banquet in Athens, Georgia. We hoped that our award would generate more interest with small airplane owners and lead to more sales of Eaglets.

Frieda and I had a great time at Mojave participating in the 2007 flight test and making side trips from Mojave to see parts of California we had not seen. At the beginning of 2008, we headed to Reno, Nevada to present a paper about our work. The paper presentation did not result in a lot of interest, and that was disappointing.

Not too far from Reno in the little town of Truckee, CA, we took a snowmobile tour into the Sierra Nevada Mountains. There had been an overabundance of snow that year. I drove our snowmobile, and Frieda had quite a bone-jarring ride sitting behind me. She was thrilled to drive the machine by herself when we got up to a large flat meadow where it was easier to steer. Our snow-filled adventure burned up a ton of calories, and we couldn't wait to get back to Truckee for dinner.

Fifty Six

Finlets on the Move

In early 2006, I developed a major physical problem. One morning while at the CAS office, I got up from my chair and started to walk out of the room. One eye went totally blind, but in about a minute my sight came back. I was scared enough to get an immediate appointment with my eye doctor. After checking my eyes, she said it was not an eye problem, and told me to get an appointment with my vascular surgeon asap. After scanning my carotid arteries, I was told one of them was 90% blocked and I needed to be admitted to the hospital.

Doctor Hafner took time to pray with Frieda and me before the surgery. We were comforted because we believed in prayer. After successful carotid artery surgery, I recovered quickly. During a follow-up visit to the doctor, I learned that since my cholesterol levels had always been normal, it must have been genetic.

Another contract encouraged by the Air Force Research Lab (AFRL) began with Bihrle Applied Research (BAR). The contract with BAR started during 2008 with creditable flight simulation engineers. It was a relationship that was going to last a long time. Apparently, AFRL had informed BAR of our CASSC software, which was proving to be a reliable predictor of post-stall aerodynamics for full-scale complete airplanes. No other software had that capability.

The most favorable software known as Computational Fluid Dynamics (CFD) fell short in predicting post-stall aerodynamics. CFD is a pre-stall solution for complex theoretical equations. BAR needed CASSC

for computing stability and control aerodynamics. Even if CFD could do the stability & control, it took days to get answers. CASSC made it work for post-stall solutions and the results took minutes on a good laptop computer.

It was a Navy Multi-Mission Maritime Aircraft that was developed and produced by Boeing from a 737-800 aircraft—modified to accomplish the missions of the US Navy. We were approached by BAR to see if we could provide the data to build a flight simulator of the P-8. Since we had been successful with predicting the data for the twin and the Bonanza, we agreed to tackle the job and add another type of airplane to our capability.

To perform the task, we needed dimensional data: (1) an accurate three view of the P-8, (2) the type or dimensions of the airfoils for the wings and tail (3) angle of attack (incidence) of between the wing root airfoil and the fuselage reference line and (4) wing twist of the wings. Once we received all the data, we went to work. A couple of months later, we had data that needed to go into the equations for the aircraft in dynamic motion, but most of our results were for static (steady state flight). BAR had to add the terms for dynamic conditions. After BAR came back to us a few times for additional data, they got the dynamic equations ready to put into the flight simulator. BAR had one of the former test pilots for Boeing to fly the simulator. He had experience in flying the real 737-800 airplane while putting it into stall and other unusual flight conditions. Much to our excitement, he said the simulator flew just like the real airplane!

We continued to work with Bihrle Applied Research through 2010. They built a wind tunnel model for us, and I attempted to build a P-8 High lift CASSC model. This meant having airfoil sections with complicated double and triple-slotted flaps. My work was too slow to finish with the time and money available. Neither BAR nor I were happy with that. He wanted a method that was much simpler, and I needed to put more of my time into the VC Finlet project.

During this time, CAS was invited to introduce the Vortex Control Finlets (VCF) concept to Warner Robins Air Logistics Command (WR-ALC/572 ACSS). They needed to find a drag reduction concept for the C-130 military cargo airplane and VCF seemed to be a good fit.

The development of VC Finlets had been proceeding quite well, and

a contract to use CASSC to predict the post-stall characteristics of the Boeing 737-800 was started in 2008. Business was booming. I had some good aeronautical engineers and Georgia Tech graduate students working with me. Good engineering and marketing contacts were necessary to get this project going.

Sam was a promising engineer who called and asked for a visit. He had worked at several aircraft companies and came highly recommended. Sam had his own company that was struggling and wanted to propose another idea. Sam knew another good marketing person named Dick who he wanted to bring onboard. Sam impressed me with his knowledge of the aviation industry and personnel.

When he suggested that we form another partnership with Sam, Dick, and me, I had some second thoughts. Sam's idea was to use the new company to market the designs of CAS and his company. Frieda and I had already been soaked by one partnership and were reluctant to get into another. They would not be partners in CAS, but we would be partners in a brand-new company. Frieda and I prayed about the new venture, and I decided to sign on. We needed their help, so we each invested equity for the company to seal the deal and AMC was born.

In the aircraft business it takes a lot of funding to develop a modification for a certified airplane. We needed backup by a larger company to be able to get large scale funding from the government. Our good report with the Air Force in Dayton, Ohio and with Warner Robins Air Logistics Command were not enough to get big contracts. Dick—one of our new partners in the company—had contacts with another company near Warner Robins through his marketing efforts.

I traveled with Dick to give a presentation which was well received. It was good enough to get a small contract from the Air Force at Warner Robins. We received a $30,000 contract to explore the use of Finlets on an AC-130U. CAS completed the contract and proved potential significant fuel savings for the airplane. The result proved to be the first real step in showing the value of VC Finlets. Our timing for getting the first contract was perfect. The Secretary of the Air Force soon issued a command to improve the fuel savings of the C-130 aircraft.

The command primarily went to Air Force Research Lab (AFRL) in Dayton, Ohio. CAS had received much respect at AFRL through our

CASSC and VC Eaglet successes. In September I received a call from a co-worker at AFRL who said, "If you are going to be up our way any time soon, come by and give us a presentation."

It took me about ten seconds to say, "I will be there day after tomorrow."

Fifty Seven

Breakthrough for Finlets

When I met with the guys at AFRL, I learned that there would be a competition for the company that could reduce the C-130 fuel savings. The Air Force Academy in Colorado had been doing research on C-130 drag reduction for a long time. I felt somewhat defeated and wondered what chance we would have against them. Soon after I got back home, I took a call from AFRL advising CAS that it had been approved to receive a $115,000 contract for further analytical study including computer modeling of the basic C-130H and the AC-130U, the gunship version of the C-130. We were to use the PMARC software, which would give us the flow field needed to use with CASSC results.

Because of government red tape, we did not get the money until a year later. Taking this long was not supposed to happen, but the task was given to an untrained person that got confused as to how to transfer the money.

I was not worried about getting the money because I had given a briefing in November 2006 to an Air Force General, commander of Warner Robins Air Logistics Command (WR-ALC). He had an extremely high interest in improved loiter time of the C-130 Gunships and requested updates on further development. During February 2008, our analytical results confirmed the predictions of C-130 drag reduction. The analytical estimate was a substantial drag reduction for the basic C-130. This large improvement kept us moving until we got the wind tunnel and flight tests to prove it.

We took time out to honor our grandson when we traveled to Scott Air

Force Base in Illinois. Our grandson, Jesse Williams, was being promoted to Air Force Sergeant. As a non-commissioned officer, he had come a long way from the eleven-year-old boy who traveled with me out West. I gladly stood up with him at the ceremony.

We also took a bus tour around Washington, DC. Two of our best friends, a couple from our church, invited us to go on that tour sponsored by a church organization. We went during the spring and enjoyed the cherry blossoms. I had been to Washington, DC many times on business trips, but that time we visited many of the places we had only seen in the news.

In August 2008, the contract was issued for (Option 1) Wind Tunnel Tests and (Option 2) Flight Tests if wind tunnel tests proved the prediction. During June 2009. The first wind tunnel test was at the Glen L. Martin Wind Tunnel (GLM), located at the University of Maryland. Only the Basic C-130 was tested. This test showed we were getting a drag reduction equal to the analytical prediction, if the bottom surface of the C-130 afterbody was clear of any protuberances.

The cargo-door pedestal was a major protuberance. The cargo door sat on the pedestal when it was open on the ground, and it was not retractable during flight. It caused flow separation of the air coming down the cargo door, and it reduced our drag reduction 40%. We tried to get the Air Force to make it retractable, but nobody wanted to spend the money. No thought was given to the large amount of fuel savings that have would more than compensated for the cost of modifying the pedestal. However, the 60% part of the drag reduction created a big savings in fuel cost. During October 2009, a second wind tunnel test was conducted at GLM. Only the Gunship version, AC-130U was tested. That version had so many protuberances it was hard to get more than about 1/2 the drag reduction of clean airplane with just the pedestal, but that gave significantly more loiter time.

Our wedding anniversary occurred during our first trip to GLM. I surprised Frieda and booked a dinner cruise on the Potomac River. The nighttime sights of Washington were beautiful with all the monuments lit up. We dined and danced the evening away before flying back to Atlanta.

With two successful wind tunnel tests behind us, plans for conducting the flight test were moving forward. A miracle occurred during the months

before the flight test began. Sam had a friend that worked with a group we will call Investors LLC. When Sam told his friend about our innovations, the investors visited our office and began negotiations.

By March 2010, we had drawn up an agreement and were signing papers. Frieda and I had attended a seminar about working with investors a few months earlier. We had learned that the inventor should not get tied up with taking a portion of the company as his payment for sales of his product. As the company grew and more money was needed, the inventor's portion would become more diluted and be worth less. Our agreement with Investors LLC was that we would get royalties only. We were on our way! This was a huge project that created a great team. Including the Air Force and the investors there were five organizations involved. The others were my company, the flight test group, and another company that provided the Finlet installation.

Since the investors had the money to pay to manufacture the Finlets, the timing for getting them on board was perfect. They felt they had to pay for getting the Finlets manufactured to protect the Intellectual Property (IP). Otherwise, the Air Force might claim it and not pay them royalties. We decided not to use the Air Force to provide the test aircraft or to use their facilities. Through my strong encouragement, we had a flight test group to test the aircraft at Mojave, our VCEaglet test site in California. I thought I would be doing this group a favor, since they had been so gracious to me with the VC Eaglets flight test. The team rented a private C-130A for the test aircraft. My hope was to make the basic C-130 flight test results agree with our wind tunnel results.

On Friday, December 10, 2010, we left our hotel in Lancaster, California and drove north into the Mojave Desert. Shades of orange, pink, and blue crept over the Eastern horizon as the sun began to rise. The flat terrain bumped against the stark mountains, and black stratus clouds hung ominously in the distance. We passed a sign indicating a Gusty Wind Zone for the next sixteen miles.

An occasional scrub bush displayed army green leaves, but everything else was the color of the terrain. Houses were painted beige, taupe pink, khaki tan, and various shades of terra cotta. Menacing Joshua Trees stood out against the desert terrain and stands of wind generators dotted the barren hills to catch the stiff winds that blew through the desert valley. The

lights of the town of Mojave appeared. We crossed the tracks and entered the Mojave Spaceport.

When we arrived, I was surprised to see the installation crew still working on the plane and to learn they had been there all night in the cold and wind. The bright orange Finlets stood out on the upswept rear fuselage of the C-130. A professional photographer was on site, and he took our picture in the cockpit of the C-130 and standing by the Finlets, which until recently we had only seen on a computer screen.

At noon the last rivet was driven through the tail and the installation was complete. The wind had picked up by the time we left for lunch, but we were still anticipating the first flight in the early afternoon. We were deflated when the mission was scrubbed due to the brisk winds, but that was par for the course. For the past few years, it had been "hurry up and wait."

On Saturday as we drove back to the Spaceport, Frieda and I discussed the fact that Christmas was only two weeks away. As we headed down the highway, we saw a sign that read Fresh Trees from Oregon. All the Christmas trees we have seen so far in the restaurants had been artificial. A real tree could not survive those dry conditions for long.

The sun rose brightly in the sky and quickly warmed the air. We started off with coats, hats, and gloves but peeled off layers as the morning progressed. The minutes ticked by, and time dragged as all the preliminaries were completed. We sat in on the pre-flight meeting as the six-member flight crew planned the details of the flight. Tiger One was the mission title for the C-130 test.

We watched as the crew climbed on board. The plane then rolled toward the tarmac. After more preliminaries, one propeller started to turn. Anticipation rose as the second prop spun into motion. The noise was loud, and the sickening smell of jet fuel permeated the air. We put blue plugs into our ears to drown out the roar of the engines. It was sweet music indeed. Frieda felt like a privileged woman to be at that place at that time. Except for Robert's wife, a test pilot, Frieda was the only woman on the premises, but none of the men seem to mind. We were not intimidated by them.

As all four propellers spun in a loud blur, the plane turned toward the runway, picked up speed, and passed the hangars. Everyone was snapping pictures and making video. The men climbed into the van to ride to the

take-off site. The roar increased as the C-130 thundered past where we stood. What a thrilling sight!

The C-130 was taxied to another runway for takeoff, and by the time we saw it again, it was airborne right in front of us. We collectively held our breath, and a shiver of delight ran through me. Louis, our project manager, and installer was so excited he sounded like a football cheerleader.

Frieda could not resist the urge to sing the Doxology.

"Praise God from whom all blessings flow. Praise him all creatures here below. Praise Him above ye heavenly hosts. Praise Father, Son, and Holy Ghost."

The pilot banked the plane as he approached the mountains, and the smoke trails streaming from the engines were clearly visible. Soon the plane disappeared in the cloudless blue sky. That day was the culmination of ten years of effort and a lot of blood, sweat, tears, and prayers.

Two flights took place the next day, and all of us gathered to watch the take-off and landing of each flight. The final descent was into a gorgeous sunset. The whole sky was filled with shades of yellow, orange, blue, pink, and crimson. A chill crept into the air, and a cold desert night descended. A crescent moon shined above our heads. A welcome home present and an exclamation point to a picture-perfect day.

Tiger One landed on Monday after an effortless fourth flight. The blue sky looked like a spider's web strung with jet streams and vortex doughnuts. The crew deplaned and everyone was all smiles. Group photos of the flight crew and all the people involved in the mission were taken. The Finlet testing was accomplished, and the number crunching began.

C-130A with Vortex Control Finlets

I was encouraged when the pilot in command said, "There were no showstoppers. Without Finlets the nose went up and with them, the nose went down." That statement indicated to me that the Finlets worked because they had increased the pressure on the afterbody and made the pitch down happen. I was ecstatic! After four successful flight tests, I knew they were working.

During the flight test at Mojave our Air Force Technical Manager from AFRL said to me, "You have stirred the pot!" I thought he was giving me a complement, and in a way he was. However, there was more in that comment than I knew. Things were happening in AFRL he could not discuss. They became a major stumbling block.

We soon learned that our biggest competitor in the military business was a large aircraft manufacturer. They had used my concept of generating small vortices with multiple Finlets or strakes along the aft fuselage to reattach the separated flow. They had made one small change that had allowed them to develop a new government patent. They could not let a small company like ours accomplish what they had tried to do for many years without success. Even though they had used my idea, I was happy to learn that their concept achieved only half the drag reduction ours did.

Epilogue

Hurry up & Wait

I chased a whirlwind for many years in my life and career. A combination of successful projects and adventures mark the years of my life. Along the way, I shared my faith with those who did not know Him. Those things continue to provide motivation for each day.

Ten years have passed since our successful flight test in the Mojave Desert. Our hopes and dreams for a quick sale of Finlets to the Air Force or a commercial airline have not materialized. However, there have been many other accomplishments worthy of mention.

The Boeing C-17 was the next military plane we tackled. The C-17 research and development was accomplished through a major cooperation called "The Technical Cooperation Program" (TTCP)—an innovation network between the United States, Australia, Canada, New Zealand, and the United Kingdom. It harnessed science and technology in support of defense and national security.

Meeting and working with a lot of great people and traveling to some interesting places for wind tunnel and flight testing was the best part of the project. We worked in Ottawa, Canada (during February—BRR!), NASA Ames High Speed Wind Tunnel in Mountain View, California, Edwards Air Force Base, California, and the Boeing Military Organization at Huntington Beach, California.

In 2016 and 2018, Frieda and I traveled to Europe to visit Italy and

France, including the Normandy Beaches. Those spectacular trips gave us a glimpse into much of the history and beauty of Paris and Rome.

I remember giving a presentation at a meeting of the TTCP contributors. It was very humbling to speak to so many people from various parts of the world. Each year the TTCP program reviews nominations for *Distinguished Service, Personal Achievement, and Team Achievement* for the year. In February 2018 I received an award along with fourteen others. The award was a beautifully designed certificate from the Technical Cooperation Program. Despite the success of the program, no drag reduction devices have been installed on the U.S. fleet of C-17 aircraft.

When the investors began working with CAS, we started to look for drag reduction on the Boeing-737-700, a commercial airplane. A wind tunnel test did not show sufficient drag reduction. Computational Fluid Dynamics (CFD) was a promising technology that had been under development for some time. We first started working with Georgia Tech and small companies that had the equipment, but the progress crawled. After the investors hired two CFD experts and an aerostructures engineer from Lockheed, we received promising results. The three engineers built and installed computer equipment in our office basement that could rapidly process CFD data. They developed a Finlet configuration that worked on the 737-700 airplane. The next step was a flight test.

Frieda and I went to Delaware during July 2018 to meet the test pilot crew and observe the flight test of the 737-700 airplane with Finlets installed. We needed to show that no stability and control problems were created by Finlets. We arrived a day before the flight test to meet all the participants. I was surprised to learn that the chief test pilot was the test pilot that had checked out the flight simulator for the 737-800 designed by Bihrle Applied Research, Inc. He knew that I had developed the computer model to predict the stall characteristics for that plane. The test pilot claimed the simulator responded just like the actual airplane. That was a significant credit to the validity of the CASSC software.

The flight test began at 4:30 after rain and wind all day. A break in the weather allowed the plane to take off and we impatiently waited for it to come back. As the pilot deplaned, he announced there were no problems with the flight. We were ecstatic when a Special Type Certificate (STC) was awarded that allowed us to put Finlets on 737-700 airplanes.

The next step was to sell the Finlets to commercial airline companies. An airline installed ten sets of Finlets on ten aircraft to test them before buying them for their entire fleet. Contract negotiations were underway, and a sale was about to become a reality. However, the worldwide COVID-19 pandemic shut everything down. The commercial airline companies parked their excess planes in the Arizona and New Mexico desert and closed most of their operations.

In August 2020, we cleaned out our CAS office in preparation for a sale of the building. Our investors could no longer pay salaries and expenses to keep our doors open. Packing up the office and cleaning out the computers kept us busy for a month. Saying goodbye to our employees was the hardest part. Much to our surprise, we sold the building quickly and went into official retirement.

My future involves continuing to study the drag reduction concept using CASSC and CFD and finding ways to improve results. I hope to double the fuel savings that we have already proven. If the Lord is willing, I will improve the concept and write a technical paper as soon as possible. In the meantime, "We hurry up and wait."

About the Author

C harles J. Dixon or Chuck, as his aviation peers call him, has over 70 years' experience in the aviation business. He earned a Bachelor of Science Degree from Mississippi State University and a Master of Science Degree from the University of Southern California both with a major in Aeronautical Engineering. He is also an Instrument Rated Pilot and has a master's degree in Business Administration. That did not come easy. Chuck's life began in 1930 during the Great Depression. Finances to accomplish all the above were not available, but his parents did teach him determination to accomplish his goals.

World War II began and ended during his school years in Whitehaven, Tennessee. He was inspired by aviation that was on the ground and in the air. During high school he joined the Naval Air Reserve. He served as an aircraft mechanic for two years during the Korean War. His first wife was a great young lady that helped and encouraged him for 44 years in his aviation career.

Chuck took advantage of the GI Bill and began studies at Mississippi State College when released from active duty. His aeronautical engineering career consisted of working for two major aircraft companies for 36 years plus 31 years with his own company. Chuck demonstrated his creative ability by being the prime inventor for five United States Patents. The last two, obtained while doing business in his own company, have been proven with full-scale flight tests. Chuck has written and published many technical papers.

Much help for this book was provided by his second wife, Frieda, and by the members of the Christian Authors Guild and Word Weavers International.

Printed in the United States
by Baker & Taylor Publisher Services